CLINKER ISLANDS

CLINKER ISLANDS

A complete history
of the
Galapagos Archipelago

Lillian Otterman

McGuinn & McGuire
PUBLISHING
Bradenton, Florida

Excerpts from *My Wicked, Wicked Ways,* copyright © 1956 by Errol Flynn.

Excerpts from "Extracts from an interview" by Thor Heyerdahl, copyright © 1961 by The New York Times Company. Reprinted with permission.

Cover illustration: Berard's "Albemarle Island", courtesy of the Mansell Collection, London.

Library of Congress Cataloging-in-Publication Data

Otterman, Lillian, 1921-
    Clinker Islands : a complete history of the Galapagos
Archipelago / Lillian Otterman.
        p.   cm.
    Includes bibliographical references and index.
    ISBN 1-881117-03-0 (pbk.)
    1. Galapagos Islands – History. I. Title.
F3741.G20869 1993
986.6'5–cd20   92-62391

AUG 1 1 1994

Dedicated to
Captain Charles H. Otterman,
Captain G. Allan Hancock,
and
all other blue water sailors who
sought adventure in
Las Islas Encantadas.

CONTENTS

1

INTRODUCTION

On Easter Sunday morning of April 22, 1962, the staysail schooner *Marpatcha* sailed into the enchanted circle of Darwin Bay, Isla Genovesa, some 650 miles west of the Ecuadorian coast. In this partially submerged volcanic crater in a lonely but lovely spot in the Pacific, I had finally arrived at the Galapagos, where, at that time, there were more volcanoes than people.

Opportunities to visit these forsaken cinder heaps were rare. Unless one owned or had access to a private yacht, a trip to the Galapagos was an expensive excursion. Even today, twenty years later, the situation has not changed much. Regularly scheduled tours operate in the area, but are by no means inexpensive.

When I learned that the ninety-nine-foot schooner would stop at several anchorages in the Galapagos before sailing to the Marquesas and Tahiti, I immediately enlisted as crew. As far as I was concerned, the Galapagos were enough for me. With jet planes flying on schedule, Tahiti no longer seems remote. But the Galapagos remained as mysterious as ever, the "faery isles forlorn."

Several of my shipmates had never heard of the Galapagos prior to this cruise. Their sights were set on verdant, tropical "South Sea Isles," and they had but little enthusiasm for these piles of ashes.

Their lack of appreciation was understandable. Except for a brief flurry of interest in 1960, when 106 Americans left the United States to colonize the Galapagos, the isles remained forgotten. Occasionally some travel magazine featured short articles about them, showing the usual pictures of bristling iguanas, giant tortoises, the barrel at Post Office Bay, and possibly a visit with Mrs. Wittmer. During World War II, an American air base gave the islands a temporary importance. My own curiosity was aroused by books written between 1924 and 1940, and I wanted to see the charmed isles myself. William Beebe had written in 1925 that the Galapagos are "the one place in the world that remains unchanged," and I wished to see whether this held true thirty-seven years later. I often wondered why so few people settled there.

More than 140 years ago, in the autumn of 1841, the whaling ship

Acushnet stopped at the Galapagos long enough to inspire a young sailor to draw from his wealth of words a magnificent but scathing description. Herman Melville painted a bleak and grim picture: "... a Tartarus of clinkers ... arrested torrents of tormented lava ... heap of cinders ... spellbound desertness ... sackcloth and ashes ... evilly enchanted ground ... hot aridities ... Apples of Sodom ... a Plutonian sight...." His most devastating remark was, "In no world but a fallen one could such lands exist."

Certainly, his forbidding account would tend to discourage visitors to this "burnt district." But then, the sheer strangeness of the place might prove attractive and fascinating. Imagine some two thousand volcanoes, some over 5,000 feet high, all crowded into the three thousand square miles of land of the thirteen major islands. Where else can one see a comparable sight on Planet Earth? On Earth's moon, perhaps. While American astronauts were bouncing around our satellite moon in their Rover, there existed right here on Earth a similar region with jagged crater rims; weird shapes; and black, buff, and gray colors. The dark flows of lava streaking down the brown slopes, hollow caves in the black-green clinker-bound coast, the rugged, rough terrain – all of this unearthly landscape seems to belong to another planet. How many submerged craters pit the bottom of the ocean near this spot, unseen in the black depths of the sea? Only the whales and porpoises know.

Despite the desolate appearance of the islands, I felt at home. The arid slopes covered with stunted trees, prickly-pear cactus, and goat trails reminded me of my last home, Santa Catalina Island, off the coast of southern California. Therefore, the scorched hills of the Galapagos did not look uninviting to me. As yet, I had not seen the green isles of the southwestern Pacific and could make no comparisons; the fugitive beachcomber from the wilds of Santa Catalina was happily content. There was promise of a lot to see: moist jungles in the interior, crater lakes, tame animals and birds, a few interesting settlers. This was a paradise for naturalists, and for escapists like myself. My only regret was that we could not linger very long here.

Our madcap crew of two women and nine men had left Salina Cruz, just south of Acapulco, on April 5, 1962, and soon we learned how the Spaniards felt in 1535 as they drifted helplessly in the doldrums, later to discover the Galapagos by accident. It was necessary for us to conserve our diesel fuel for running the compressor and generators, and so we were at the mercy of light and variable winds, and victims of whimsical currents. The skipper had been here before and knew what to expect; our first mate was baffled. He had the strange idea that cursing and foul language would help us move along, but it did not bring us any closer and angered the crew. He made short tacks, argued with the skipper, and was quite dismayed when his short tacks got us nowhere. We lost by current what we had gained by wind. The humidity was oppressive. All of our spare clothing and leather goods mildewed. The suffocating atmosphere drained any remaining vestiges of vitality out of us.

About the same time that we arrived near the Galapagos, an elderly American, Mr. Kaul, was also becalmed in this area in his little thirty-six-foot ketch, the *Qui Vive*. He was sailing alone with "no dorg nor no cat" from Panama to the Galapagos. Strong currents threatened to dash his tiny vessel against the lava cliffs, so he blithely proceeded on his lonesome journey toward the Marquesas without bothering to anchor or go ashore in the Galapagos. The intrepid navigator recounted his adventures to us on May 29, 1962, at Taiohae, Nuku Hiva Island, in the Marquesas. Our sailing time from Salina Cruz to the Marquesas was thirty-eight days, not counting our two-week stay at the Galapagos. A safari hunter by previous occupation, Mr. Kaul had been at sea for eighty days between Panama and the Marquesas without setting foot on shore.

Early navigators had experienced worse problems; they had incorrect charts to follow. The unreliable winds and strong vexatious currents had made the Galapagos difficult to chart. There were mysterious indrafts which, like the legendary Scylla and Charybdis of the Mediterranean, sucked vessels toward the rocky cliffs. Though a ship sailed at four to five knots, the irregular currents were strong enough to divert the vessel from its course. As late as 1750 A.D., there was the mistaken belief that two clusters of islands, leagues apart, existed in this area, because the islands seemed to appear and disappear. Small wonder the early Spaniards thought the islands bewitched and bedevilled! Also, strange unearthly creatures, the giant tortoises and dragon-like iguanas, added to the sense of black magic, casting a brooding spell over this lava spewn out of the ocean. So, for sufficient reason, the superstitious mariners named them "Islas Encantadas," the Enchanted Islands.

A more popular name used then and today is "Galapagos" (from an old Spanish word, galapago, meaning saddle or leather shield), bestowed by the Spanish to honor the lumbering land tortoise with its saddle-shaped vaulted shell – a grotesque species peculiar to these islands. The official name for the group of islands is "Archipielago de Colon." However, even in mainland Ecuador the island cluster is called Galapagos.

Ecuador annexed the islands in 1832, but for centuries before that the islands were busy places with a lively history. Activity decreased there when the seas were freed from buccaneers and when petroleum replaced whale oil.

Each island has its own stories to tell, many of which are tragic tales involving shipwrecks, and deaths by crime, thirst, and drownings. Others tell of settlers who found happiness through hard work in a desolate land. There was a notorious murder in the 1930's which excited worldwide attention, and there were several social experiments which failed miserably, including the 1960 American fiasco. There are tales of hermits, cruelty, depredation, and buried treasure.

Scientific expeditions learned much here; Darwin's observations led to the formation of his basic theories of evolution. Thus, these forgotten, outcast islands really helped to revolutionize man's thinking about his past and origins. For this reason alone, the Galapagos Islands should be preserved as much as possible in their natural state, as a monument. Fortunately, steps are being taken by the United Nations and the government of Ecuador to save the unique flora and fauna from annihilation.

Rising from the sea, these volcanoes – some dead, some dormant, some spectacularly active – have defied the centuries; they are lands of "silence and slow time." It was not until man arrived that their peacefulness was disturbed and nature's orderly cycle disrupted.

Man was not welcome here. Unbenign forces strove to keep him out as if he did not belong here. Most attempts at permanent colonization ended in failure, tragedy, and disillusionment. Even today, life on the islands is a struggle, and of the many who go there to visit, few elect to stay. Dr. Eibl-Eibesfeldt reported in 1960, "Life is hard, even miserable, and most of the Europeans suffer – whether they admit it or not – from boredom at the monotony of their existence and from the lack of a cultural stimulus."

Improved and regularly scheduled transportation has made the islands more accessible, but until recently growth has been slow. From 1,346 residents in 1950, there was an increase to nineteen hundred in 1960. Some were descendants of convicts who came here not by choice; others were part of a military garrison. In 1970, the population numbered about fifteen hundred.

Of the Galapagos, Melville (1856) had written, "Ruin itself can work little more upon them." But eventually the Great Polluter will cause further havoc. The flora is being uprooted or chopped down, the precious fauna more and more herded into small, crowded sanctuaries.

Towns will grow out of the shabby villages; substantial homes and hotels will replace the humble houses; roads will replace the goat and burro trails. All the loneliness and mystery that added to the enchantment will be gone.

2

ORIGINS: THE PRE-SPANISH ERA

The Archipielago de Colon consists of ten major islands plus a large number of minor islets and rocks, scattered over a vast watery expanse of 23,000 square miles, with a total land area of about 3,000 square miles. The group lies directly on the Equator approximately 900 miles southwest of Panama and about 650 miles west of the coast of Ecuador. Professor Howel Williams claims they may represent the most active volcanic field in the world. The disastrous Peruvian earthquake of May 31, 1970, was centered somewhere between Peru and the Galapagos Islands in an historically active seismic region.

The largest island, Isabela, possesses six major volcanoes, several of which are almost a mile high; San Cristobal and Santiago have two each; most of the other islands have one apiece. The main islands have both Spanish and English names – the latter persist in literature. In order of diminishing size, the larger islands are listed in Table 1-1.

The generally accepted view is that the Galapagos Islands were never an actual part of the mainland of South America. Studies indicate there never existed a land bridge to Central or South America. In one of his books, William Beebe had drawn the Galapagos as connected to Cocos Island with a great plateau which is a submerged extension of the continent. Horneman, the Norwegian geologist who had lived many years at Academy Bay, made a study and concluded in 1931 that this was "stuff and nonsense" because the water between Cocos and the Galapagos is 2,000 fathoms (12,000 feet) deep; a tremendous lowering would have been required of the ocean floor. It is true that a submarine ridge extends northeast from the Galapagos and connects with the Cocos Ridge (running from Costa Rica), but at an extreme depth.

Within the last thirty years, an intensive mapping of the ocean floor in the Galapagos region was made by the Scripps Institute of Oceanography, the U.S. Bureau of Commercial Fisheries, and the Institute of Marine

Table 1-1
Official and former names of the 16 largest islands of the
Galapagos in decending order of size.

Official Name	Former Names
1. Isabela	Albemarle
2. Santa Cruz	Indefatigable, Chavez, Norfolk
3. San Cristobal	Chatham
4. Fernandina	Narborough
5. San Salvador	James, Santiago
6. Floreana	Charles, Santa Maria
7. Marchena	Bindloe
8. Pinta	Abingdon
9. Española	Hood
10. Santa Fe	Barrington
11. Genovesa	Tower, Quito Sueno
12. Pinzon	Duncan
13. Baltra	South Seymour
14. Rabida	Jervis
15. Wolf	Wenman
16. Darwin	Culpepper

Resources, University of California. In a summary of their work, George
Shumway (1963) reported:

> The volcanic islands of the Galapagos do not rise directly from
> the deep sea floor, but are perched on a platform elevated a
> thousand fathoms or more above the surrounding deep sea
> floor . . . . The steep side of the platform lies close to the west
> and southwest sides of Fernandina Island and Isabela Island,
> with depths of 1,700 fathoms being found within 6 to 8 sea-
> miles of the islands.

Horneman had said to Von Hagen (1935):

> Darwin believed, and I think he was right, that the Galapagos
> rose from the bottom of the sea, that by successive outpourings
> of lava, they rose finally above the sea and in some cases, like
> Albemarle, they coalesced to form one island. Also, the Ga-
> lapagos show elevation – some local subsiding and breaking
> down of the craters due to the action of the sea. Academy Bay
> is the mouth of a crater broken at one end.

Durham confirmed this in 1965 when he reported that, with the exception of

Isabela and San Cristobal, all of the major islands had formed from "a single large volcano and its accompanying satellites." However, he states that the buildup of lava from the sea floor was not a simple process: "There have been local uplifts, submergences, tilting and erosion; nevertheless, no evidence indicating regional uplift or subsidence of the islands as a whole was found." All of the bedrock is purely volcanic material (basalt), but at several places beds of limestone indicate submarine deposition which in turn is overlain by thin basalt flows; granite has yet to be found.

As to the age of the archipelago, Kuschel reported in 1963, "Geologists unanimously believe that the islands cannot possibly be older than the late Pliocene – that is to say they are not much more than 10 million years old – very recent, geologically speaking."

It seems that some major upheaval in the earth's center caused hot liquid rock to boil up through weak spots in the earth's crust, building cones that rose above the surface of the steaming waters. The molten material cooled, leaving slag-like deposits which were exceedingly hot and active for ages. Then the activity decreased until only a few craters remained alive, erupting from time to time. (Narborough Island has had many eruptions even in recent years.) Meanwhile, temperature changes and the relentless action of wind and water broke down the tough volcanic slag until it weathered slowly into thin layers of soil.

Life began to make its appearance: seeds and insect eggs were carried in the plumage of birds, or came with debris washed to the shores; spores were carried by air currents and storms. A good example of this occurred late one evening as the *Marpatcha* skimmed along in the Gulf of Tehuantepec in April of 1962. Reflected in the beams of our searchlight, fairly large particles were being blown seaward by strong gusts of wind. We were experiencing a dust storm at sea, 200 miles out from land! Though the Galapagos are remarkably free of squalls and storms, winds capable of lifting seeds and spores probably do occur, especially about every seven years when the little-understood "El Niño" phenomenon occurs. (The El Niño is a warm surface current accompanied by rain storms.)

Melville mentioned "wide levels of multitudinous dead shells, decayed bits of sugar cane, bamboos and cocoanuts washed upon this other and darker world from the charming isles to the westward and southward-fragments of charred wood, mouldering ribs of wrecks . . ." This he saw in 1841, possibly before any coconuts were planted in the Galapagos. There are no palms native to the islands. At Cormorant Bay, Santa Maria Island, we saw bamboo (which the Skipper said came from the South and Central American coast), coconut trees and husks, and other driftwood and lumber windrowed on the yellow sand beach.

Another curious natural phenomenon occurs near the Galapagos which helps bring debris from distant places. Beebe refers to it as "current rip"; on the *Marpatcha* we called it a riptide, where at the confluence of currents the water becomes extremely choppy and frothy. We met one rip about five degrees North and ninety degrees West; several days later we skimmed through another as we rounded the northernmost tip of Isabela. In his previous trips to the Galapagos, our skipper had met the rip at various places; he saw one near Wreck Bay. We saw an abundance of fish and seals here, but I was too busy to notice any debris in the water; my eyes were glued to the shore and to the fantastic outline of Isla Isabela.

Beebe (1926) commented on the rip which he met about two hundred miles southeast of Cocos Island, two-and-a-half degrees North, eighty-five degrees West:

> I saw a very distinct line in the water to the north . . . It was a wall of water against which all the floating jetsam for miles and miles was drifted and held . . . On our side, the South, the water showed dark and rough, but much lighter and smoother to the North . . . .

> When the *Arcturus* was at last actually astraddle of the rip, I saw it as a narrow line of foam, zigzagging across the placid sea, with spouting whitecaps shooting up through the froth that marked the meeting place of the great ocean currents
> . . . .

> Birds followed along the line of foam . . . Some were perched on floating logs . . . Here was a concentration of organisms – the minute so abundant that in places they were the consistency of soup, . . . billions of living creatures clinging to the central line of foam.

A clue to the origin of the drifting mass was given by one single log which yielded fifty-four species of small beings, most of which are those found on the coast of Mexico and Panama: trigger fish, crabs, seven-inch worms, jellyfish, mollusks, tiny luminescent creatures – all were tropical, not of the kind usually borne by the cold Humboldt Current. Beebe continued:

> There passed log after log, sticks and solid pieces of wood, besides three bits of wreckage from ships – bamboos up to five inches in diameter, soft pine-like wood, sections of palm trunks, and a cocoanut in the husk – all rotten, all alive with living creatures catching a ride . . . .

The fact that one can see the above debris on any of the shores of the Galapagos is proof enough that seeds, mangrove roots, ants, spiders, and other involuntary immigrants could easily have been transported to the archipelago with the floating debris, perhaps on "floating islands." In 1936, Von Hagen reported finding a huge tree trunk 100 feet long and 2¹/₂ feet in diameter on Abingdon Island.

Strong currents certainly could have brought the giant tortoises, which are not long-distance swimmers, but are extremely buoyant. Fossils of these huge creatures have been found throughout the world, especially in the United States, South America, and Cuba. They disappeared from the mainland, but managed to survive in the Galapagos as remnants of the ancient Age of Reptiles.

The current also could have brought the land iguanas. They cannot breathe under water, but their eggs (or the small animals themselves) could have come with the debris. The marine iguanas occur nowhere else in the world, and there is some speculation as to whether the land type evolved into a sea-going type. Being powerful swimmers, the marine species could have arrived from the mainland, except that none are found there. In a journal entry dated September 9, 1835, Darwin observed:

> Of toads and frogs there are none: I was surprised at this, considering how well suited for them the temperate and damp upper woods appeared to be . . . The absence of the frog family in the islands is the more remarkable, when contrasted with the case of the lizards, which swarm on most of the smaller islands. May this difference not be caused, by the greater facility with which the eggs of lizards, protected by calcareous shells, might be transported through salt water, than could the slimy spawn of frogs?

Frogs themselves require pure and unsalted moisture to survive and would easily have perished on any ocean voyage, even of short duration.

Large birds like the albatross, frigate-bird, booby, and cormorant landed upon the Encantadas in the course of their migrations, and stayed. The abundance of fish, insects, plankton, and crabs as food, and the absence of predatory enemies, made the islands an ideal place to nest. The cormorants may have come from the coast of South America ages ago, and in time developed into a flightless, bulky bird, much larger than its counterpart on the mainland. Von Hagen (1935) noticed that only land birds of a more northerly distribution inhabited the islands. There were no hummingbirds, parrots, toucans, or other jungle residents.

One exception was the tropical pink flamingo, which has the cold-loving penguin as his unlikely neighbor.

Penguins, fur seals, and sea lions were unexpected visitors from colder regions. They may have been brought to the Equator by the Humboldt Current which sweeps northward along the western coast of South America, then turns sharply west to the Galapagos with temperatures fifteen to twenty degrees colder than normal equatorial waters. Perhaps the penguins could not return to the Antarctic against the two- to four-knot current, or maybe they liked the environment; they stayed, and in time were modified to become the smallest and most northerly penguins in existence.

It is likely that other small, warm-blooded animals besides the birds arrived, but perished due to lack of fresh water and particular kinds of food. The only four-legged creatures that could live under the parched coastal desert conditions, tortoises and iguanas, survived on land. Snakes occur on four islands and are each of a different species; all are nonpoisonous. Sporadic eruptions may have wiped out other newcomers and creatures already established. The greatest challenge in colonizing an island is not getting there, but becoming established.

The isolation of the islands caused the closely inbred species to develop uniquely, forming a scientific wonderland unequaled in any other part of the world. Dr. Eibl-Eibesfeldt wrote in 1957, "Out of the 89 species and subspecies of birds that nest on the islands, 77 exist nowhere else in the world." And there are other zoological oddities like four-eyed fish, and two species of finch which sometimes obtain their food with sticks.

The curious menagerie thrived in harmony. There was plenty of "lebensraum" and food for all – seaweed for marine iguanas, fish and insects for birds, algae for crabs, cactus and other greenery for tortoises and land iguanas. Reptiles, birds, and crabs fed peacefully side by side. Fear of man was unknown. Even today, many of the creatures regard a human being with indifference or curiosity. The extreme tameness of the so-called "wild" life may be another proof of the absence of human inhabitants on the Encantadas before the arrival of the Spanish.

It is possible that a few South American Indians could have been swept accidentally to the Galapagos Islands. Before the Spanish introduced the use of the sail to them, the Indians propelled their canoes and balsas by paddles, and hugged the coast. If any reached the Galapagos, they perished and left no trace. Despite Thor Heyerdahl's controversial conclusions based on his visit of 1953, most anthropologists agree there were no permanent settlements on the isles before 1535 A.D. Also, it is not likely that the adventurous Polynesians arrived at these shores because the prevailing trade winds blew against them, from southeast to northwest. Also, unfavorable currents prevented Polynesian migrations to the Galapagos vicinity.

So, for millions of years, the tortoises and iguanas enjoyed each other's company and went about their business undisturbed on these clinkered shores. It then took Man, the deadliest animal, only three hundred years to bring the tortoises and land iguanas close to extinction.

3

INCAS AND CONQUISTADORES

ௐணௐணௐணௐணௐணௐணௐண

In 1524 A.D., the aged Inca chief, Huayna Capac, at his fortress residence at Incapirca, Ecuador, received news from post-runners that two great ships had arrived at the river which the Spanish later named San Juan. The galleons of Francisco Pizarro had reached the western coast of South America.

Scarcely ten years before, the Aztec ruler, Montezuma, had died at the hands of bearded white men, and intertribal communications had spread this tragic news from the Aztecs in Central America to the Incas of Peru and Ecuador.

An unusual number of omens of evil portent, like earthquakes and falling stars, had made the old chief apprehensive. With the powerful white warriors close at hand, and sensing danger to his people, Huayna Capac divided his empire between his two sons. Soon the half-brothers were warring against each other; Pizarro's conquest was made easy in a divided land. Only a handful of men were required to subdue a million people, panic-stricken at the sight of guns and horses. By 1533, the highly advanced Inca Empire was crushed as Cuzco fell.

After looting treasure from the sun temples and palaces, the Spaniards exploited the rich silver and gold mines with brutality and ferocity. In a short time, there began a steady procession of Spanish galleons, laden with plunder, journeying from Peru to Panama. There was silver from the fabulous mines of Potosi; gold was mined on the slopes of the Andes; intricately carved emeralds came from Colombia. In return for these wordly goods, the heathens received heavenly treasures from the Church, "owing to the Catholic desire," wrote Darwin, "of making at one blow Christians and Slaves." Monks, priests, and nuns arrived to convert the natives, and, by 1534, a sumptuous church was built at Quito, Ecuador.

Tomas de Berlanga, third Bishop of Panama, set sail for Peru on

February 23, 1535. By royal decree he had been sent to report on the progress and conditions in the conquest of Peru, and to place limitations on Pizarro's power. Several days out of Panama, the ship encountered a long spell of calm and was swept out to sea by powerful currents. Sixteen days later, on March 10, the ship drifted within sight of some islands not recorded on the meager charts. Desperately low on water, the crew landed on a small island. They found no water, nor grass for the horses, only seals, turtles and "such big tortoises that could carry a man on their back, and many iguanas like serpents."

The Spaniards saw another island, "larger than the first and with great sierras," possibly Isabela. Before they could get near it, they were becalmed for three days; the ship lay motionless and the water rations were entirely consumed before a wind arose strong enough to propel them closer to shore to effect a landing. Their thirst was so great, they tried "a leaf of some thistles," the thick leaves of the prickly-pear cactus. The sap from the juicy pads "looked like slops of lye, and they drank it as if it were rosewater." After two days of search they found a ravine containing much water and filled eight hogsheads and all available barrels and jugs. Too weak to benefit by the fresh supply, one man and ten horses died. Thus, the first of many graves was dug in this desolate land.

Of one island, Berlanga wrote, "On the whole island I do not think there is a place where one might sow a bushel of corn, because most of it is full of very big stones, so much so, that it seems as though God had showered stones." On the beach he found some small stones which at first he thought were diamonds (either quartz or feldspar) and yellow stones which he said resembled amber.

More islands were sighted but no attempts were made to land. After nineteen days of sailing, with water almost gone and subsisting on wine, the crew joyously sailed into the bay and river of Caraques, Ecuador, on April 19, 1535. The journey from Panama had lasted forty-five days, but the men considered themselves fortunate, inasmuch as another vessel had taken eight months. Seven days later, Berlanga dispatched his report, with a pilot's map, to King Charles of Spain, who placed it in the archives of Seville. The "steel-clad bishop" had claimed the islands for the Viceroyalty of Peru, but did not bother to name them, considering them worthless.

Another Spanish vessel drifted to the Galapagos in 1547. Twenty-two men under Captain Diego de Rivadeneira had seized a ship in Peru after a revolt against Gonsalvo Pizarro. Unable to rescue their leader Centeno, they sailed into the Pacific with neither map nor compass, hoping to reach New Spain, which is now Nicaragua. After twenty-five days at sea, they sighted some high-peaked islands, where they searched for water without success. Nevertheless, by spearing fish with harpoons made of their spurs, and by collecting rainwater, they managed to survive and eventually reached Guatemala. They reported having seen giant tortoises, iguanas, sea lions, and flamingoes, but found the islands absolutely devoid of human beings. After a few more ships strayed involuntarily into this area, the Spanish christened the islands "Las Islas Encantadas," the Bewitched Islands. Of this period, Beebe remarked, "Navigation was more an art than science."

Until 1563, the Spanish continued to hug the coast of South America. Then, guided by pilot Juan Fernandez, they learned to take advantage of the winds away from the coast. By standing broad out from land, where winds were more favorable for getting to the South, and by running east with the trades, the galleons could return to the coast without difficulty. The Galapagos were visited more often.

Just about this time, the Spanish became intrigued by a legend which they linked with the Galapagos. The story claimed that in 1408 A.D., the great Inca, Tupac Yupanqui, having conquered the provinces around southern Ecuador, encountered at the port of Tumbez some Indian merchants who had just returned from a long journey on balsa rafts. They spoke of two islands to the west, well-peopled and rich with gold: Hahuachumpi (Fire Island) and Ninachumpi (Outer Island).

Tupac Yupanqui then consulted his chief necromancer Antarqui. After a certain amount of professional hocus-pocus, Antarqui assured the Inca that these islands did indeed exist, and that a mission against them would be highly successful.

The greedy Inca then built a fleet of huge balsa rafts floated on inflated sealskins and reputedly equipped with large rectangular sails and great rudders. Father Cabello later wrote of them: "They were made of certain particularly light logs strongly lashed to one another with a platform of interwoven canes above, making a very safe and commodious sort of vessel of the kind called Balsas."

Twenty thousand warriors sailed on this daring voyage. After a year, and already despaired of as lost, the conquerors returned to Cuzco in triumph, bearing "Indian prisoners, black in color, much gold and silver, and the hides of animals, like horses." Best of all, they had a throne of copper and gold.

Pedro Sarmiento de Gamboa, who was writing a history of the Incas, jumped to the conclusion that Bishop Berlanga's mysterious islands and those of the Inca legend were identical. He disregarded the fact that Berlanga found no inhabitants there, nor any precious metals. Gamboa seemed unaware that the Incas confined their rafts to rivers and the coast. They could not have coped with the doldrums and currents, which confused even the clever Spanish. Moreover, the currents were against them on the return voyage.

The legend may have pertained to other islands, or it may have been a pure invention by the wily Incas to persuade the Spanish to go elsewhere. Anyway, de Gamboa believed the tale, claiming the booty had been stored in the fortress at Sacsahuman in Peru, and found 42 Inca witnesses to corroborate the story. He then persuaded the Viceroy of Peru to give him two ships and 150 men. Under Alvaro de Mendana de Neyra, 70 soldiers, 50 sailors, 4 Franciscan friars, and some slaves left Callao, Peru, on November 19, 1567, and set sail for the treasure islands of the Galapagos. The expedition eventually ended in the Solomon Islands, some 6,000 miles from the Galapagos, which they had missed entirely, possibly having sailed through their midst without seeing them. The Galapagos are strewn like petals over a vast expanse of ocean, often obscured by fog and mists.

In 1570, the Flemish mapmaker, Abraham Ortelius, made a set of charts called "Theatrum Orbis Terrarum," a sort of atlas of the known world. In the section called "Peruviae Auriferae Regionis Typus," he engraved the islands in their true position and labeled them "Insulae de los Galapagos," having read Bishop Berlanga's report. About 1589, the name was changed on the charts to "Las Islas Encantadas."

In 1602, a Spanish vessel is said to have been shipwrecked in the archipelago. Three years later, a bearded, tattered, and emaciated survivor was rescued. Having meditated upon his sins with the threat of imminent death always at hand, he became a penitent Christian during his lonely isolation. After rescue, the former legate of Santo Domingo became Fray Martin Barranga, stalwart member of the Church.

In the "Historia General de los Hechos de los Castellanos" (General History of the Exploits of the Spaniards), written by Antonio de Herrera in 1607, the "Islas Galapagos" appear in the general map of South America. However, no reference was made to them in the text, although Berlanga's voyage was mentioned in some detail.

Meanwhile, except for the usual occupational hazards of scurvy, fevers, and malnutrition, the Spanish galleons proceeded unmolested in the Pacific waters – but not for long. On the heels (or rather, sterns) of the Spanish came the English, Dutch, and French buccaneers.

4

BUCCANEERS

Disregarding the rights of the native inhabitants to prior possession, and on sole merit of discovery, Spain appropriated the southern New World as her exclusive treasure trove, jealously excluding all other nations from participating in the flow of wealth. Having slaughtered most of the peaceful and timid natives of the West Indies by overworking them in the gold mines of Haiti and Puerto Rico, the Spaniards concentrated on the more lucrative plunder of the continent.

Gold and silver were stolen from the cities and extracted from the mines of Mexico and Central America. Mule trains carried the booty from Mexico City to Acapulco, then to Panama. Unspeakable cruelties and treachery accompanied the raids, so that Burney (1816), in his *History of the Buccaneers of America*, had said, "It was as if the discovery of America had changed the religion of the Spanish from Christianity to the worship of gold with human sacrifices."

Rich silver mines were discovered by the hundreds in Chile and Peru in 1546. Solid bars of silver and silver coin in the form of pieces of eight (eight Spanish *reals*) were hauled to Panama by the Silver Fleet. The loot was sent over the Isthmus by land caravans to the waiting Spanish Armada. Spain now held a monopoly on precious metals which were exchangeable only for Spanish merchandise.

Spanish galleons also carried vast treasure from the Philippines in small vessels which travelled a great circle from the East Indies, down the coast of California, south to Acapulco, and back to the Philippines. The great *Manila Galleon* generally arrived at Acapulco from late November to early January after a voyage of about five months and carried a cargo of gold, spices, silk, ivory, amber, perfumes, and precious stones. On its return to the west, it usually carried a large fortune in silver. The Manila trade increased tremendously: from 1 million pesos carried on China-bound vessels in 1586, to 12 million in 1596.

The galleons commonly had three masts, two decks, wide beam, low waist, high poop, and high forecastle. And while they increased in number, all took the same route during the same time at the end of the year. Because of the large amount of cargo, there was no room for artillery, and the clumsy ships went unarmed and unescorted – a fact which did not escape the notice of freebooters.

French, English, Dutch, and Portuguese pirates who scourged the Caribbean were increasingly repulsed and thwarted by Spanish warships. Nevertheless, some like John Oxnam in 1576, managed to cross the Isthmus of Panama and ravaged Spanish colonies on the Pacific, waylaying treasure ships along the coast of Mexico and Peru. Most of the buccaneers had an implacable hatred for the Spanish and exterminated them with a vengeance. (Oxnam was captured and executed at Lima, Peru, not for piracy but for heresy.)

Meanwhile, the Galapagos Islands remained undisturbed and unvisited, as all the piracy was concentrated closer to Panama. Although pirates Sir Francis Drake and Sir Thomas Cavendish ravaged the coast of Chile, Ecuador, and Peru, the first Englishman known to visit the Galapagos was Sir Richard Hawkins who, in 1594, found the islands a safe refuge when fleeing the Armada. In his *Memoirs* he wrote, "Some forescore leagues to the westward of this Cape [Cape Passeos] lyeth a heap of Islands the Spaniards call Illas de los Galapagos; they are all desert and beare no fruite." Returning to the mainland, he burned four Spanish vessels, but his own ship *Dainty* was captured. Hawkins was imprisoned at Lima and released on payment of ransom. Both he and Cavendish were classed as privateers indulging in legalized robbery because England and Spain were now at war.

For the next fifty years, piratical onslaughts on the Spanish coast were carried out by Dutch raiders called *Pechelingues*. The first expedition to cross the Horn in 1599 ended miserably, plagued by scurvy and hunger and attacks by Chilean Indians. Only one ship captured a prize, then sailed west toward Asia. Van Noort and De Lint had slightly more success in 1600, as did "Black Anthony" in 1603. In 1615, Speilbergen defeated the Spanish fleet at Peru, then sought Cocos Island in vain. In 1624, a fleet of ships under Schapenham destroyed the port of Guayaquil, but won no significant prizes except a black name for their inhuman treatment of Spanish prisoners. The last effort was a Dutch expedition to establish a trading colony in Chile in 1643. Captain Hendrick Brouwer sailed home after failing in his attempt to instigate an Indian revolt against the Spanish in Chile. Dutch privateering ended when a treaty was signed in 1649 between Holland and Spain.

It is not known how many pirates stopped at the Galapagos during this time, but evidence indicates they were a favorite rendezvous. Here they had a "secure retreat, an undiscoverable hiding place but little traversed, surrounded by islands of unhospitable aspect – and yet within a few days sail of the opulent countries which they made their prey," wrote Melville. A steady supply of fresh meat was available, not only from the tortoises, but from the goats and pigs with which the buccaneers had deliberately stocked the islands. Their raids on the mainland had given them an excess of loot which they cached at the Encantadas.

Except for vessels captured by buccaneers, no Spanish ships frequented the Galapagos, either out of superstitious fear of the bewitched Encantadas or because it was unsafe to get near them. The Galapagos had become the exclusive domain of the buccaneers.

James Island

Centrally located in the Galapagos Archipelago is a large island which became known as James, San Salvador, and, later, Santiago. Roughly rectangular, it is about ten miles wide and twenty miles long, and lies fifteen miles south of the Equator. A huge mountain at the northwestern end, 3,020 feet high, forms the main mass of the island; a smaller crater occurs at the southeastern end. Numerous small parasitic craters are distributed over the island. One of them has a circular lake of salt covered with several feet of water; it is the saltcellar of the archipelago. Green vegetation appears in the higher central regions.

James is a typical Galapagos island of lava and rock, with patches of green on the otherwise barren brown slopes. It has numerous harbors and coves, and some fresh water may be found. In the northwestern corner is a semicircular indentation known as James Bay; it is protected from rough seas by little Albany Island, and surrounded by weird pinnacles above and spooky caves below. It was here in Buccaneer Cove that the pirates dropped anchor to refresh themselves and to refit and careen their ships. In fact, a Spanish map of 1747 calls this island "Carenero" – named after the interesting process in which a ship is heeled over to one side for cleaning and repairs to the hull. Spare sails, casks, and spars were stored here, also.

Of James Island, Colnett wrote in 1797:

> This Isle appears to have been a favourite resort of Buccaneers, as we found seats, which had been made by them of earth and stone, but a considerable number of broken jars scattered about, and entirely whole, in which the Peruvian wines and liquors of that country are preserved. We also found some daggers and nails and other implements. This place is, in every respect, calculated for refreshment or relief of crews after a long and tedious voyage, as it abounds with wood, and good anchorage, for any number of ships, and sheltered from all winds by Albemarle Isle. The watering place of the Buccaneers was entirely dried up, and there was only found a small rivulet between two hills running into the sea.

And what did Melville think of the "fine old ruins of what had once been symmetric lounges of stone and turf . . . , a sofa as the poet Gray might have loved to throw himself upon . . ."? He claimed that the buccaneers were not all unmitigated monsters. Since they rarely erected dwelling houses on land, "it is hard to impute the construction of these romantic seats to any other motive than one of pure peacefulness and kindly fellowship with nature. That the buccaneers perpetrated the greatest outrages is very true – that some of them were mere cut-throats is not to be denied; but we know that here and there among them was a Dampier, a Wafer, and a Cowley, and likewise other men, whose worst reproach was their desperate fortunes – whom persecution, or adversity, or secret and unavengeable wrongs, had driven from Christian society to seek the melancholy solitude or the guilty adventures of the sea."

"But," he added, "I found old cutlasses and daggers reduced to mere threads of rust, which doubtless had struck between Spanish ribs ere now. These were the signs of the murderer and the robber; the reveler likewise had left his trace." Centuries later, the fragments of broken jars of marmalade and Peruvian Pisco spirits were used by Thor Heyerdahl to support his highly controversial notion of pre-Spanish occupation of the islands.

Melville also remarked, "After the toils of pirate war, here they came to say their prayers, enjoy their free-and-easies, count their crackers from the cask, their dubloons from the keg." He knew that religion was strangely blended with their vices; they often began their enterprises with a prayer. Captain Watling began his command by ordering observance of the Sabbath; Captain Sawkins once threw the dice overboard when his men gambled on that day.

In the entire history of the Galapagos, it is a curious fact that missionaries do not play any part and are never mentioned, unlike the case with most Pacific islands. The Spanish found no indigenous, savage, or heathen population here to convert to the niceties of civilization: piracy, plunder, slaverunning, and blackbirding. This was all for the best, because "wherever the European has trod, death seems to pursue the aboriginal," wrote Darwin. Melville concurs: "No sooner are the images overturned, the temples demolished, and the idolaters converted to nominal Christians, then disease, vice, and premature death make their appearance." Both Darwin and Melville had ample firsthand knowledge of this, as they visited islands in the Pacific between 1830 to 1850.

Batchelors' Delight

The treaty of 1670 between Spain and England should have ended buccaneering in the Caribbean, but piracy continued, though on a smaller scale. French and English authorities kept one eye (sometimes both) closed to a business so profitable to the colonies.

On April 5, 1670, a band of 331 rogues, mostly English, including such impressive names as Bartholomew Sharp (the leader), Basil Ringrose (author), Lionel Wafer (author and surgeon), William Dampier (author, naturalist, explorer), John Coxon, Richard Sawkins, Peter Harris, and Edward Davis took on the ambitious project of crossing the Isthmus of Panama. With the help of sixty-eight Indian canoes they reached the Bay of Panama and seized a Spanish vessel of thirty tons. Five more vessels were taken later, loaded with specie, flour, wine, brandy, poultry, gunpowder, and shot. In July of 1681, the *San Rosario* was seized; it contained silver plate, coins, and 620 jars of brandy "with which we made very merry," wrote Ringrose.

Unfavorable winds prevented them from getting to the Galapagos, so they sailed along the coast, where another Spanish ship was captured. Prisoners were put ashore, prize money was divided, and all ships were abandoned except the huge *Trinidad*, which very obligingly carried valuable maps and charts of all the ports and harbors of the entire western coast of South America. All men boarded this vessel, renamed *Trinity*, and elected Watling as captain. They sailed to Juan Fernandez Island, 2,300 miles south, but had to leave quickly when three armed Spanish ships approached. Inadvertently, a Mosquito Indian boy named William was left behind, hunting goats on shore.

The *Trinity* returned to the Isthmus of Panama, where the band split into two groups. Sharp and his men returned to Peru to cause an estimated damage of four million pesos and the destruction of twenty-five ships, while Dampier, Cook, Wafer, and Davis returned to the West Indies. By this time, 1683, war had been declared between France and Spain.

The four last named adventurers joined a vessel under a Dutchman named Yanky, captured several French ships, and sailed north to Virginia. After selling their prize goods, they kept an eighteen-gun ship which they christened *Revenge*. Ambrose Cowley joined this group of seventy men, pretending he was ignorant of the nature of the voyage, and signed on as navigator or pilot.

The frigate *Revenge* left Chesapeake Bay on August 23, 1683, under Captain John Cook, with Lionel Wafer as "Chyrgeon" (surgeon), William Dampier as an officer, and Cowley as pilot. "These were no ordinary buccaneers," observed Melville, "but rather gentlemen with literary pretensions who were not averse to turning a fast dubloon."

Off the coast of Africa they encountered a huge Danish ship of thirty-six guns. Pretending they were a merchant vessel, the crew of the *Revenge* hid below deck until they were close enough to surprise and capture the Dane. The prisoners were put ashore to shift for themselves.

The *Revenge* was burned and scuttled, "that she might tell no tales," and the large Danish prize was rechristened *Batchelors' Delight* by the merry rogues, a most appropriate appellation. One authority claims that the *Revenge* was traded off the African coast for sixty young black girls who later perished miserably, one by one, in the cold climate near the Antarctic.

They reached the Straits of Magellan on February 14, 1684, and while choosing valentines "and discoursing of the Intrigues of Women, there arose a prodigious Storm, which did continue till the last day of the month, driving us into the latitude of 60 degrees and 30 minutes South, which is further than any ship hath sailed South; so that we concluded the discoursing of Women at Sea was very unlucky and occasioned the Storm," wrote Dampier.

Safely on the Pacific side of the Horn, they soon met the frigate *Nicolas* under Captain Eaton. Both ships sailed to Juan Fernandez, where the Indian boy William was rescued after three years of being marooned. Selkirk was not the first "Robinson Crusoe" of that island.

Cautiously they sailed northward, keeping well off the coast. In May, they captured a Spanish ship carrying timber from Guayaquil to Lima. From the officers of the Spaniard, the bachelors learned that the Spanish authorities were well aware there were freebooters in these waters. In fact, the Viceroy of Peru had issued an order that all Spanish vessels were to be burned if the English were sighted in any port. Moreover, dogs were landed on many of the islands to kill the goats and pigs which earlier pirates had stocked as a reserve food supply.

To avoid a hot reception on the mainland, and with their prize in tow, the *Nicolas* and the *Batchelor's Delight* stopped at the Lobos Islands to clean their fouled vessels. Captain Cook was ill, as were others of the crew. Shortly after, they chased and captured three more galleons, one of which carried eight tons of quince marmalade in native pottery, plus a large cargo of flour. There was very little silver plate or gold bullion on the prizes because 800,000 pieces of eight had been taken ashore when it became known that the enemy was near.

Cowley wrote, "We stood away to the Westward to see if we could find those Islands called Galipagoes, which made the Spaniards laugh telling us that they were enchanted Islands and that there was never any one but Captain Perialto that had ever seen them but could not come near them to anchor at them, and that they were but Shadows and noe real Islands . . . when after three weeks of sail we saw Land, consisting of many islands . . . . I gave them all distinct Names . . . . This island maketh high land, that which I called King Charles's Island; and we had sight of three more which lay to the northward of this, the next I called it Crossman's Island; the next to that Brattle's, and the third Sir Anthony Deane's Island . . . . We came to anchor at Duke of York's Island. There lying to the eastward of that (a fine round island) which I called Duke of Norfolk's Island . . . lieth another curious island, which I called Duke of Albemarle's; in which a commodious bay is where you may ride Landlock'd; and another island which I called Sir John Narborough's; and between York and Albemarle's lieth a small one, which my fancy led me to call Cowley's Enchanted Island . . . . It appeared always in many different forms, sometimes like a ruined Fortification . . . Great City, etc.''

The date of first sighting was May 31, 1684, and the small fleet anchored at what is now Conway Bay, near the northwestern side of Indefatigable. They stayed only one night because two of their prizes could not get in to anchor. The ships were so heavily burdened with plunder that they had fallen too far to leeward and could not follow the other ships into the same anchorage. Here the crew found sea turtles and land turtles, but the next day sailed northwest to neighboring James Island and anchored in James Bay.

Dampier wrote, "It is steep all around this island and no anchoring at this place . . . . The ground is so steep, that if an anchor starts it never holds again . . . . These isles of the Gallipagos have plenty of salt. We stayed here but twelve days, in which time we put ashore 5,000 packs of flour for reserve."

The ailing Captain Cook was hospitalized in a tent on land while the crew provisioned the ship with fresh meat. This was an easy task, as there was a plentiful supply of land tortoises and sea turtles. Crude storehouses were built for the supplies cached on shore. Cowley's account differs from Dampier's: "We laid up, and put on shoar at Albany Bay and other Places, 1,500 Bags of Flower, with Sweetmeats." The "sweetmeats" probably referred to the eight tons of quince marmalade captured off the coast.

The navigator, Ambrose Cowley, busied himself with his charts, disregarding all Spanish names which the islands may have had. Of their anchorage he said, "This Bay or Harbour in the Duke of York's Island, I called Albany Bay; and another Place York Road. Here is excellent good sweet Water, Wood, etc. and a rich Mineral Ore." He drew anchors on the chart to mark the places where they had stopped. He named one island after the Duke of York, but a year later, when Cowley learned that a Stuart had become James II of England, he renamed it James Island.

The former king, Charles II, had decreed that piracy was to be suppressed, because England and Spain were no longer at war. However, the authorities at Jamaica, Nassau, and Bermuda enforced the law half-heartedly or not at all. Cowley showed his gratitude for the laxity of enforcement by naming islands after some of these officials, no doubt for favors previously received or exchanged.

Bindloe was named after a member of the Jamaican council, Colonel Robert Bindloss, brother-in-law to the pirate Henry Morgan. Wenman and Brattle were named after Lords Wainman and Nicolas Brattle. Dassigney's Island (now Chatham) was named after Sir Philip Dassigney. A northern island, fairly large, Cowley named Earl of Abingdon's Island, which name is still used today.

Three small islets off the coast of Norfolk (Indefatigable) were named Guy Fawkes Islands, in admiration for the man who attempted to blow up

Parliament in 1606. Von Hagen remarked, "I know not what inspired this appellation unless the islands were in eruption at the time."

A small island between James and Norfolk was christened Sir Anthony Deane's Island, after a shipbuilder to Charles II. He was incarcerated in London Tower for questionable practices regarding booty taken in battle, and therefore had won the black hearts of fellow plunderers.

The largest island was named after the First Duke of Albemarle, George Monk, a general who restored Charles II to the throne. The barren isle next to Albemarle honored the famous navigator, Sir John Narborough, who, in 1669, made an exploratory voyage to the South Seas.

In all, Cowley had made fifteen folio maps, drawing in perspective the prominent landmarks to distinguish each island. An artist in England copied them, making one general map for the entire group plus individual maps, elaborately ornamenting the compass points and cartouches in gold leaf.

Sufficiently refreshed and rested, the merry bachelors and their prizes left the Galapagos on June 12, 1684, and headed north toward New Spain. Off Cape Blanco, Captain John Cook died of a fever, and Edward Davis became the new commander of the *Batchelors' Delight*. For a pirate, he was a decent chap who restrained the ferocity of his companions and did not stain his character with acts of cruelty.

Ambrose Cowley threw in his fortunes with Captain Eaton of the *Nicolas*, which departed for the Ladrones after an argument about the division of spoils. The *Batchelors' Delight* continued to raid the coast of New Spain from Baja California to Guayaquil, and the French and English joined forces.

The buccaneer fleet at Panama now consisted of 960 men in ten vessels of assorted sizes. The Spanish fleet numbered fourteen sails, of which six were armed with cannon. When the two fleets met, they circled each other for two days in a very bloodless affair. The buccaneers knew that all the Spanish treasure had been unloaded on shore, and so were not anxious for a fight. Overcome with discretion, the Spanish fleet sailed away.

The adventurous William Dampier left his gay companions and joined Swan on the *Cygnet* because it was sailing to the East Indies. Thus, the *Batchelors' Delight* lost another of its literary gentlemen. Somehow, between fighting and sailing, Dampier managed to find enough time to write a fascinating journal of scientific value and great human interest. Byron called him "the mildest-mannered man that ever scuttled a ship or cut a throat." Fortunately, the bachelors still had surgeon Lionel Wafer to chronicle their adventures. His writing was interrupted at this time when an epidemic of spotted fever broke out among the crew of 130 men.

At the end of 1684, the *Batchelors' Delight* returned a second time to the Galapagos to pick up 500 sacks of flour which were found in poor condition – the "turtle doves" had pecked away at the bags. In June of 1685,

Lionel Wafer, possibly referring to James Island, wrote, "We found a great many tortoises of that sort which we used to call Hecate . . . there we Careen'd our ship . . . . Turtle doves and other birds would light upon our Heads and Arms. Here are some Guano [iguanas] very plentiful which are good food. There grows a sort of wood in this isle very sweet to smell [palo santo] . . . full of sweet gum."

Until the end of 1686, Davis plundered towns and captured more Spanish ships before he again reached Juan Fernandez Island, preparatory to sailing home around the Horn. However, many of the merry bachelors found that they had lost all their dubloons at gaming and refused to leave the South Sea empty-handed. It is unlikely that they had buried treasure at the Galapagos because they were homeward bound. The paupers resolved to return to Peru; the lucky ones embarked for the West Indies under Captain Knight, via the Horn.

The luckless residue of sixty Englishmen and twenty Frenchmen, under Captain Davis, sailed to Guayaquil, Ecuador, and found the town being attacked by English and French. Adding thirty-six guns to the fight, they helped secure a ransom of 42,000 pieces of eight, also gold and flour, which was divided among the ships. All ships, excepting the *Batchelors' Delight*, returned north to Panama.

Having a ship sturdy enough to sail around the Horn, Davis decided to sail for home, but first he made a third trip to the Galapagos in the autumn of 1687 for the main purpose of dividing the booty among his men. The system of distribution was unique: all the pieces of eight were divided among the men; other items were auctioned off to the highest bidders; the silver realized from the sales of the auction was re-divided a second time.

On this last visit, the *Batchelors' Delight* was careened and victualed at Charles Island, known then to the Spanish as Santa Maria del Aguada. Tortoises and flour were taken aboard as well as sixty jars (each of eight gallons capacity) of oil from the land tortoise, which they considered not inferior to fresh butter "to eat with doughboys or dumplins." Water was found three miles inland.

On the way to Juan Fernandez, Davis spotted an island south of the Galapagos leading to unsolved controversies of the future as to whether "Davis's Land" was the present Easter Island. It is very likely that a ship, in making a passage through the southeast trades, could come upon Easter Island. Wafer recorded, "We saw a range of high land which we took to be islands, for there were several partitions in the prospect . . . . I and my men would have made this land, and gone ashore, but the Captain would not permit us . . . . The small island bears from Copiapo [Chile] almost due west five hundred leagues, and from the Galapagos, under the line, is six hundred leagues . . . ."

The *Batchelors' Delight* came to Juan Fernandez Island but found meager supplies of goats, as huge dogs and been landed here by the Spanish to destroy the buccaneers' supply of fresh meat. The bachelors ran into ice at the Horn, then steered too far east and had to double back west to get to the South American coast. According to Lionel Wafer, the ship reached Philadelphia in May of 1688, after four years at sea, and from there the *Batchelors' Delight* passed into obscurity. Dampier, Cowley, and Wafer returned to England where their journals became best sellers. Of the three, Dampier had the most adventurous trip and was destined to visit the Galapagos again.

In 1708, France and England were at war in the War of Spanish Succession. The merchants of Bristol fitted out the *Duke* and *Duchess* for privateering against both French and Spanish. William Dampier came along as pilot for Captain Woodes Rogers. They rounded the Horn in December of 1708 and sailed to Juan Fernandez Island.

Four years and four months earlier, Alexander Selkirk, a Scot, had been marooned here by Captain Stradling of the *Cinque Ports*, at the same time that Dampier was here as master of another ship. The *Duke* found Selkirk dressed in goat skins, bearded, and in good health. Dampier vouched for him, and "Robinson Crusoe" was made skipper of a captured ship.

Dampier commanded the artillery at the sack of Guayaquil and collected 30,000 pieces of eight for ransom of the town. On May 8, 1709, the *Duke* and *Duchess* and four prize vessels sailed to the Galapagos when 140 men became ill with a fever. Years before, Dampier had stated, "The Galapagos, by and large, are extraordinarily good places for ships in distress to seek relief at."

On May 21, 1709, one ship under Captain Hatley disappeared mysteriously in the Galapagos. "Here are very strange Currents amongst these Islands," said Rogers. "We fir'd Guns all Night, and kept Lights out, in hopes he might see or hear us, and resolv'd to leave these unfortunate Islands, after we had viewed two or three more to Leeward. We pity'd our five men in the Bark that is missing, who if in being have a Melancholy Life without Water, having no more but for two days, when they parted from us. Some are afraid they run on Rocks, and were lost in the night, others that the two Prisoners and three blacks had murder'd them when asleep; but if otherwise, we had no water, and our men being still sick, we could stay little longer for them."

The *Duke* and *Duchess* returned to the South American coast, but came back to the Galapagos once more on September first to search again for Hatley and his men. The ship had vanished; no trace was ever found. Dampier returned to England in 1711 and published another book which brought very little money. He died in obscurity.

In 1713, an English privateer named Captain Charpes sailed round South America with three or four ships. His own crew consisted of forty-eight Irishmen and twenty blacks. After looting Payta in Peru and capturing two prizes, they ran across to the Galapagos, then to Panama for three more prizes, and careened at Cocos Island.

In 1715, John Clipperton reappeared in these waters, was captured by the Spanish, and later released. In 1720, he came again in the ship *Success* where he spent most of his time drunk in his cabin. He took several Spanish prizes and joined forces with the pirate Shelvocke, then fled to the Galapagos when pursued by three Spanish warships. After scrubbing ship at James Island, he went north of the Galapagos where he took the *Prince Eugene*; aboard was the president of Panama, whom he kept for ransom. After once more raiding the coast of Peru, he returned to the Galapagos a second time, then sailed to Cocos to take on fish, wood, and water. There he marooned three Englishmen and eight blacks, all badly ill with scurvy. The unmitigated monster had a small atoll, just two miles square, named after him.

In 1747, the Spanish acquired a new map of the Galapagos from Don Jorge Juan de Ulloa, showing the islands in relatively correct positions, but some had acquired new names: Albemarle was called Ysabel; Chatham had become San Clemente; James was Carenero; Culpepper and Wenman were known as Los Dos Hermanos; and Abingdon was Quito Sueno (Nightmare). Later this name of Nightmare Island was transferred to Tower by some writers.

In 1789, Captain Don Alfonso de Torres, of the Spanish Royal Armada, stopped briefly at the Galapagos on his return from an expedition seeking the Northwest Passage. Bindloe Island was renamed Isla de Torres.

Perhaps the first scientific expedition to reach the Galapagos was that of Captain Alesandro Malaspina, exploring the Pacific to the Bering Sea and the South Seas. The ships *Descubierta* and *Atreuida* arrived in the Galapagos in 1790, and a botanist made a study of the Galapagos flora. His report was buried in some ancient archives in Spain.

Some of the last pirates in the Galapagos were the two corsairs, Buchard and Brown, nefarious partners in Argentine waters. They came to the Galapagos in 1816 to divide their spoils and dissolve their partnership. In the same year, the brig *Colonel Allen*, under Captain David McLennan, stayed a few days at the Galapagos on a smuggling expedition and witnessed an eruption on Isabela Island.

Piracy was now being replaced by the growth of commerce; the Galapagos changed from a pirate rendezvous to a whaling station.

5

COMMERCE AND WAR ARRIVE

The Whalers

At the beginning of the eighteenth century, oil of the sperm whale was recognized as being far superior to the oil of whalebone whales for the lamps, soap, and candles of the world. Great demand and high price for the oil spurred the whalers to extend their spermaceti whale fisheries to larger areas of ocean. By 1780, there were numerous disputes over whaling grounds in the Atlantic Ocean between England and the newly-independent nation, the United States.

The British sperm whalers were the first arrivals in the Pacific in 1788. Several years later, the first American whaler to reach the Pacific was the *Beaver*, under Captain Paul Worth, from Nantucket. In one-and-a-half years off the Chilean coast, their cetacean harvest yielded 1,100 barrels of sperm oil and 200 barrels of whale oil.

The merchants of the city of London, ever alert for new mercantile possibilities, commissioned Captain James Colnett of the English navy to investigate anchorages in the Pacific where whalers could refit and victual their ships. The Spanish still jealously guarded their harbors along the South American coast, allowing few foreign vessels to enter. However, they were quite indifferent to the Galapagos Islands, which were located in some of the best whaling waters.

Colnett sailed from England in the H.M.S. *Rattler* in January of 1793, and anchored in the Encantadas in June. Guided by Cowley's charts and the reports of Dampier, Colnett made an exhaustive study not only of the harbors, but also the plant, animal, and bird life. His extensive report, published in 1798, described the usefulness of the Galapagos to the whaling fleets: whales were abundant, the harbors were excellent for beaching vessels, and "the woods abound with tortoises, doves and iguanas, and the lagoons with teal."

"We searched with diligence," writes Colnett, "for the mineral mountain mentioned by Dampier . . . but were not so fortunate as to discover it; unless it be that from which the heavy sand and topazes were collected, and of which I ordered a barrel to be filled and brought away.''

Colnett also improved upon Cowley's map, renaming the islands which he could not identify or locate. One island which did not appear on the chart he called Barrington, after Sir Samuel Barrington, Admiral of the Blue.

Sir Philip Dassigney's Isle became Chatham, after William Pitt, first Earl of Chatham. Sir Anthony Deane's Island became Duncan, after the famous British admiral, and two smaller islands were christened after Lord Hood and Admiral Jervis. Colnett then proceeded north to Cocos Island and to the coast of Mexico.

The whalers soon discovered that Colnett's report did justice to the islands, and the Galapagos became even more popular with the whalemen than they had been with the buccaneers. The square-sided, blunt-nosed, unlovely whaleships, lacking both grace and speed – floating oil factories of a money-minded industry – became a common sight in the harbors of the Encantadas. Seamen insisted that the whaleships were built by the mile and sawed off in desired lengths. Americans soon took monopoly of the whaling industry and came to the Galapagos in ever-increasing numbers.

There seemed to be no end to the supply of whales; the same held true for the blubber-hunters. By 1840, huge clouds of smoke, blackening the sails, billowed from the brick tryworks of 675 malodorous American whaling ships, as well as from 230 ships of other nations. In 1841, when the Fair Haven whaler *Acushnet* was near Rodondo Rock north of Isabela Island, Herman Melville described ''a fleet of full thirty sail, all beating to the windward like a squadron in line. A brave sight as ever man saw . . . . But there proved too many hunters for the game. The fleet broke up, and went their separate ways out of sight, leaving my own ship and two trim gentlemen of London. These last, finding no luck either, likewise vanished.''

The American fleet reached a maximum of 729 vessels in 1846, manned by 15,000 men. Despite all this frenzied activity, it can be said that the sperm-whale fishery was the only venture that did not end because of over-fishing. The discovery of petroleum in Pennsylvania in 1859 ruined the price of whale oil, and the seizure of many vessels during the Civil War helped the dissolution of the whaling business. Some seamen also found a more lucrative (and less dangerous) occupation, dealing in sealskins, dried sea slugs, edible birds' nests, turtleshell, mother of pearl, guano, and other novel and exotic cargos which they sold at fabulous prices in Canton, San Francisco, New York, and Europe.

Whaling was a bloody occupation which did require extreme courage and skill. Many brave men died fighting the huge mammals, which at least had a sporting chance of escape in their natural element. Meanwhile, another bloody, but more sordid, industry preyed in these waters upon the hapless fur seal.

The Sealers

A lucrative but short-lived industry in the southern waters began about 1784 in the Falkland Islands, an archipelago east by north of the Straits of Magellan. The prey this time was the innocent fur seal, a charming creature, tame and trusting, easily captured on land because of its clumsiness in getting around outside of its natural element. It lived in herds on rocky coasts. Each herd was an independent, self-perpetuating unit which did not intermingle with other herds; this factor helped in its extinction on many islands.

In the early years of the nineteenth century, millions of seals were systematically hunted down on all the islands and coastal seal rookeries in the southern hemisphere. As many as nine hundred per day were clubbed to death on small islands. Their skins were stripped for sale in Canton markets, where they brought handsome prices – not always in coin, but in exchange for teas, silks, and porcelain. Prices ranged from thirty-five cents to five dollars, but generally averaged about one dollar. The huge profits stimulated whole-sale slaughter, until all accessible seals were hunted down and exterminated, regardless of their sex or age. By 1800, they were extinct on the Falklands and other islands around South America.

At this time, there were about sixty vessels in the sealing fleet, representing the United States and five of the leading European nations. One of these vessels was the *Perseverance*, a sealer and general trader, commanded by the old Boston sea captain, Amasa Delano (ancestor of Franklin Delano Roosevelt), who made three voyages to the Galapagos.

Killing off the seals also meant a shortage of food supply for the aboriginals of Tierra del Fuego, whom Delano described as "a race of poor half-starved miserable beings, who are very little removed from brute creation. They live on fish and seals' flesh when they can get them. They eat the seals raw and nearly-rotten. Their numbers are but small."

The *Perseverance* arrived at the Galapagos during the rainy season and took on a plentiful supply of water at James Bay. The crew amused themselves in watching the solemn pelicans, whom they named the Russian Army. The more numerous boobies became Napoleon's Army. A lovely white bird with a clear, sweet whistle they christened "Boatswain's Mate." We know it now as the bosun bird, or tropic bird. They also witnessed a minor eruption of a volcano on Isabela Island, and picked up some Spanish deserters. Delano wrote, "I have been at almost all ports on the coast of Chili repeatedly, and seldom but when I carried in more or less Spaniards who had been prisoners of war, or otherwise distressed. I have taken them off the Gallipagos Islands, after they had run away from English ships, and gone on shore to prevent being carried to England.''

In 1835, Darwin, who visited the salt lake on James Island, wrote, ''A few years since, the sailors belonging to a sealing vessel murdered their captain in this quiet spot; and we saw his skull lying among the bushes.''

Fur seals probably were not as numerous in the Galapagos as in the colder waters near Cape Horn. But even so, Eibl-Eibesfeldt (1957) wrote that between 1816 and 1897, 17,485 fur-seals were taken from the Galapagos Islands. Today, only a few hundred are left on Tower and James Islands. Sea lions, with their less valuable fur, are abundant on all the islands. The remnants of the fur-seals surviving in the Galapagos, at Guadalupe, on the Crozet Islands of the Indian Ocean, and on some islands in the South Atlantic, owe their existence to the inaccessibility of the rocky shores they inhabit.

Post Office Bay

A delightful custom which survives to the present day originated in the days of the whalers. Due to protracted voyages, often lasting anywhere from one to five years, the sailors found it expedient to establish a sort of postal service, wholly unofficial and friendly, but not on regular schedule.

An anchorage at Charles Island was selected for this mail service, and the bay was appropriately named Post Office Bay. It is said that the bay was known earlier as Hathaway's Post Office, after Colnett set up a large barrel there in 1749. This spot was a favorite place for both the pirates and whalers, because it had a wide flat beach with water springs nearby, and a plentiful supply of tortoises, pigs, and goats, as well as numerous caves for caching supplies.

Before this place was selected, messages were left on various of the islands. They were placed in bottles which were corked and sealed, then tied to a stake. Sometimes the stake rotted and collapsed before a ship stopped to collect the notes.

The ''mailbox'' on Charles Island at first consisted of a box nailed to a post or a keg tied to a tree in a conspicuous place near the beach. Vessels that had just rounded the Horn, and which had several more years at sea ahead of them, would deposit letters to and from home. Ships that were homeward bound gathered up the mail and delivered it to the first port where mail service was available. Many of the letters never reached their intended destination; some may have been lost at sea, either awash in a storm or lost with the ship. There is record of one woman who penned a hundred letters to her sailor-husband in the course of a three- year cruise; he received but six of them.

Not all messages were letters to and from home; many were left for the benefit of other fishermen and were reports as to what luck was encountered in whaling or tortoise hunting. Some were letters of distress, like those of the Ritters at the end of 1929.

From time to time, the mailbox was replaced or refurbished by grateful sailors who appreciated this unique service. From a box or cask tied to a tree, it evolved to a barrel perched on a post. Today, it is a barrel, gaudily painted in red, white, and blue; it has a hinged door on the side and a roof to protect it from rain. Cattle skulls, and wooden plaques with ships' names, ornament the post, which is imbedded in a cairn of lava rock. Passing yachts collect the mail from the barrel and post it at their next port of call. In 1962, the author took forty-one pieces of mail from the barrel and posted them in Papeete, Tahiti.

Captain David Porter

British whaling in the Pacific was seriously crippled by a United States naval officer who raided the British merchantmen in the vicinity of the Galapagos.

During the War of 1812, American whalers from Nantucket and New Bedford were harassed in the Pacific by British whalers and their Peruvian allies. Unaware that the war had begun, the unarmed American vessels fell easy prey to armed British privateers and armed whalers. This wholesale destruction by the British eventually brought about their own undoing.

Captain David Porter of the U.S.S. *Essex*, without orders from his superiors, sailed his frigate round the Horn in the winter of 1812, with the intention of destroying British shipping. The *Essex* herself was formerly a British whaler taken as a prize and converted to an armed cruiser.

Porter scouted the southern waters, and at Payta, Peru, recaptured the American whaler *Barclay* which had been taken by a Peruvian privateer. Together they sailed for the Galapagos and sighted Chatham Island on April 17, 1813. Finding no ships at Chatham or Hood, they headed for Post Office Bay on Charles Island. All things being fair in war, they took the British mail out of the box nailed to a post. From the papers thus obtained, Porter was able to make a list of about twenty English ships cruising in these waters.

Suspecting that most of the whalers would be found at the westernmost end of the archipelago, the *Essex* sailed around the southern end of the largest island, Isabela. After rounding what Porter named Essex Point, the armed vessel passed Elizabeth Bay and waited near Tagus Cove for an appearance of the enemy.

At daylight, Porter sighted a large British whaleship heading west. While chasing the vessel, he spotted two more. Quickly, he seized the unarmed *Montezuma*, put his own officer and crew on it, then pursued the other ships. The *Georgiana* and the *Policy* surrendered. The three vessels obtained with so little effort were estimated to have a value of a half-million dollars to England. The *Montezuma* had 1,400 barrels of spermaceti oil. All three vessels "had supplied themselves with those extraordinary tortoises of the Gallipagos, which properly deserve the name elephant tortoises," recorded Porter in his "Journal of a Cruise made to the Pacific Ocean."

The *Essex* remained in the Galapagos from April 18 to June 8 of 1813 during which time five more ships were captured. The "Journal" records strange sea battles and games of hide-and-go-seek. Many times the crew of the *Essex* was exasperatingly becalmed while just a few miles away an enemy ship sheared through the waters under full canvas. The strong currents also proved to be enemies, and the *Essex* struggled against them as they seemed invariably to set in a direction opposite to the one Porter wanted.

The *Essex* had been at sea a long time, and supplies and equipment were exhausted or worn out. From the captured prizes, she was completely refitted with cordage, canvas, paints, tar, and ship's stores. To prevent the British from recognizing her, the *Essex* was constantly being repainted, and disguised with the construction of false parts. Her sides were painted to give the appearance of a poop like that of a Spanish merchantman. The captured prizes also were painted and repaired for future sale to the Spanish on the mainland. During the repairs, all prisoners were allowed ashore as much as they desired, because many were ill with scurvy.

All of the officers of the *Essex*, including the chaplain and doctor, were given command of the prize vessels. The only remaining midshipman on the *Essex* was a twelve-year-old boy, David Farragut, whom Porter had adopted in New Orleans, and who would later distinguish himself as admiral. At his tender age, the boy was given command of the *Barclay*, much to the chagrin of its erstwhile skipper, the old sea dog, Gideon Randall. Many of the seamen on the British vessels were Americans who had been unwillingly impressed as crew, and gladly worked their ships under Porter after capture.

All the naval engagements seemed to be rather bloodless affairs. Porter lost only two men in the Galapagos, one of whom was Doctor Miller. The other seaman died, not on the field of battle, but on the field of honor in a duel. Porter wrote, "I have now the painful task of mentioning an occurrence which gave me utmost pain, as it was attended by the premature death of a promising officer . . . . I shall throw a veil over the entire proceedings and merely state that the parties met at daybreak on shore without my knowledge, and at the third fire Mr. Cowan fell dead. His remains were buried on the same spot where he fell, and the following inscription was placed over the tomb: 'Sacred to the memory of Lieutenant John S. Cowan, of the U.S. Frigate ESSEX, who died here, anno 1813, aged 21 years.'"

Twenty-eight years later, Melville saw this epitaph and wrote, "Upon the beach of James Isle, for many years was to be seen a rude finger-post, pointing inland – the stranger would follow the path till at last he would come out in a noiseless nook and find his only welcome, a dead man – his sole greeting the inscription on a grave.''

Another finger-post was left at James Bay, from which was suspended a bottle with the touching message: ''The U.S. Frigate ESSEX arrived here on the twenty-first of June, 1813, her crew much afflicted with the scurvy and shipfever . . . out of which she lost forty-three men . . . . The ESSEX leaves this in a leaky state, her foremast very rotten, and her mainmast sprung . . . . Should any American vessel, or indeed a vessel of any nation put in there, and meet with this notice, they would be doing a great act of humanity to transmit a copy to America, in order that our friends may know of our distressed and hopeless situation, and be prepared for worse tidings . . . .'' A list of forty-three names of the ''dead'' was appended to the note. The message was a trick to mislead the enemy.

It was also on James Isle that Porter left one male and three female goats ashore to graze, but they disappeared during the night. Their descendants roam the island today, and are a source of food for present-day settlers.

At Charles Island, the *Essex* took aboard over four hundred tortoises, which they called ''Gallipagos mutton.'' Here they also laboriously took on 2,000 gallons of water which was found one-and-a-half miles inland. It was carried in ten-gallon kegs for this long distance, emptied into barrels on the beach, and rafted through high seas and heavy currents to the ship anchored six miles away. Of the water, Porter said it was of a ''filthy appearance, having a bad taste and smell, and filled abundantly with slime and insects. But to us it was a treasure too precious to lose, and the greatest industry was used to save every drop of it, for fear that the sun, which was evaporating it rapidly, should cheat us of our prize.''

At the foot of the mailbox at Post Office Bay, Porter buried a bottle containing instructions to Lieutenant Downes, the new Captain of the prize *Georgiana*, concerning where to meet next.

Five years before, this same *Georgiana* had anchored there to bury a seaman, and a mound of stones had been heaped over his grave in a shady spot. The crew of the *Essex* used this grave as a table and drank toasts for the repose of the poor soul underneath. The grave board had the following verse:

> Gentle reader, as you pass by,
> As you are now, so wonce was I;
> As now my body is in the dust,
> I hope in heaven my soul to rest.

Herman Melville gives this version of the verse, which he placed on Chatham Isle:

> Oh, Brother Jack, as you pass by,
> As you are now, so once was I.

Just so game, and just so gay,
But now, alack, they've stopped my pay.
No more I peep out of my blinkers,
Here I be – tucked in with clinkers!

On June 6, 1813, Porter witnessed a volcanic eruption on Isabela Island. He sailed north of Abingdon and dispatched Lieutenant Downes to sell the four captured prizes, plus the barrels of whale oil, at Valparaiso. Porter returned to Isabela to capture four more ships.

During these last sea battles, Nature too was staging a spectacle. Four craters were smoking on Narborough and one at the southern end of Isabela, while a furious eruption took place on Charles Island.

Having destroyed a million tons of enemy shipping, practically sweeping the British whaleships from the seas, and dealing such a blow to their Pacific fishery that it never recovered, Porter proceeded to the Marquesas for further adventures. Eventually, he was captured by two British warships.

Upon his return to the United States, Porter was suspended for six months without pay and was reprimanded by Congress for having exceeded his orders in rounding the Horn at all. However, he did deserve censure for his activities in the Marquesas. His unprovoked attacks against the Marquesans tarnished somewhat the glory earned for previous exploits.

6
NATIVES AND VISITORS

Land Tortoises

While Captain Porter of the *Essex* was exterminating the British whaling industry in Galapagos waters, another form of devastation was occurring on land: the giant tortoises, after which the island group had been christened, were systemmatically being slaughtered by the whalers.

Earlier, a heavy toll had been exacted by the buccaneers, who rhapsodized over tortoise meat. "No Pullet eats more pleasantly," wrote Dampier. However, the total number of buccaneer ships from the years 1593 to 1720 was infinitesimal compared to the huge fleets of whalers that swarmed the South Pacific from the years 1791 until after the American Civil War. Pirate ships were small; there was precious little storage space for the bulky tortoises. The pirates hardly made a dent in the huge supply of tortoises which were to be had for the taking. However, the goats, pigs, rats, and dogs left ashore by the buccaneers also destroyed many of the eggs and young of the tortoise family.

Dr. Townsend reported that over 200,000 tortoises were taken from the Galapagos Islands in thirty years. This figure was obtained from a study of whaleship logs from the years about 1830 to 1860. Almost a quarter of a million tortoises is not a high estimate considering that there were on average over 500 vessels in the waters per year, and each ship took over 100 tortoises apiece. From the years 1831 to 1868, seventy-nine American vessels alone carried off 13,000 tortoises. Some of the entries read:

> Hector – 237 taken at Charles Island in 1832
> Isabela – 335 taken at Hood Island in 1831
> Luna – 224 taken at Charles Island in 1837
> Abigail – 132 taken at Indefatigable Island in 1834
> Bengal – 200 taken at Charles Island in 1834

The tortoises were called "turpin" on the whaleships' logs – a contraction of the word terrapin. The whalers also pronounced the name of the archipelago as Galapaygos. The correct Spanish pronunciation is Galapagos, with the accent on the second syllable.

An old timer in the business since 1795, the *Barclay*, about which we read in connection with Porter, had these entries:

> July 17, 1835 – Two boats went a-turpining. Three of the men deserted. Boats returned without them 7 o'clock with 30 turpin.

> July 18, 1835 – Caught the three runaways and put ringleader Caleb Halstead in irons and kept him below. Ship Gideon Barstow left. Ships Baleaner and Washington of New Bedford arrived.

There is no record of how many turpins were removed by whalers, sealers, and warships in the years not included in Dr. Townsend's study, but the numbers must have been staggering. Darwin reported in 1835, "It is said that formerly single vessels have taken away as many as 700, and that the ship's company of a frigate some years since brought down in one day 200 tortoises to the beach."

And what was so special about the land tortoise that made it so desirable? Why were these relics, which Melville called "Roman Coliseums in magnificent decay," in such great demand?

The main reason: they were excellent eating. Whaling skippers termed the meat far more delicious than chicken, pork, or beef. Captain Porter wrote, "After once tasting the Gallipagos tortoises, every other animal food fell greatly in our estimation. These animals are so fat as to require neither butter nor lard to cook them. The oil is superior in taste to that of the olive. The meat of this animal is the easiest of digestion." Darwin wrote, "The breast-plate roasted, with the flesh on it, is very good; and the young tortoises make excellent soup; but otherwise the meat to my taste is indifferent." Even Melville "made a merry repast from tortoise steaks and tortoise stews" after discoursing at length upon the creature's ghost – the "spectre-tortoise," dark and melancholy. Other whalers thought, if there was better eating than turpin, it was turpin liver. Turpin oil, pure and fine as butter, was greatly prized by the housewives of New Bedford and Nantucket.

Another reason for their popularity was that the behemoths provided a continuing supply of fresh meat. Live tortoises could be dumped in the hold and forgotten until needed. They could remain alive, above or below deck, a whole year without food or water without detriment to the quality of the meat. The whaleship *Niger* mislaid a tortoise in its hold for two years, but it survived. Beebe wrote, "The tortoise was the equivalent of a cold-storage room in those days . . . . In the hold the tortoise continued to exist after the unemotional manner of their kind, without apparent distress." Thus, the scurvy-threatened crews had ever-present fresh meat, neither pickled nor salted.

A third feature of the galapago important to the thrifty New England skippers was that the tortoises were free. Also, being entirely defenseless against man, they were easy to obtain. The larger beasts were overturned and dragged with ropes; those weighing seventy-five pounds or less were carried upon a man's back. For ease of carrying over the rugged volcanic country, the smaller ones were usually selected. Those too big to be moved were slaughtered for their fat or water sacs, or sometimes left alive, a date inscribed upon their backs for the edification of hunters who would arrive perchance a hundred years later.

The smaller islands were stripped first, and only those creatures survived that penetrated the haunts which man could not reach: either the dry desert country where only cactus grows, or the impenetrable upper jungles. Sometimes the men who went "a-turpining" wandered too far. If gone too long, they were abandoned to be picked up later by other ships.

The large island, Isabela, and the rugged Indefatigable, continued to yield tortoises long after the reptiles became extinct or rare on other islands. To find them, the hunter had to search for their track: a straight line in the dust where the lumbering beast dragged his tail. Another clue was the path of broken branches, bushes, and trees which the armored tank knocked down as he passed by. Melville wrote, "I have known them in their journeyings to ram themselves heroically against rocks, and long abide there nudging, wriggling, wedging, in order to displace them, and so hold on their inflexible path . . . . Their stupidity or their resolution is so great, that they never went aside for any impediment . . . . At sunrise I found one butted like a battering-ram against the immovable foot of the foremast, and still striving, tooth and nail, to force the impossible passage."

In 1936, the naturalist Von Hagen made a study of the life habits of the tortoise, which he reported in his book *Ecuador, the Unknown.* It is the main source of the information that follows:

Sixty million years ago, the Chelonian type of tortoise had spread throughout all of the Americas: North, Central and South. The largest fossil specimen at the American Museum was a monster tortoise weighing over two thousand pounds. Equally large specimens were found in India; during the Age of Reptiles, giant tortoises existed everywhere on earth. Today, they are extinct except for two places on the globe: the islands of the Aldabra group in the Indian Ocean, and the Galapagos in the Pacific Ocean. The remoteness of both island groups, and freedom from mammalian predators, contributed to the survival of these antideluvian creatures.

For sheerest monotony of existence, the land tortoise takes the prize. He awakens at dawn, daintily browses on cactus (the sharp spines don't bother him one bit), munches on fallen tree leaves, grass or lichens, then takes a siesta at noon. In late afternoon he awakens for another meal, then seeks a place to sleep for the night. Imagine doing only this for not twenty or thirty years, but century after century for over two hundred. "Penal hopelessness," wrote Melville.

Once in a while, if living in the desert, the tortoise gets thirsty and is obliged to travel great distances to higher elevations where water collects in craters and vents during the rainy season. Crawling slowly and ponderously with heavy elephantine steps, he can cover eight miles in two or three days. Darwin clocked him doing sixty yards in ten minutes, and claimed a tortoise travels night and day when moving purposely toward any point. Taking the same path for centuries, the tortoises wear smooth the lava rock upon which they drag their heavy carapaces. To find water, the Spaniards learned to follow these well-worn paths.

Darwin found the tortoises to be "very fond of water, drinking large quantities, and wallowing in the mud." If the water is deep enough, they immerse themselves completely, swallowing large gulps, and storing as much as two gallons of water in a large sac in the lower part of the shell. After three or four days at the water-hole, they laboriously wend their way whence they had come.

Another break in the utter monotony is the mating season, when the hardly animate creature loses his lethargy for a few weeks. Being of a polygamous nature, the huge male guards his harem from would-be intruders. With roars and bellows, the fighting males bite each other's shells, trying to overturn one another. They groan and push and churn the earth, stopping only when darkness comes.

The male differs from the female mostly in size and greater length of tail. The male breast-plate is concave; the female is convex. The male grows to wondrous immensity, over five hundred pounds, and the top of his dome-shaped shell can be three or four feet above the ground when he is walking, higher than a table top. A monster like this furnishes two hundred pounds of meat and has a neck two feet long. His shell is an impregnable fortress, and, if not killed by man, he will either die of old age or from a fall off a precipice. The adult tortoise has no enemy except man.

After painfully digging a hole with her long-nailed front claws, the female deposits eight to twenty eggs of ping-pong ball size into the cavity, then tamps down a hard crust.

If not eaten by rats or pigs, the eggs hatch in four months. The little two-ounce tortoise, about two inches long, works his way out of the sand. If lucky, he will survive being gobbled up by buzzards, rats, cats, pigs, goats, and dogs. He is not safe until he is about fifteen inches long, when his shell hardens enough to withstand the teeth of a wild dog. He draws in his head and legs with a deep hiss when attacked or disturbed, falling to the ground with a heavy thud.

The young tortoise grows two inches per year, shedding the thirteen five-sided plates of his shell. Underneath the detached plate is a new one, larger in size. After his twenty-fifth birthday, he slows down to half an inch growth per year. Eventually, from a modest beginning of two ounces, he grows to the colossal size of five hundred pounds, or four thousand times his original weight, provided he escapes the soup pot of a hungry settler.

Beebe confirmed the fact that tortoises can swim, paddling with their front legs. However, the giant tortoise does not enter the ocean of his own free will, nor does he swim from island to island.

One specimen is recorded to have lived 140 years in captivity, wrote Roydon Bristow, who spent nine months in the Galapagos in 1931. He was impressed by their great age: "I hated the horrid work of butchering . . . . A life which may have begun several hundred years ago had ended." He continued, "Even if the head is shattered by a bullet, the vitality of the creature is so great that there will be movement in the legs fifteen minutes after the body has been completely removed from the shell. Butchering these creatures is made more unpleasant by the fact that one cannot help thinking they are alive when cutting them up. I saw the heart, which had been removed and thrown aside, pulsating strongly twenty minutes later.

"We killed these creatures only when we had no other means of getting other fresh meat. It always seemed vandalism to me; I could not help reflecting on what the American told me of their great age, and I wondered if one of these fellows had been alive in the days of the old buccaneers."

Aside from the gory aspect of killing these truly wondrous creatures – "none of your school-boy mudturtles" – some persons would be squeamish for another reason. "Most mariners," wrote Melville, "have long cherished the superstition, not more frightful than grotesque. They earnestly believe that all wicked sea-officers, more especially commodores and captains, are at death (and, in some cases, before death) transformed into tortoises; thence-forth dwelling upon these hot aridities, sole solitary lords of Asphaltum."

And what happens to ordinary seamen? Good or bad, all who die at sea become porpoises, the merry, carefree hoboes of the oceans.

Hunilla, the Chola Widow

While on the subject of whalers and tortoises, one is reminded of a story related with great feeling and sympathy by Melville concerning Santa Cruz Island, "a spot made sacred by the strangest trials of humanity."

Melville often altered or invented facts to create a better story. He read Colnett's account of James Bay and transported it to Barrington; he also transferred the Hermit Oberlus from Charles Island to Hood Island. However, his tale of Hunilla, the Chola widow, is too detailed to have been a pure invention. Melville claims that in 1841, his ship, *Acushnet*, rescued a Chola widow stranded on the lonely island of Norfolk, now known as Indefatigable and Santa Cruz. She had drawn their attention by waving a white handkerchief as they sailed a half mile offshore.

It seems that the half-breed Hunilla, her Spanish husband Felipe, and her brother Truxill, had left Payta, Peru, in 1838, aboard a French whaler. With two favorite dogs, tools, a chest of clothing, cooking utensils, kegs, and a crude apparatus to render out the oil from tortoises, the three entrepreneurs were landed on Norfolk Island. The French whaler promised to return after four months to remove them to the mainland. Meanwhile, they would procure tortoises, from which they would extract the precious oil and store it in kegs until the Frenchman returned.

After two months of successful hunting, they built a rude Indian raft. On a fishing trip, as Hunilla watched from the shore, the raft was dashed against a reef. Felipe's body was washed ashore; Truxill's was never found. The grief-stricken widow and her dogs had two more months to wait for the French ship. It never came.

Hunilla neglected her rude calendar and lost all sense of time. Her sustenance was fish, sea-fowl eggs, and tortoises. After being assaulted by whalers, she hid in a secret cove where she built a crude shack. Melville wrote, "The roof inclined but one way; the eaves coming to within two feet of the ground. And here was a simple apparatus to collect the dews . . . , which in mercy or mockery, the night-skies sometimes drop upon these blighted Encantadas . . . . All along beneath the eaves, a sheet was spread . . . . A small clinker weighed its middle down, thereby straining all moisture in a calabash below." Sometimes she obtained three quarts of water overnight. For three years she shared her water and food with her dogs, which had increased to ten. Then, one day, upon a mysterious presentiment that a friendly ship was near, she emerged and signalled the *Acushnet.*

Hunilla, two of the dogs, her chest, and two kegs of oil were taken aboard, together with live tortoises which she presented to the captain as a gift. She sat motionless and never looked back at the eight howling dogs which had to be abandoned on the beach near her husband's grave. After a long passage, the ship reached Tumbez; the kegs of oil were sold; the silver, to which was added a contribution from all hands, was given to the silent passenger. The lone Hunilla passed from their sight, riding a small donkey homeward to Payta.

Solitaries

"Probably few parts of earth have sheltered so many solitaries," wrote Melville. "A sullen hatred of the tyrannic ship will seize the sailor, and he gladly exchanges it for isles, which though blighted by a continual sirocco and burning breeze still offer him . . . a retreat beyond the possiblity of capture."

Others were thrust ashore by inhuman captains. Captain Porter relates this story of a castaway at Tagus Cove:

"There was erected a hut, built of loose stones, but destitute of a roof. In the neighborhood of it were scattered in considerable quantities the bones and shells of land and sea tortoises. This . . . was the work of a wretched English sailor, who had been landed there by his captain, destitute of every thing, for having used some insulting language to him. Here he existed for a year on land tortoises and guanas, and his sole dependence for water was on the precarious supply he could get from the drippings off the rocks . . . . He provided himself with two sealskins, with which, blown up, he formed a float; and after hazarding destruction from the sharks . . . he succeeded at length in arriving along side of an American ship early in the morning, where his unexpected arrival not only surprised but alarmed the crew. His appearance was scarcely human; clothed in the skins of seals, his countenance haggard, thin and emaciated, his beard and hair long and matted, they supposed him a being from another world."

Some unfortunates were lost while tortoise hunting. Melville recounts how one man, lost on Narborough, saved himself by drinking the blood of seals until rescued. He wrote, "Woe betide the straggler at the Enchanted Isles! The impatient ship waits a day or two; when, the missing man remaining undiscovered, up goes a stake on the beach, with a letter of regret, and a keg of crackers and another of water tied to it, and away sails the craft." On October 19, 1835, when the *Beagle* returned to pick up Charles Darwin from an excursion on Isabela, Captain Fitz-Roy reported, "The day we re-embarked Mr. Darwin, there was a man missing, belonging to an American whaleship, and his shipmates were seeking for him. Men have been lost hereabouts, and it is said that some of the bodies were never found."

At the Whaling Museum in New Bedford, there is a log of the whaler *Chili* which has this entry: "Albemarle Island, September 25, 1841. Two boats came in with twenty-two tortoises. Lost a man. Could not find him. Left bread and water and directions in a bottle if anyone should find him."

In some places, crude basins were hollowed out by miserable runaways or castaways to catch the precious dew which might drop from upper crevices. Other signs of vanishing humanity were gravestones or graveboards set to mark the burial of some seaman. Melville claims that ships used the Encantadas as a convenient potter's field; burial at sea was done only when land was far astern.

Isla Isabela

Just as James Island was the favorite resort of the buccaneers, so did Isabela Island (Albemarle) become the rendezvous of the whalers.

Isla Isabela is the largest of the islands in the Galapagos archipelago and contains more than half of the total land area of the entire group. Shaped like a boot with a narrow ankle and a broad foot, it consists of five principal volcanoes, and at one time its neighboring island, Fernandina (Narborough), may have been a sixth.

The volcanoes are spread equally through the eighty-five mile length of the island and are extremely high. Mount Whiton, the northernmost, is an impressive 5,500 feet high; its neighbor thirteen miles south, Mount Williams, rises to 4,600 feet. The awesome Cerro Azul (Blue Mountain), at the southern end, looms 5,540 feet into the clouds. These mountains are especially impressive because they rise directly from the sea.

Five distinct species of tortoise on Isabela prove that the main volcanoes at one time were separated from each other by the sea. They coalesced later, either because the land was elevated or because enough lava flowed from the craters to fill the gaps between them to join their bases.

Isabela presents a scene of utter desolation, especially at the northern end: gaping craters, both peaked and truncated; cones; and smoking fumeroles. Eruptions as recent as 1948, 1953, and 1957 choked whatever vegetation grew between times, leaving areas gaunt and naked. From the sea, Isabela appears lifeless, but actually it harbors tortoises, sea lions, wild dogs, and, on its western side, two unique birds: the Galapagos penguin and the flightless cormorant. It also has numerous flamingo rookeries, ducks, herons, gulls, and both terrestrial and marine iguanas. There are forests, bathed in garua (mists), which support vines and orchids. Many thousand head of cattle roam the southern end of the island. Vicious wild dogs, looking like a cross between a collie and a shepherd, attack turtles, birds, and cattle. "They have grey eyes like wolves," says Von Hagen, and "travelling in packs they attack tortoises, rob eggs from flamingo and cormorant nests, slaughter penguins and cormorants, and even swim out to sea after the sea iguanas." In 1934, William Robinson of the *Svaap* was attacked by a canine family group. He had taken one of their pups to give to the yacht *Stranger*, and the parents protested with such violence that Robinson was forced to shoot them in order to remain at the camp where he was filming a penguin colony.

Until 1957, Ecuador maintained a penal colony at the southern end of Isabela, composed of destitute and unhappy beings. The island is actually one enormous ranch, operated by a private owner to whom the government had given complete concession. A small fishing fleet is based at the south shore at Villamil. Four miles inland from the port is the village Santo Tomas.

Near the northern end of Isabela is Roca Rodondo, a dangerous table-topped rock about eighteen miles offshore, 200 feet high and a quarter mile in circumference. The barren monolith is visible at a distance of thirty miles, and is often mistaken for a sail due to the "birdlime streaks of a ghostly white staining the tower from sea to air," wrote Melville. The shelves along its sides teem with sea fowl; the deep waters (thirty fathoms at a quarter-mile away) abound with rock-cod and whales.

Tagus cove occupies a crater in Isabela, open to the sea through a breach in its southern wall. Names of visiting vessels are painted on its steep cliff walls, a custom much deplored by Dr. Robert I. Bowman, who terms it a defacement of the landscape. However, huge luxury ocean liners make Tagus Cove their only stop in the archipelago for the sole purpose of viewing these names. It is a thrill for boatmen to see names they recognize, and to realize that the archipelago has had many visitors, though seemingly unknown to the general public. Somebody does bother to sail to this wondrous place.

Many ships of the United States Navy had been here: U.S.S. *Erie, Jade, Babbitt, Barnegat, Charleston, Trenton, Bowditch,* and *Concord.* Tuna boats and pleasure yachts had registered here. Some had made repeated trips: Vanderbilt's *Ara* in 1926 and 1928, Leon Mandel's *Carola* in 1938 and 1941, Commander Baverstock's *Inca* in 1940 and 1950, seven trips for Irving Johnson's *Yankee* between 1933 and 1961, and five trips for Astor's *Nourmahal* between 1920 and 1938.

Some had come a long way: *Cyprus* from New York in 1931; *Phoebe* from Africa, 1960; *Hildur,* Toronto, 1957; and *Rundo,* Oslo, 1958. The *Zaca* had been here in 1932 and 1935 with the Templeton Crocker Expedition of the California Academy of Sciences. Near the head of the bay was the name *Albatross,* March, 1961: the ill-fated vessel sank in a squall off Florida just two months after registering at Tagus Cove.

There are names smacking of adventure: *Norseman, Windjammer, Tondelayo,* J.P. Morgan's *Corsair,* Mellon's *Vagabondia,* Vanderbilt's *Pioneer,* Otterman's *Invader,* and others too numerous to mention. Captain Otterman's *Marpatcha* appears highest of all, and near to his *Explorer* on an eastern cliff, but no record of his *Gloria Dalton* was located, although the schooner had been there in 1954.

Tagus Cove had been a meeting place for whaling ships and was known to them as Rendezvous Bay, or the Basin. It was a perfect but gloomy anchorage, a nook sheltered with high wall-like cliffs coming straight down into the sea, with deep water at the foot of the black walls. The only landing place was a ravine at the head of the narrow cove.

Across the ridge is Tagus Crater Lake whose rim is a half-mile wide and 400 feet high on the highest side. The lake floor is below sea level, and sea water has percolated through the thin wall of ash to form a salt water lake. It is colored a vivid green by filamentous green algae. Silver-white fish, an ocean species, are found in this lake and may have been dropped into the lake by birds. At a ledge overhanging a sort of cave, more names appear on the rock wall. Among them is deeply chiseled *St. George,* 1924. It represents the

English Expedition whose geological studies were published in a Bishop Museum Bulletin.

There are many flightless cormorants at Tagus Cove, sitting on their low nests of seaweed. One of the rarest birds on earth (a 1972 estimate was merely 800 pairs), this cormorant can be found only on Isabela and Narborough islands. The birds have a reptilian aspect: an S-shaped, snake-like neck, cold greenish-blue eyes, dusky plumage, dark, and a long powerful beak. Seafood is so abundant in the Galapagos that the cormorants confined their food-getting activities to swimming; flight was unnecessary. As their wings grew smaller, their bodies evolved into a larger and heavier type than those of the continent. Eibl-Eibesfeldt's book *Galapagos* gives a delightful account of their courting activities.

Solemn dignified pelicans crash into Tagus Cove water "like sacks of coal." Melville called this dull-gray bird, powdered over with ashy cinders, "a penitential bird fitly haunting the shores of the clinkered Encantadas." Wild dogs can be heard howling during the night.

The saucy pigmy penguins of Tagus Cove have grown wary of man. They paddle close enough to satisfy mutual curiosity, but do not permit themselves to be caught. Early voyagers were puzzled by these ambiguous creatures who stand erect on shore like little men with black dress suits, white waistcoats, and yellow spectacles. In 1669, Captain Woods commented, "We have already mentioned those birds called penguins to be about the bigness of geese; but upon second thoughts to call them Fowls I think improper, because they have neither Feathers nor Wings, but only two Fins or Flaps, wherewith they are helped to swim." The Galapagos penguin does not measure more than twenty inches long.

Elizabeth Bay is the crescent bay formed by the curve of Isabela around Narborough. Whales come here at certain times of the year to calve. The whalers would blockade the wide entrance with their ships, "and so had the Leviathans neatly in a pen," wrote Melville. They preferred to hunt "off this greater isle, away from the intricacies of the smaller isles, for here is plenty of sea-room – though even here the current runs at times with singular force, shifting with singular caprice."

At the southwest corner of Isabela Island, the grim Cerro Azul (Blue Mountain) is almost always obscured by clouds and has had recent eruptions. Shipwrecked men have died trying to get around it to the village of Villamil. Dr. Schmitt called this westerly projection "the weirdest of all – a Valley of the Moon." It is a perilous place, avoided by craft without an engine. No fisherman cares to risk his life there; the many wrecks have given the name Wreck Point to this place. Huge rollers carry everything to shore. Winds are fickle, and landmarks confusing. The small craters that pit the shore look very much alike from any angle. Heavy fog and dampness add complications. In this vicinity, it took the schooner *Marpatcha* four days to travel by sail a distance which could have been covered in about six hours by a powerful motor cruiser like the *Explorer*. One learns to expect such things in the bewitched Encantadas.

7

VISITORS AND COLONIES

∽∞∽∞∽∞∽∞∽∞∽∞∽∞∽∞

Floreana

At the southern end of the archipelago there is a roughly circular island with a diameter of about eight miles, known variously as Floreana, Charles Island, or Santa Maria. The highest peak is 2,100 feet high, and, like all the other hills scattered over this island, has been rounded by erosion over eons of time. Small islets and rocks (Watson, Gardner, Caldwell, Enderby, Champion, and Winslow) lie close to shore. The best anchorages are along the northern and northwestern sides of the island at Cormorant Bay, Post Office Bay, and Black Beach.

Rain is rare on the beach and lower slopes. However, at higher elevations inland, the vegetation is green. Fertile soil supports a jungle of lime trees and a pampas of coarse grass. Avocado, papaya, guava, and orange trees, introduced by early settlers, thrive well. Rain is frequent, and permanent springs bubble out of the rock.

The buccaneers introduced goats, pigs, cats, and dogs; later settlers brought the larger animals: cattle, horses, and burros. The island is well stocked with domestic creatures gone wild, but the "wildlife" is tame. Land tortoises are extinct. Small birds are friendly and curious.

In the hills about a half mile inland are "pirate" caves – probably volcanic gas pockets – in the soft, easily worked stone. Frances Conway remarked, "Everything of ancient and uncertain origin is automatically charged to the pirates." The caves may have been enlarged by settlers as permanent residences. The largest cave is twenty by fifteen feet, with a fireplace and benches chiseled out of the walls. Smoke is carried off through the thin ceiling by a chimney ten feet high and a foot in diameter. The entrance is screened by saplings, and a spring bubbles only sixty feet away. A rock basin, two feet deep, collects the water, and the overflow forms a bog on a lower level. Fruit trees grow near the cave. What an ideal place for a hermitage! Because of its very hospitable aspect, Floreana attracted permanent settlers.

The Hermit Oberlus

The first-known permanent resident of Floreana was a rascally Irishman named Patrick Watkins, who is reputed to have killed his captain with a marlin spike. Having escaped from an English ship about 1800 A.D., he settled at Black Beach, which at that time became known as Pat's Landing. A mile inland, he built a miserable hut near a spring (later known as the Ritter Spring), and started cultivating two acres of ground.

Pat succeeded in raising a fair quantity of potatoes, tobacco, and pumpkins, which passing whaleships gladly accepted in exchange for rum spirits or dollars. Business was good, though infrequent; Pat managed to procure enough rum to keep himself insensible a good part of the time. Porter described his appearance as "the most dreadful that can be imagined: ragged clothes, scarce sufficient to cover his nakedness, and covered with vermin; his red hair and beard matted, his skin much burnt from constant exposure to the sun, and so wild and savage in his manner and appearance that he struck everyone with horror."

"The only company of Oberlus," wrote Melville, "were the crawling tortoises; and he seemed more than degraded to their level, having no desires for a time beyond theirs, unless it were for the stupor brought on by drunkenness . . . . The long habit of sole dominion over every object around him, his almost unbroken solitude, his never encountering humanity except on terms . . . of mercantile craftiness . . . all this must have gradually nourished in him a vast idea of his own importance."

With an old musket, he intimidated a black who had come ashore from an American ship. Proposing to make the prisoner his slave, Pat marched him into the interior. However, the sailor overpowered his would-be master, tied him, and carried him to the ship.

The captain of an English smuggler then in port, desirous of stealing Pat's few dollars, whipped him, and with him returned to the hut, stole his money, wrecked the shack, and destroyed the garden. Pat escaped into the impenetrable wilds where he plotted deep revenge against all men.

Soon Pat recultivated his garden, vessels once more bought his produce, and his signal revenge took form. Every now and then he would ply a visiting sailor with rum until the man was insensible, then would conceal his victim until the ship's departure. When Pat had thus procured five slaves, completely dependent upon him and intimidated by "that shocking blunderbuss," he stole an open boat and sailed for Ecuador with his prisoners.

In his hut, Pat left a note stating: "On 29th of May, 1809, I sail from this enchanted island in the *Black Prince* bound for the Marquesas,'' (signed) Fatherless Oberlus. The prisoners, too, managed to leave a note in a keg at Black Beach making known their enslavement and the rogue's villainy.

Pat arrived alone at Guayaquil, presumably having slain his prisoners. At Payta, Peru, he wound himself into the affections of a tawny damsel, prevailing upon her to accompany him to his Enchanted Isle.

However, his ''extraordinary and devilish aspect,'' and his attempt to steal a small vessel, caused his arrest by the authorities, who promptly clapped him into one of their unwholesome jails. When Captain Porter arrived at the Galapagos three years later in 1812, Patrick Watkins was still languishing in his jail of sun-burnt brick. Whether he died in prison or was released is unknown. Von Hagen claims he was cut to pieces in a barroom brawl.

Revolution in Ecuador

With the departure of its singular solitary settler, the archipelago continued as a ''no man's land,'' visited by transient whalers, sealers, warships, and privateers. The Viceroyalty of Peru neglected its little possession in the Pacific; too many events were happening at home. About 1809, a revolt against the tyrannical Spanish rule started brewing in Quito, Ecuador. The Ecuadorian war of independence attracted a Creole named José Villamil, who had left New Orleans, Louisiana, after the Louisiana Purchase of 1803. He distinguished himself as a general in the army of combined forces under Simon Bolivar. The liberated provinces of Ecuador, Colombia, and Venezuela formed the Federacion of Gran Colombia and busied themselves with post-war affairs. The Galapagos, in the meantime, remained unwanted and forgotten.

Sir Basil Hall

The year 1822 brought to the Galapagos Islands a young British naval officer, an adventurous romantic who had served in the Napoleonic wars, interviewed Napoleon at St. Helena, written accounts of his travels to the Far East, and explored Korea before he was thirty-two years old.

Now on duty in Pacific waters between 1820 and 1822, Sir Basil Hall arrived at the tiny island of Abingdon aboard the frigate H.M.S. *Conway.* Abingdon is the most northerly of the larger islands of the archipelago. Hall brought with him the Kater pendulum, a valuable contribution to physics as well as to the science of mapmaking. It employed a principle of Huygens, in which centers of oscillation and suspension were interchanged.

Various experiments were conducted in the hills with this invariable pendulum while the group camped on shore at the southern end of the island.

Some time was spent studying the great tortoises peculiar to this island. However, after nine days of discomfort due to lack of water, they left.

In 1923, William Beebe was puzzled by the mystery as to when the name "Indefatigable" was applied to one island, previously known as Norfolk, later as Porter's Island and Santa Cruz.

After leaving Abingdon, the H.M.S. *Conway* probably sailed to a bay at the north end of the island in question. Being engaged in mapmaking, it probably was Hall who christened the bay Conway Bay after his ship, and named the island Indefatigable. Years later, Zane Grey thought this name quite appropriate, as it required someone quite "indefatigable" to traverse the lava-strewn, tangled, mosquito-infested jungle of this island. It has also been called "Inexcusable."

At any rate, in 1835 Darwin used the name "Indefatigable." Sometime between 1812 and 1835, this curious appelation appeared on an English map. It may well have been Sir Basil Hall who put it there in 1822.

Benjamin Morrell

Captain Benjamin Morrell had made two visits to the Galapagos – first in 1823 and then two years later, searching for new sealing grounds. On February 14, 1825, his small topsail schooner, *Tartar*, lay anchored in a cove of Bank's Bay on the western side of Isabela Island, directly across from the northeastern point of Narborough.

At two o'clock in the morning, the complete stillness of the night was interrupted by a sudden terrific explosion of one of the volcanoes on Narborough, about ten miles away from the *Tartar*.

Morrell wrote, "The whole hemisphere was lighted up with a horrid glare . . . . The heavens appeared to be in a blaze of fire, intermingled with millions of falling stars and meteors, while the flames shot upward from the peak of Narborough to the height of at least two thousand feet in the air."

Two-and-a-half hours later "the boiling contents of the tremendous cauldron had swollen to the brim and poured over the edge in a cataract of liquid fire. A river of melted lava was seen rushing down the side of the mountain." The molten lava travelled a distance of three miles to the sea, raising clouds of steam as the water "boiled, roared and bellowed."

Though ten miles from the erupted cone, "the heat was so great that melted pitch was running from the vessel's seams, the tar dripping from the rigging." The air was hot and stifling, and the gases caused extreme faintness among the crew. A breeze finally arose, and the *Tartar* moved southward through the almost boiling water, until the ship was fifteen miles from Narborough where the water temperature was still 102 degrees Fahrenheit.

The *Tartar* was anchored at the southern end of Elizabeth Bay for the night. The next morning Morrell decided to abandon the bay entirely, as the volcano's activity continued unabated. The ship rounded the western end of Isabela and sailed for Floreana. From here, at a distance of eighty miles, "the crater of Narborough appeared like a coloured beaconlight, shooting its vengeful flames high into the gloomy atmosphere, with a rumbling noise like distant thunder." Lightweight pumice stone littered the seas all over the archipelago.

Seven months later, the *Tartar* returned to Elizabeth Bay and found the volcano still active and burning.

During the *Tartar's* stay in the Galapagos, the crew collected 187 tortoises at Indefatigable Island.

A Funeral Procession

A month after Morrell witnessed the sudden eruption on Narborough, the frigate *Blond* anchored at Tagus Cove on March 25, 1825. It was on a strange mission: to fetch home the bodies of the king and queen of the Sandwich Islands (Hawaii).

In 1824, leaving Queen Regent Kaahumanu to mind the kingdom, the dissipated King Liholiho and his favorite wife embarked on a cruise to England aboard the English whaleship *L'Aigle* whose Captain Starbuck was an American.

The royal pair were regally and lavishly entertained in London, but the festivities were marred when their majesties caught the measles and died. The seventh Lord Byron (next in line after his cousin, the poet George Gordon) was commissioned to escort the bodies (in teakwood caskets) to their native land. With a royal guard of English officers and the native retinue, the H.M.S. *Blond* left England September 24, 1824, under the command of Admiral Lord Byron.

The voyage from England around the Horn, then north to the Galapagos, took seven months. Here they hoped to find water, but, as Beebe wrote, "Everyone who ever came to the Galapagos arrived thirsty; most voyagers left the islands in the same condition."

Lord Byron was quite impressed by the Encantadas: "The place is like a new creation; the birds and beasts do not get out of our way; the pelicans and sea lions look in our faces as if we had no right to intrude on their solitude; the small birds are so tame that they hop upon our feet; and all this amidst volcanoes which are burning round us on either hand. Altogether it is as wild and desolate a scene as imagination can picture .... Our party at Narborough Island landed among an innumerable host of sea-guanas, the ugliest creatures we ever beheld. They are like an alligator but with a more hideous head and a dirty sooty black color, and sat on the black lava rocks like so many imps of darkness."

First Colony

On May 30, 1830, Ecuador seceded from the Columbian Confederation to become an independent republic under its first president, General José Flores. Two years later, General José Villamil sent his lieutenant, Colonel Ignacio Hernandez, to take formal possession of the Galapagos Islands for the newly created republic.

On February 12, 1832, in the presence of the crews of several whaleships that happened to be at Charles Island, Colonel Hernandez hoisted the yellow-blue-red tricolor and declared the islands to be the property of Ecuador.

General Villamil had conceived the idea of colonizing the islands. As a reward for his important services rendered during the war for independence, he was granted a concession to begin a settlement on Charles Island.

Villamil obtained pardon for eighty soldiers who had been sentenced to execution for plotting a rebellion against the new government. They were freed on condition that they become workers in the new colony. Quite enthusiastically, the reprieved rebels and their families moved to Charles Island with their pigs, burros, horses, and cattle, and began to clear the land at a thousand-foot elevation, about five miles from shore. Their village was called "Asilo de la Paz" – Asylum of Peace – and was near springs which provided sufficient quantities of water. They planted fruit trees – lemon, orange, banana, papaya – and grew assorted vegetables. One hundred years later, the orange trees would be sixty feet tall, bearing the most delicious oranges in the archipelago, and some claim the best in the world.

These first colonists were soldiers, not criminals. The colony thrived and had a promising future, until Ecuador made the mistake of augmenting their numbers to 300 with convicts and other miscreants. The Asylum of Peace degenerated, and within three years descended into the miserable state in which Darwin found them.

General Villamil lost interest after the island became a penal colony. After five years of originally enthusiastic work and dedication, he resigned as governor. He was succeeded by a villain named Colonel Williams, who set himself up as a tyrannical dictator. He was still in power in 1841, when Herman Melville arrived in the Galapagos aboard the whaler *Acushnet*.

Years later, Melville published the story of "Charles's Isle and the Dog King," in which he related how "King" Williams freely lessened the census of the isle by his murderous dispensation of justice, and was forced to exchange his human bodyguard for a dog regiment. He encouraged sailors to desert their ships and join his army, but "these lawless mariners, with all the rest of the [former] bodyguard and all the populace, joined forces into a terrible mutiny and defied their master. He marched against them with all his dogs and a deadly battle ensued upon the beach. It raged for three hours . . . .

Three men and thirteen dogs were left dead upon the field, many on both sides were wounded, and the king was forced to fly with the remainder of his canine regiment . . . into the interior . . . the victors returned to the village on the shore, stove in the spirit casks, and proclaimed a republic.''

The fugitive later returned from the hills, was promptly banished, and sailed away on the next ship to Peru. He left in 1842, and by this time the colony was reduced to eighty persons, most of whom were transferred to Chatham Island. In 1849, twenty-five men were left on Charles Island, but the herds had vastly increased and gone wild.

In 1851, with the failure of their colony at Charles, Ecuador toyed with the idea of settling its debt to England by selling the Galapagos to that nation. Peru, France, and Spain protested so vociferously that the matter was dropped.

By 1852, the community at Charles Island was reduced to a mere handful of desperate folk, including a certain Briones, the pirate of Guayaquil. He was exiled to Charles in 1852 with seven of his confederates who lost no time in plotting an escape from their island prison. The opportunity came when the American whaler, *George Howland*, dropped anchor in Post Office Bay. The ruffians seized the ship and sailed for Chatham.

General Mena, an aged man, was spending his declining years conducting an agricultural experiment at Chatham Island. He and five other men were seized and later slain by Briones.

Meanwhile, trouble was brewing on the mainland. The former president, General Flores, was in Peru planning a revolt against the existing government in Guayaquil. He recruited an expedition which was to overthrow the incumbents, and, with sixty or seventy volunteers, boarded two sloops and sailed for Ecuador.

Briones, on his way to Guayaquil, intercepted and attacked one of the sloops, savagely slaughtering its entire crew of twenty-nine. The second sloop beached ashore on the mainland while Briones sailed to Guayaquil. The cut-throats expected to be received with honors for having ''destroyed the vanguard of Flores.'' Instead, all of them were hanged.

International repercussions arose in 1854 as the United States sought reparations of $40,000 for the loss of the whaler *George Howland*. During the negotiations, the United States offered Ecuador $3 million for exclusive rights to collect guano from the islands. The offer was refused by Ecuador after England, Peru, and Spain protested. Actually, their protest did the United States a tremendous favor, because the report of huge guano deposits on the Galapagos islands was completely unfounded. The archipelago never had enough guano for commercial exploitation.

During the American Civil War, Ecuador offered the Galapagos to the United States as a coaling station, but the United States was not interested. This offer was not as ridiculous as it may seem, considering that there was no

Panama Canal in existence, and American warships had to sail around South
America if needed on the opposite coast of the United States.

Second Colony

A second attempt to colonize Charles Island occurred in 1870, and,
according to Melville, "furnishes another illustration of the difficulty of
colonizing barren islands with unprincipled pilgrims."

The patron of this second settlement was Señor de Valdizian, whose
main interests were agriculture and also the gathering of the orchilla moss
(*Rocella tinctoria*), which furnishes a dye that was commercially important.
At first, the colony prospered and flourished, but as happened before, the
government unloaded more undesirables into the colony. In 1878, the convicts murdered Valdizian and sacked the village in a drunken orgy. The
peaceful settlers fought back and killed all but one of the convicts in a fierce
battle. The colonists then scattered despite attempts of Captain Thomas
Levick, master of Valdizian's ship, to restore order. Charles Island was
abandoned, and in 1892 the Italian corvette, *Vettor Pisani,* reported that not
one inhabitant remained, though the orchards, vineyards, and cattle were in
excellent condition.

During that same year of 1892, to commemmorate the four-hundredth
anniversary of Columbus's discovery of America, the entire archipelago was
rechristened *Archipielago de Colon* (Islands of Columbus). Charles Island
now became Floreana to honor President Flores. Albemarle became Isabela
and Narborough became Fernandina, after the queen and king who financed
Columbus's voyage. James was changed to San Salvador, the navigator's
landing place in the New World; Hood became Española after Spain. Abingdon was named Pinta after one of the ships; and Duncan was changed to
Pinzon, probably to honor Vicente Yanez Pinzon, close friend to Columbus.

Chatham Island was rechristened Isla San Cristobal, after St.
Christopher, patron saint of travellers; Indefatigable was named Santa Cruz
(Holy Cross), while Barrington was called Santa Fe (Holy Faith). Bindloe
and Tower were respectively named Marchena and Genovesa.

A third attempt to colonize Charles Island was made in 1893 by a Señor
Antonio Gil. However, his main purpose was to exploit the cattle herds for
their hides. After four years at Charles, he transferred his settlement to
Isabela, where cattle and tortoises were more numerous.

Villamil, Isabela Island

In 1897, Señor Antonio Gil founded his new settlement near the southeastern point of huge Isabela Island, near tiny Tortuga Isle (Brattle), a
crescent-shaped clinker. The port by which the island colony was reached

was named Villamil. The little village located four miles in the hills was called Santo Tomas, after a volcano on the island.

Besides raising cattle for hides, Señor Gil and his son also shipped tortoise oil to Ecuador in vast quantities. A small profit was made from mining sulphur found in a volcanic crater and by burning coral on the beach for lime. The proprietor hired some of his laborers; others were government convicts.

In 1905, there were about two hundred people at Santo Tomas despite the shortage of water. Potable water was obtained from brackish water holes near the coast and from coconuts which were planted here and thrived. By 1923, however, the population had dwindled to sixty persons.

In 1902 a small military garrison was stationed at Santo Tomas, but living was a struggle even for the soldiers, let alone the mistreated peons and convicts. In 1904, eleven soldiers deserted into the interior. Most of Isabela Island is unexplored, and the deserters were confident of finding water. They probably had intended to cross the island to the western side, in hopes of being rescued by some fishing boat. Many days later, one of these men staggered back into Santo Tomas, almost dead of hunger and thirst. He told how the soldiers had scattered in a desperate search for water, never to meet again. The other ten were never found; it is quite certain they perished.

Señor Gil had certainly selected an inhospitable location, although his ranch survives to the present day. Besides lack of water, remote location, and dangerous reefs and seas near the port of entrance, there is the additional hazard of frequent volcanic eruptions. In 1911, the largest volcano erupted, but the ranch managed to survive the poisonous gases.

The year 1911 also marked a different sort of outburst. The United States put forth a proposal to establish a maneuver base for the American Navy in the Galapagos. Because of the islands' strategic position, only 900 miles from the nearly completed Panama Canal, the United States wished to fortify this vulnerable "Achilles' Heel of the Canal." To reinforce the Caribbean approaches, negotiations were underway with Denmark to purchase the Virgin Islands, and now the United States was willing to pay $15 million for a ninety-nine year lease of the Galapagos, to protect the "backdoor" of the canal. The request was unfavorably received by the Ecuadorians, and after quite an uproar by the general populace, the proposal was dropped.

Soon afterwards, one Ecuadorian president offered the islands in secret to the United States as security for a loan of $10 million. When the American State Department demanded full title to the archipelago until the loan was paid, negotiations came to an end. The publication in 1909 of private papers of a former president of Ecuador revealed that Ecuador had made previous attempts to sell the islands to France and Britain for cash, but there were no buyers. In 1917, to foment a revolution, pamphlets were circulated in Ecuador claiming that the archipelago had been sold to the United States.

Towards the end of World War I, an American enterprise launched from California was interested in the economic development of the Galapagos, in cooperation with Ecuadorians. The reaction to this "American penetration" was so adverse that the Ecuadorian government forbade the American steamship *Witasboro* to clear the port of Guayaquil with supplies for the islands.

Apparently, the Encantadas were now being kept by Ecuador mainly for prestige value. The little republic did nothing to develop the islands, and the bountiful harvests of tuna and other fish were being reaped by other nations.

8

NATURE AND NATURALISTS

The ecclesiastical fact that the Encantadas were discovered by a bishop had no permanent effect upon the type of men who followed. Since 1535, disreputable men like pirates and convicts frequented the lonely isles. Then came the whalers and sealers to despoil the islands of their curious beasts. Warships cruising in the area augured war and destruction.

It was not until 1835, exactly 300 years after Berlanga's discovery, that a different type of visitor came, not to plunder and kill, but to enrich his mind and that of mankind.

Charles Darwin

The H.M.S. *Beagle* left England on December 27, 1831, for a long voyage to survey the South American coast and take meridian observations around the world. Captain Fitz-Roy, himself a genius at navigation and hydrography, selected a young man "of promising ability" to gather natural history specimens and information that would "confound the geological skeptics who impugned the literal truth of the Bible." Little did the captain realize that this young naturalist would someday cause quite a stir among scientific and religious circles with his unorthodox and rather notorious book, *On the Origin of Species.*

Darwin was only twenty-six years old when the 100-foot *Beagle* reached the Galapagos, but the last four years spent in studying the tropics, plains, and snowy summits of the eastern and western coasts of South America had sharpened his powers of observation to an accuracy and acuity rarely equaled.

The *Beagle* anchored on the leeward side of Chatham on September 17, 1835. After the parched deserts of Chile and Peru, Darwin found the Galapagos equally uninviting. Everywhere were heaps of black basaltic lava and "a few fragments of granite curiously glazed and altered by heat." He immediately noticed that the southern sides of craters were quite broken down, and lower than the northern rims. "As all these craters have apparently been formed when standing in the sea, and as waves from the trade wind and the swell from the open Pacific here unite their forces on the southern coasts of all the islands, this singular uniformity in the broken state of the craters, composed of the soft and yielding tuff, is easily explained," he remarked. These same trade winds also bring the moisture which condenses on the southern, windward slopes of larger islands at above one thousand feet. The northern coasts and slopes are bare.

Darwin was disappointed with "such wretched-looking little weeds," which were more likely found in arctic than equatorial climates. He found lava blown into great bubbles whose tops had fallen in, leaving circular pits with steep sides. The slag heaps of Chatham reminded him "of Staffordshire, where the great iron foundries are most numerous."

On Charles Island, Darwin hiked upward to the settlement four-and-a-half miles inland, passing from cactus to greener areas and finally to thriving vegetation of trees and ferns at one thousand feet, but he "saw nowhere any member of the Palm family, which is more singular, as 360 miles northward, Cocos Island takes its name from the number of cocoa-nuts."

The vice governor of the colony on Charles Island happened to be an Englishman, a Mr. Lawson, who was delighted to serve as guide. The black mud and rich earth at Charles was a pleasant surprise to the travellers, who missed the tropics of Brazil. Here, too, they saw "mosses, ferns, lichens and parasitical plants." It was Lawson who told Darwin that the tortoises differed on each island, and that from the shape of any tortoise, Lawson could with certainty identify the island from which it came. This remark prompted Darwin to label the tortoises, as well as other specimens, as to the island on which they were found. Had he commingled the species, the all-important evidence of variation would have been lost in later classification of the finds. Even Dampier, as far back as 150 years before, had noticed four different species of tortoises on four separate islands.

Darwin spent six days on Charles Island, diligently collecting all the animals, plants, insects, and reptiles he could find, stating, "It will be interesting to find from future comparison to what district or centre of creation the organized beings of this archipelago must be attached."

At Isabela Island, the *Beagle* anchored in Bank's Cove in the northwestern section of the island. During the short stay here, Darwin did not see the pigmy penguins or flightless cormorants – both excellent examples for his theory of natural selection.

To Darwin, the "miserably sterile" islands of Isabela and Narborough were "great caldrons" from which the lava had poured "like pitch over the rim of a pot in which it had boiled." He visited a little crater lake in the center of which another crater formed a tiny islet.

The surgeon of the *Beagle*, Benjamin Bynoe, had camped with Darwin on the shore of James Island for a week while the *Beagle* left to get water. Here they busied themselves skinning and preserving bird and lizard specimens. Several Spaniards from Charles Island were here also, drying fish and tortoise meat. At a height of two thousand feet, about six miles inland, two men were living in a shack, employed in catching tortoises. Darwin stayed with them a while, dining on tortoise meat. Then he visited a salt lake where "the water is only three or four inches deep, and rests on a layer of beautifully crystallized salt." The *Beagle* returned with water, but it was not obtained from the parched islands. "We should have been distressed if an American whaler had not kindly given us three casks of water and made us a present of a bucket of onions," acknowledged Darwin.

The extreme tameness of the birds surprised Darwin, who caught them with his cap. Of land birds he collected twenty-five species, "all peculiar to the group and found nowhere else. To the eleven waders and water birds, he could have added flamingoes, which he did not see.

Darwin was impressed by "a most singular group of finches . . . of which . . . the most curious fact is the gradation in the size of the beaks." It was this drab group of finches which gave him the idea that species are mutable and subject to modification for different ends. The thirteen species he saw had the same common ancestry as shown by their similar plumage and body build, yet their beaks were shaped differently. Some had huge beaks for crushing kernels; other beaks were curved for probing into flowers; an elongated beak was suitable for probing into crevices for insects; there were beaks for splitting small twigs, for cracking open shells of crabs, or for pulling tails off lizards.

Darwin probably ran himself ragged; never was a collector more eager or avaricious. Captain Fitz-Roy, with patience and resignation, often smiled at the cargoes of apparent rubbish Darwin hauled aboard ship. "Of flowering plants there are 225, of which I was fortunate to bring home 193," Darwin complained. Out of these, 100 were new species, yet had an undoubted western American character. "This archipelago, though standing in the Pacific Ocean, is zoologically part of America," Darwin wrote. He drew up a chart listing the species of plants, which led him to summarize, "We have the truly wonderful fact that in James Island, of the thirty-eight Galapageian plants, or those found in no other part of the world, thirty are exclusively confined to this one island." He found the plant life of Isabela, Chatham, and Charles Islands to be similarly unique.

The tortoises differed significantly from island to island, not only in size but in other characteristics. Those of Hood had shells turned up in front like a Spanish saddle; those of James were rounder and blacker, and better tasting. It seemed as though each island, depending on height and location, harbored life peculiar to it, and prompted Darwin to remark, "I never dreamed that islands, fifty or sixty miles apart, and most of them in sight of each other, formed by precisely the same rocks, placed under a quite similar climate, rising to a nearly equal height, would have been differently tenanted.'' The conclusion he drew from this was that isolation and environment can effect a mutation in living species. This isolation is caused by the strong currents, which separate the southern islands from the northern. However, the most important factor to Darwin was the profound depth of the channels between the islands which ''render it highly unlikely that they were ever united.''

To Darwin, who had not visited Mexico or the Central American coast, there was enough similarity between the Galapagos and South America to cause him to write, ''It was most striking to be surrounded by new birds, new reptiles, new shells, new insects, new plants, and yet by innumerable trifling details of structure, and even by the tones of voice and plumage of the birds, to have the temperate plains of Patagonia, or the hot dry deserts of Northern Chile, vividly brought before my eyes.''

Perhaps the best summation he gave was that ''the Galapagos Archipelago should be called a group of satellites, physically similar, organically distinct, yet intimately related to each other, and all related in a marked though lesser degree to the great American continent.'' To Captain Fitz-Roy, the queer moonscapes and bizarre creatures led to the remark that the Encantadas are ''a fit shore for Pandemonium.'' In Milton's classic *Paradise Lost*, Pandaemonium was the capital of Hell.

The five short, busy weeks at the Galapagos enabled Darwin to pierce the mysteries of creation. Here in this archaic land, still belching smoke and fire, he found living fossils that belonged to another age, another time. Darwin's ''little world within itself'' haunted him. The differences from island to island, the modifications due to environmental factors, and the curious relationship with the mainland raised puzzling speculations in his mind. The fossils he had unearthed in South America, too, had similarities to living creatures. The only solution to the enigma was that species do change, not only in the Galapagos, but everywhere else.

The final conclusion he drew was so strange and disturbing that Darwin hesitated for years before publishing his doctrine that all living things, including man, ''have descended from some one primordial Form.''

Amblyrhyncus, the Swimmer

Millions of years ago, huge reptilian monsters swarmed over land and sea. Then suddenly, through some cataclysmic change, the dinosaurs and plesiosaurs vanished – almost.

In the ''lost and forgotten world'' of the Galapagos, however, are miniature ''dragons'' which retain a fearsome prehistoric aspect. Darwin said, ''It is eminently curious that these volcanic cinder heaps should have been the last refuge of the extinct iguanid Mesozoic reptiles.'' These remnants of the Age of Reptiles managed to adapt themselves to new conditions, and one marine species is found on at least twenty-three of the islands and islets of the Galapagos. "The species are not numerous," wrote Darwin, "but the number of individuals is extraordinarily great." Of these lizards, he noticed "there are two species, resembling each other in general form, one being terrestrial, the other aquatic."

The marine lizards, or sea iguanas (*Amblyrhyncus cristatus*), are very abundant on the rocky coasts of the larger islands. They do not live in the sea; they are called marine because they are the only species of lizard in the world which feeds solely on seaweed.

The amphibious *Amblyrhyncus* can hold his breath under water and is a powerful swimmer, yet prefers to live on the rocky shore and actually spends very little time in the water. When not basking in the sun, he spends his time munching on the sea algae which festoon the rocks and lie exposed on the beach at low tide. He never ventures inland, and stays within ten yards of the water's edge. Each iguana has his own little rock crevice or burrow.

The marine iguana returns from the cold sea to a well-defined territory on shore, where he can slowly restore the oxygen depleted from his body and raise his body temperature. In underwater tests in 1970, Jacques Cousteau learned that the iguana can live one hour without air and can dive to an amazing depth of ninety feet, a zone of immense pressure. His heartbeat slows from forty-five beats a minute to four or five beats underwater, and he can exist without a heartbeat for three minutes without apparent damage. The iguana has no gills and originally was not meant to be a diver. Cousteau believes that the marine iguana was a land animal that returned to the sea because of the scarcity of food on land.

There are many strange anomalies about *Amblyrhyncus*. At first sight, he presents a fierce and dreadful appearance: twenty clawing talons of equal length, horny spines from head to tip of tail, formidable sharp teeth in a short, broad head, and a body measuring as much as four feet overall. Darwin wrote, "It is a hideous-looking creature, of a dirty black colour, stupid and sluggish in its movements." George Banning called him a "reddish-black hippogriff with spiked crest, horny head, and a face as green as mildew . . . . So flashing red was his wide-open mouth that he might have been gargling fire."

However, beneath that savage exterior beats a gentle heart. Ambly does not bite or claw or lash his tail, and he is "much less dangerous than the big scarlet crabs that live with him," wrote Darwin. He does not attack his neighbors; he permits crabs and birds to walk over him, removing ticks from his scaly armor. Small iguanas nonchalantly walk over his head without his batting an iguanid eyelid. Even fighting males do not bite each other; they push their heads against each other like two billy goats, and the loser surrenders before he can be bitten. Eibl-Eibesfeldt gives a fascinating description of the chivalrous "dragons' joust," and the preliminary formalities and rules of the iguana duels, in his book *Galapagos*. When extremely frightened, the iguana will spurt twin jets of vapor from his nostrils, like any proper old-fashioned dragon should.

Another puzzling feature is the protective coloration which seems wholly unnecessary; it may not be for protection at all. The jet-black color of the young iguanas is a perfect camouflage against the black lava; yet, until the arrival of man, the iguana had no enemy on land except the Galapagos hawk. Even now, despite the pigs and rats destroying the eggs and young, the iguana is quite abundant on all islands except in the vicinity of the human settlements. The marine iguana is edible, and the skins, when cured, are made into belts, pouches, and other items for sale.

The hind feet are partially webbed between the third and fourth toes. This is another curious aberration, since the feet are not used for swimming. The legs are folded close to the body, streamlining the creature so that it is a superb swimmer, propelling itself with sidewise motions of the long tail. Large iguanas have been seen crossing wide stretches of water; however, only the older iguanas have less fear of sharks, possibly because of their more powerful swimming ability. They will occasionally go out to sea for the more plentiful seaweed on the bottom.

It was Darwin who first observed that a sea iguana, when frightened, will not enter the water. If thrown into the water, it will return like a living boomerang to the spot from whence it was thrown. Darwin reports, "As often as I threw it, it returned in the manner above described. Perhaps this singular piece of apparent stupidity may be accounted for by the circumstance, that this reptile has no enemy whatsoever on shore, whereas at sea it must often fall prey to the numerous sharks. Hence, urged by a fixed and hereditary instinct that the shore is its place of safety, whatever the emergency may be, it there takes refuge."

William Beebe caught an iguana and jerked him into the air, then loosed the noose and set him free. "He offered no resistance at being caught again and swung into space. Six times I repeated this, and if anything he was tamer after the rough treatment than before, in the face of a series of experiences which would have driven any ordinary creature insane with fright."

Between November to February, the female lays her annual two eggs in the sand, a little above high tide. The young hatch soon afterwards, depending on the amount of heat from the sun.

Early attempts to breed *Amblyrhyncus* in captivity resulted in failure. Unlike his cousin, the land iguana, the marine iguana (whom Banning called a "stubborn little non-resistant Pacifist Mahatma Gandhi hunger-striker") could not be kept alive in captivity even by force-feeding. However, in recent years, scientists learned how to retrain the iguana to accept a varied diet.

Melville was completely justified in calling the iguana "that strangest anomaly of outlandish nature."

Conolophus, the Cactus Eater

The land iguana, *Conolophus subcristatus*, is heavier and larger than his marine cousin. He cannot breathe under water and his toes are not webbed. He has perfect powers of diving and swimming, but never willingly enters the water.

Conolophus prefers to stay inland because he is a cactus eater; grass, herbs and anything green are acceptable, also. With his wide-angled jaws he clamps down on a cactus pad and chews off a large bite, which he swallows with almost no mastication. His stomach and intestines take care of the digestive process. With his claws, he does scrape off some of the larger thorns from the juicy cactus, but his soft reddish tongue seems unaffected by the remaining prickly spines. Occasionally the creature will climb into the low scrub trees for a change of diet to acacia leaves and berries.

In comparison with the sea iguana, *Conolophus* has a shorter, but more rounded, tail; no bony ridge on his back; a longer head; a wider and pointed snout; and is far less active. Lazy and torpid, *Conolophus* will slowly crawl out of his burrow only on sunny days, numbed by the chill of the night. His gait is awkward as his whole body moves from side to side at each step. He hugs the ground with his belly, and this characteristic reveals his primitive ancestry. The position of his legs – well out to the sides of his body – labels him an archaic leftover. The iguanas of the continent were, at one time, heavy and weaklegged, but, to escape their numerous enemies, they evolved into faster creatures with strong legs that lift them well off the ground for easier escape; the short-legged iguanas died off in the process of natural selection.

The land iguana lives in a deep hole dug with his huge claws. These cavern burrows are so numerous on some islands that hiking is difficult, because the earth gives way and the hiker plunges into a deep nest of lizards. Darwin wrote, "I cannot give a more forcible proof of their numbers, than by stating that when we were left on James Island, we could not for some time find a spot free from their burrows on which to pitch our single tent."

The land iguanas were found confined to the central part of the archipelago only on six islands: Isabela, James, Indefatigable, Barrington, Narborough, and South Seymour and also the Las Plazas Islets off the eastern coast of Indefatigable.

Darwin saw these terrestrial lizards only on Isabela and James, but he surmised correctly that each island had its own form. However, the difference seems to be only in the coloring; their habits are identical. Indefatigable has a species that is brick-red and golden, like an antique tapestry with a brocade of old gold. Barrington has a rare pale yellow species called

Conolophus pallidus. Narborough and Seymour have yellow-crested types. The other islands have a species that is brownish-red above and yellowish-orange beneath. Most are a yard long and weigh about ten to fifteen pounds.

If improperly handled, this miniature monster will bite and hang on with a tenacious grip like that of a bulldog. Correctly handled, they are harmless and make good pets. Iguana tail is highly esteemed as a food, being considered a cross between chicken and fish by those "whose stomachs soar above all prejudices," says Darwin. The elongated oval eggs are eaten by Ecuadorian settlers.

Conolophus will face his pursuer with "blood in his eye." His eyes actually do turn from light grey to blood red. When cornered, he will puff up, hiss and spit, and put up a big bluff, but prefers flight to fight. He tolerates finches hopping on his back, and is not as tough as he pretends to be.

The female lays about seventeen eggs in a burrow, but the young are rarely seen after they hatch, possibly to keep out of sight of the hawks.

The land iguana will live in captivity. When some species were placed aboard the *Velero III* in 1933, at first they galloped blindly in hysterical panic. Soon they became accustomed to their surroundings, and stoically accepted their ultimate destiny in a zoological park, where they exchanged their cactus menu for such delicacies as lettuce and bananas.

Isla Genovesa (Tower)

A mere speck in the watery vastness which surrounds it, Tower Island is roughly circular with a diameter of three miles and a huge crater lake toward its center. It is 200 feet high with steep cliffs rising sheer out of the ocean. Of these aged rocks, scarred and seamed, Beebe had written, "So silent, so hard, so immutable were these, that no continent seemed more permanent than this tiny island in midsea. Surely, when the world first cleared its face, these eternal iron cinders were here – cold, motionless, black as night, . . . dead cinders of the world's end."

There was a large crater at the southern end, but the incessant pounding of the surf had crumbled one-fifth of the southern rim. The ocean waters rushed or seeped through the jagged gap to fill the deep pit, forming a circular bay about one-and-a-half miles wide with a narrow entrance. In 1923, William Beebe was surprised to find this bay, almost hidden from view, "There seemed but one name for such a find as this, so then and there I called it Darwin Bay." This name appears on all charts now, but Beebe was not the first to discover the bay. Others had been here before him: explorer-naturalist Rollo Beck visited the bay in 1902 and 1906.

The entrance to Bahia de Darwin is encumbered by reefs only three-quarters to two-and-three-quarters fathoms below the water surface. Actually, this is the submerged, broken rim, and care must be exercised when entering the bay. The black reefs can be seen in bright sunlight; it is dangerous to enter in late afternoon when the water is dark. There are depths of 100 fathoms in the center of the bay; only one northern spot is shoal.

In April of 1962 the schooner *Marpatcha* dropped anchor in about thirty fathoms of water near the head of the bay, facing the rock walls on which were printed names of ships: *Ara*, 1928; *Director*, 1935; *Carola*, 1941; *Utopia*, 1957; *Norseman*, 1940; *Observer* (Krieger Expedition), 1953; *Goodwill*, 1957; *Gracious*, 1958; *Dubloon*, 1958; Captain Hancock's *Velero III*, 1932; *Collegiate Rebel*, 1960. The last-named vessel had been to the Galapagos several times before when Captain Otterman owned her under the name of *Gloria Dalton*. There were many other names, some very old and illegible, others very recent.

Having rowed ashore, an exploring party soon crunched up the white coral beach, revelling in the splintery, grating noise as they kicked up coral chunks; coral is rare in the Galapagos, except here and on Isla Isabela.

On every bush was a bird; nests littered the ground. Unafraid, the birds allowed the human intruders to approach and touch them. A baby pelican, fuzzy and all alone, screeched away. Another baby frigate bird bravely hissed from between mama's legs as mama nonchalantly ignored the visitors. Bluefooted boobies (bobo is the Spanish word for clown) waddled around.

Nature really ran wild with her paintbrushes as she colored the birds here on Genovesa: blue beaks, pink beaks, red eyes, orange feet, blue feet, pink feet, and black, gray, white, and brown feathers. Tropical reds and greens were absent in the plumage. The bright red balloons of the adult frigates were so large as to almost conceal the entire body, and were horribly grotesque. These birds have a wingspread of about six feet and are called man-o'-war birds because they attack other birds, especially boobies, and force them to drop their fish catch in flight.

A strange incident occurred. An ancient and wrinkled frigate bird, startled at the visitors' approach, stood erect, flapped his wings, then grew limp and died, right before their eyes. He was old, and died a natural death. Such deaths seem common at Darwin Bay; there were many carcasses of old birds, recently deceased, lying undisturbed. They have no natural enemies here, except starvation; we saw no evidence of wild dogs, goats, pigs, cats, or other animals which prey on the birds or their eggs. Beebe said this was not a normal country – no caterpillars, no bees, no flies, only one wingless type of beetle, and only a few mosquitos. There are ants, grasshoppers, and crickets, though.

Bird sounds are incessant: whistles, croaks, screams, honks, pleasant notes, and chirps. Melville called it a "demoniac din," and it takes a while for one to get accustomed to the racket. The air is usually filled with gulls, boobies, petrels, bosun birds, and terns, besides the frigate bird which seemed to be in the majority here.

Going inland over a gradual slope, one arrives suddenly at the crater lake which Beebe named Arcturus – a circular hole about a half mile across, olive-green in color at the shallow part, darker green in the center. White guano, not sand, rims the salt water, and there is a fringe of mangroves beyond the narrow strip of white beach. Beebe said the salty water is extremely buoyant, and the muddy shore has an overpowering smell of rotting matter, vegetable and animal. Only a dyed-in-the-wool naturalist like Beebe would venture into it.

The cove itself is astonishingly beautiful, its emerald green water and white beach contrasting sharply with the jutting black reefs on either side. Slate-colored iguanas bask in the sunshine and allow themselves to be caught with a looped stick. Their firm and solid bodies are dry, not slimy. Fiery red and orange crabs scurry about; their only mortal enemy is the bittern, a pale-blue shore bird with a short, strong beak.

The white beach was clear of debris, perhaps because of the sheltered nature of the cove. Along the foot of the cliffs around the bay, Beebe had reported seeing "barrels, boards, carved wooden posts, wicker baskets, pieces of chests, cabin doors and companion ladders – wreckage of old and forgotten ships."

Northern Islands

The islands known as Genovesa, Marchena, Pinta, Wenman, and Culpepper are the five islands in the archipelago which lie north of the equator. Tower (Genovesa) has been described, and is the easternmost of the five. Culpepper (Isla Darwin) is the most northerly of the group and is about twenty miles from Wenman (Isla Wolf). Known to the Spanish as "Los Dos Hermanos," these two islands are about eighty miles from the main body of the archipelago. Geologist Shumway reported in 1963:

> Darwin Island and Wolf Island are isolated from the Galapagos platform by about 60 sea-miles of water deeper than 1,200 fathoms; in this respect they are not part of the Galapagos group.

Culpepper is about a mile in diameter, 550 feet high, and has sheer cliffs which rise vertically to 400 feet from the sea. The first human beings known to set foot on top of the island were members of an expedition which arrived by helicopter in January of 1964. They found a large concentration of sea birds: boobies, frigate-birds, noddies, fork-tail gulls, shearwaters, white tropic birds, and petrels. The island also happens to be the only nesting place in the Galapagos for the sooty tern. Finches are plentiful.

The island supports only a dozen species of plants; small flies and beetles are abundant. There are no butterflies, no land mammals, no snakes, no land iguanas. Tiny mockingbirds feed on the plentiful supply of twelve-inch long centipedes.

Wenman (Isla Wolf) is over a mile long, a half-mile wide, 830 feet high, and has several smaller islets adjoining it. It is seldom visited because of the dangerous anchorages and 20-foot swells. Explorers who arrived by helicopter found the island covered by scrub vegetation such as low croton bushes and opuntia cacti. The scalesias (tree-sunflowers) also grow here as small shrubs. All vegetation is covered with orange, green, gray, or white lichens.

Wenman boasts of several queer inhabitants. A peculiar order of insects – embiids – was discovered for the first time in the Galapagos by David Cavagnaro. Recently, Dr. Bowman reported on the blood-eating habits of some nasty little finches that feed on the blood of boobies, solely on this particular island. There are no owls or hawks here to molest the finches. The isolation of this small island, and the small variation in its finches, is helpful in the study of evolutionary patterns.

Marchena (Bindloe), ten miles at its widest point, has a central peak 1,160 feet high. Utterly barren and desolate, and almost completely covered by ash-gray lava flows, it is surrounded by extremely deep water abounding in a species of rock-cod. The island's only claim to fame is the discovery of two mummified bodies on the beach in late 1934.

Isla Pinta (Abingdon) is northwest of Marchena and twice as high, but only half as large in land area. One of its two high peaks reaches 2,500 feet into the clouds, and thus attracts moisture which supports life in the dense growth of the highlands. At the 800-foot elevation thrive rich grass, large cacti, and leafy trees covered with orchilla moss.

Finches, gulls, and pelicans abound here; there are no rats, pigs, or dogs, but goats are common to the southern side. Dr. Bowman reports that the rare Abingdon tortoise is now extinct. Jagged craters on the northern end of Pinta smouldered in 1936.

Scientific Expeditions

With the decline of the whaling industry during the latter part of the nineteenth century, the Galapagos lost their importance as a whaling station. However, the lonely isles were not entirely forgotten by the world. Ships other than whalers had been making brief stops, mostly out of curiosity, and continued to come in ever-increasing numbers.

In 1841, the French frigate *Venus*, under Du Petit Thouars, stopped here on her cruise around the world. In the same year, Sir Edward Belcher, of the H.M.S. *Sulphur*, added to the scarce literature about the islands. In 1852, the first Norwegian warship ever to cruise the world, *Eugenie*, visited the archipelago; Professor Anderson, a botanist on board, wrote a paper on the Galapagos flora.

During the California gold rush, some of the gold seekers sailed in huge clipper ships around the tip of South America. A few of these fast passenger ships put in at the Galapagos for repairs or provisions. In August of 1849, Joseph Kendall aboard the clipper *Canton* wrote of Chatham, "The greater part of the island is utterly scorched by the sun . . . . It is all of volcanic matter, like burnt black cinders, which rattle like a bell at every step one takes."

While at the islands, the *Canton's* passengers enjoyed turtle soup and tortoise steaks three times a day. When the craft set sail, her decks were cluttered with sixty giant tortoises destined for the steak pan. Two other passengers, but of the two-legged variety, had been picked up after being stranded in the Galapagos for nine months. The Yankee seamen had deserted a New Bedford whaler and managed to survive in these wastelands. None the worse for wear after their adventure, they happily boarded the *Canton* for San Francisco.

After Darwin's *On the Origin of Species* was published in 1859, the Galapagos became a showplace of evolution. Here was found the visual demonstration of Darwin's theory, and the islands became a major scientific attraction. The 3,000 square miles of the Encantadas were to be visited by more scientists than any other area of comparable size in the world. Indeed, as Von Hagen wrote, "The H.M.S. *Beagle* has given the Galapagos scientific immortality."

In 1872, the United States Coast Guard steamer *Hassler* dropped anchor in the Galapagos while conducting scientific investigations in nearby waters. Aboard was Louis Agassiz, the famous naturalist and geologist who had been an uncompromising opponent of evolution. Darwin hoped that this trip would give Agassiz the same insights which Darwin obtained in 1835. Conceding that each species was not created independently, Agassiz was still puzzled as to how transmutation could have occurred in what he termed the "recent" geological occurrence of the islands. Of course, at that time it was not known that dominant traits could change populations in a relatively short period of time, and very little was known about mutation. Agassiz left the islands impressed by the "startling array of facts," but the die-hard skeptic was unconvinced. His visit coincided with a severe drought in the Galapagos and Agassiz reported 1,200 head of cattle dead on Charles Island.

In 1875, the German geologist Theodor Wolf was retained by the Ecuadorian government to make a geological survey of the islands. Dr. Wolf made a serviceable map of the islands and returned in 1878 for further work. The small northern islet of Wenman was renamed "Isla Wolf" to honor this scientist. Culpepper, too, was rechristened "Isla Darwin."

The island of Abingdon was visited by the English warship *Petrel* in 1876. Commander Cockson found an unusual type of tortoise, which he sent to England for identification and comparison with other specimens. The yellow-headed tortoise was an unusual saddle-backed type with a curious flange over the neck of the shell. It had a close resemblance to a species on the northern end of Isabela, which is separated from Abingdon by extreme depths of 1,600 fathoms. The two islands also share a few plants in common, even though the possibility of a land connection in the past is remote.

The United States Fisheries steamer *Albatross* came to the Encantadas in 1888 under the leadership of Alexander Agassiz, the marine zoologist and specialist in marine oceanography and son of Louis Agassiz. The younger Agassiz had been in the Galapagos before, on the *Hassler*, and was amplifying knowledge learned in the first trip. The *Albatross* was exploring the waters of the Pacific from Panama to the Galapagos.

Soundings were taken between the Galapagos and South America, proving there had not been any connection between the islands and the continent. However, no clear or conclusive evidence was found as to the connection between the Galapagos and Central America.

Eighteen tortoises were taken alive for the National Museum in Washington, D.C. Unfortunately, all of them died in the cold climate. The *Albatross* returned to the Galapagos in 1891, seeking information to be used in the fur seal arbitration meeting to be held in Paris. A distinguished member on board was Charles Haskins Townsend, who later was to publish some interesting studies regarding the extinction of Galapagoan tortoises.

When the schooner *Lila and Mattie* arrived in August of 1897, the members of the Webster-Harris Expedition witnessed an eruption on James Island when a crater opened on the southeastern side of the island.

In 1902, the schooner *Mary Sachs* brought a party of scientists sponsored by the Honorable Walter Rothschild. Fifty tortoises were brought to San Francisco, then shipped to London; the heaviest in the group weighed 593 pounds. A member of this expedition, Rollo H. Beck, returned to the Galapagos in 1905 as master of the eighty-five-foot schooner *Academy*. The vessel had been purchased by the California Academy of Sciences, and its crew consisted of young men who later became professional scientists: E. W. Gifford, Joseph R. Slevin, and F. X. Williams. They contributed much to the scientific literature on the Galapagos Islands.

The Academy left San Francisco in June of 1905 and remained twelve months in the Galapagos, where 266 tortoises were rounded up by the nine scientists on board. Academy Bay on Santa Cruz Island was named after the schooner.

Beck was quite dismayed at the slaughter of tortoises on Isabela Island. He had spent two weeks at the ranch of Señor Gil, collecting and studying the tortoises. The creatures were very abundant in the higher regions, despite the fact that they were being slaughtered in wholesale numbers for their oil, which sold for nine cents (American) per pound. Beck saw 400 gallons in casks being loaded onto a ship, while 800 more were stored on the beach. With each tortoise yielding from 1 to 3 gallons of oil, these casks represented at least 500 animals slain. In addition, Beck saw many skeletons of tortoises killed by wild dogs; most of these tortoises were female, being the smallest and easiest to attack.

The flightless cormorant was at last discovered in 1907.

Several expeditions noticed the tool-using finches. E. W. Gifford watched a finch on Isabela Island feeding in a dead tree. He wrote, "It was apparently searching for insects, for it inspected every hole carefully. Finally, it found one too deep for its bill. It then flew to a neighboring tree and broke off a small twig, about a half-inch in length. Returning to the hole, the bird inserted the little stick as a probe, holding it lengthwise in its bill. It proceeded to examine other holes by the same method. Mr. Beck and Mr. King said they noticed similar instances elsewhere."

In this phantasmagorical land where wild creatures act tame, and domesticated creatures run wild, where sea lions climb mangrove trees and miniature dragons feed on cactus and seaweed, and where Antarctic penguins paddle around on the Equator, the sight of twig-using birds is not surprising after all.

9

MOSTLY CHATHAM ISLAND

∽∽∽∽∽∽∽∽∽∽∽

Chatham Island

The Galapagos island closest to the South American mainland, only 580 miles away, is Chatham. Its official name of San Cristobal is seldom used in older literature.

The singular blessing bestowed upon this fortunate island is an abundant and dependable supply of fresh water. An extinct volcanic crater acts as a natural reservoir, and on the southern side of the island, facing the trade winds, is a fifty-foot waterfall which pours the precious commodity into the sea. This is at Freshwater Bay, which can only be reached with great peril due to the heavy surf that batters ceaselessly against the dead volcano.

Elliptical in shape, about twenty-five miles long and eight miles wide, Chatham has a central hump that is 2,490 feet high. The pirates called it Mount Morgan, but its present name is San Joaquin. Actually, Chatham is a series of craters upon whose slopes and valleys is an undulating country with patches of sugar cane, coffee bushes, lime and orange trees, grazing cattle, and wild horses. The soil is a rich red loam bathed by the heavy garua (mist), and is almost stoneless. During a heavy rain, it turns into soft mud.

This fertile country supports the small village of Progreso, named in a moment of sheer recklessness or optimism, on a plateau which is a five-mile hike, or one-hour's ride on horseback, from the single port on the island.

Puerto Chico (later renamed Baquerizo Moreno) is located at Wreck Bay on the southwestern end of Chatham. The bay lies between two recognizable landmarks, Dalrymple Rock (named after a British naturalist) and Wreck Point. The entrance channel is only 300 yards wide, with Lido Point to port and the dangerous submerged Schiavoni reef to starboard. Huge rollers break upon the reef with thunderous roars. The inner bay is quiet and has a good anchor-holding ground of firm white sand. About a half mile inland is a lagoon which swarms with ducks.

For many years, the one and only lighthouse in the Galapagos archipelago was located here in the port at the head of the bay; it was an oil lamp atop a steel pole about twenty-five feet high, and usually was lighted only when the locally-owned trade schooner was due to arrive.

A prominent feature north of the midpoint of Chatham is Kicker Rock, a gray wedge which rises 486 feet straight up from the sea. Its walls are absolutely vertical, and the summit is crowned with grass. It derives its name from its appearance, which resembles a shoe or ankle-length boot, and contains in its center a deep channel about twenty-five feet wide. The Spanish call it "Leon Dormiente," because it also has the shape of a sleeping lion.

The Cobos Empire

A handful of settlers lived on Chatham as far back as 1850 when General Mena, later killed by the pirate Briones, had been conducting agricultural experiments. Some land was cleared, and orchilla moss was gathered for sale to France for dye manufacture. In 1870, there were about fifty settlers.

After the murder of Señor Valdizian on Charles Island, 100 penal colonists were transferred to Chatham. In 1880, Señor Manuel J. Cobos started a sugar cane plantation, then planted coffee and imported some cattle. He needed cheap labor, and the Ecuadorian government very obligingly supplied him with convicts promptly forgotten. Many overstayed their sentences; once at Chatham there was little hope of freedom.

Cobos ruled his 300 wretched prisoners with a brutal hand. With the help of a governor and a small military detachment, Chatham was a veritable Devil's Island, seldom visited by anyone except the Cobos trading schooner.

Convict labor constructed a road of stones banked with red earth, about five miles long to the open savannah at a 1,500-foot elevation. Here a sugar refinery was built, with a corrugated iron roof, to house the machinery brought from Glasgow, Scotland. The huge boiler was lowered from a steamship into the bay and floated to shore, pulled with shore lines. A team of sixty oxen, plus manpower, dragged it from the beach to firm land and up to the factory, requiring one full month of arduous labor.

The plantation brought a fortune to Cobos. He made his own money – purported to be either copper or rubber coins of oval shape – and ruled like a despotic potentate over his prisoners. He appointed a "priest" to perform marriage ceremonies. Women of questionable morals had been imported from the mainland, and these were "married" to as many as seven husbands. Rumors of cruelty drifted to the mainland, but the government was not interested in checking on the fate of the unfortunate convicts.

For minor infractions, the prisoners received extreme punishments. Six men were flogged to death, five were shot by the firing squad, some were shoved into caves to be eaten by rats, and four others were marooned on remote islands. Of these, three perished of thirst, but one escaped. Unable to endure the desperate situation any longer, the prisoners revolted in 1904. The unarmed men persuaded the plantation manager, crazed by fear, to kill Cobos.

In an unguarded moment while eating lunch, Cobos laid aside his habitual revolver, only to be shot. Wounded slightly, he seized his gun and jumped over a fence, breaking his leg. As the mob slashed away with machetes, he staged a desperate battle, killing an incredible number before falling on the lava "black as his own heart." His henchman, the governor, was slain also.

Cobos had a small sloop hidden in another part of the island. The rebels found it and christened it the *Liberty*, then sailed to Colombia. The seventy-seven men and eight women on board were detained by Colombian authorities, as there were no ship's papers. Slowly, their story was extracted from them. Returned to Ecuador, they brought terrible charges against Cobos during their trial, and were set free after an investigation. The gunboat *Cotopaxi* was sent to Chatham, and found conditions worse than had been expected. A party set out immediately to search for a man marooned three years before at Indefatigable.

Camilo Casanova had been left on the beach with a little water, a small knife, a machete, a few matches, and several pieces of clothing. He lived on raw turtles and iguanas, and drank their blood. After several attempts into the impenetrable interior to search for water, he returned to the beach and allayed his thirst by chewing cactus pads. Twice he begged English sailors to remove him from the island, but they refused, leaving him biscuits, matches, and cigarettes. Their seemingly heartless refusal was explained later, when the *Cotopaxi* found a signboard on the other side of the island, stating in English and Spanish: "Do not take this man away. He is twenty times a criminal." Casanova was found alive, and removed from the island.

Another prisoner, Raimundo Guardado, was not so lucky. His skeleton was found on James Island in 1897 by a scientific expedition from the schooner *Lila and Mattie*. At that time, his finders considered his remains as that of a ship-wrecked sailor, unaware that he had been marooned by Cobos.

The evil spirit of Manuel J. Cobos was said to abide in his stone dwelling on a high rocky point. The stone hacienda had gates of ironwork at each door, and was strongly built like a fort. No peon dared enter the ruins. Years later, the building was torn down and rebuilt by his son.

For many years, Cobos' black shade also haunted the decrepit old trading schooner which he named after himself.

Schooner *Manuel J. Cobos*

There is a great deal of mystery attached to the origin of the squat 80-foot schooner which the villain Cobos employed between Chatham and Guayaquil. Some Ecuadorians say it was a pirate ship. Others contend it had crossed the Pacific bringing a human cargo of Chinese coolies to labor and die in the guano islands off the coast of South America. It may have carried some of the loathsome fertilizer around the Horn.

At any rate, Señor Cobos acquired the vessel just about the time that the guano deposits were exhausted. From about 1880, it began to make irregular trips to and from Chatham carrying assorted cargoes of passengers, cattle, dried fish, and other produce. Sometimes it left Guayaquil and then returned a few days later unable to locate the islands; the bewitched currents of the Encantadas were at work. Murderers and thieves, bound for the penal colony at Chatham, lounged on her decks. Badly prepared cowhide, smelly dried fish, nauseous blocks of sulphur, and fly-covered oranges and bananas often filled her holds on the return trip to the mainland.

Ecuador had an almost non-existent navy in the early years of the twentieth century, and the *Manuel J. Cobos* served as the only link to the Galapagos, carrying supplies and what little mail there was. The only residents were at Chatham or at the cattle ranch at Isabela. From Isabela it carried not only cattle and hides, but also tortoise oil which was still being obtained in large amounts on the largest islands.

After the death of the elder Cobos in 1904 at the hands of the convicts, Ecuador gave the entire island of Chatham to the three heirs: a young son named Manuel Augusto Cobos, a daughter, and her husband, Señor Alvarado. The prisoners became free men and Chatham was no longer a penal colony. Many of the descendants of the former convicts continued to live at Progreso. Life on the mainland did not have much more to offer.

Young Manuel Cobos had spent most of his boyhood in Europe, and was educated in Paris. After four years of gay life in that city, he marooned himself at Chatham, calling it his purgatory. Mindful of his father's tragic death, Manuel was armed to the teeth at all times, even when entertaining guests in the privacy of his home. He carried a sheathed dagger in the top of his riding boot and wore a revolver strapped to his waist. The peons carried razor-sharp machetes, but their relations with the new heir were friendly.

While Manuel managed the huge plantation, his brother-in-law, Alvarado, sold the produce in Ecuador. Alvarado maintained a home in Guayaquil and travelled back and forth every few months on the indestructible schooner.

Shortly after the death of the elder Cobos, a tragedy befell another ship, not quite as fortunate as the schooner *Cobos*.

The Bark *Alexandra*

There are two versions of the tale of the *Alexandra*. One was told to William Beebe by a New York taxi driver in 1923, a Dane named Christiansen who had been a nineteen-year-old able seaman on the *Alexandra* in 1906. The other version is the story recorded in the ship's log by Captain Petersen and published in Norway in 1915.

The three-masted Norwegian bark *Alexandra* had left Newcastle, England, with goods for Australia and a cargo of coal for Panama. There were twenty men on board: Captain Emil Petersen, a First Mate, Second Mate, cook, and sixteen seamen, two of whom were Americans. Having rounded South Africa, they proceeded eastward and left New South Wales on November 6, 1906. At the beginning of March, they sighted Galera Point near Guayaquil, but the curse of the equatorial doldrums struck.

The ship lay becalmed for weeks; it began to drift westward, trapped in the strong Humboldt Current. Day after day, week after week, they drifted in a windless calm. Food was running short, even though the *Alexandra* had originally carried enough food to last 140 days for what should have been a 70-day journey.

Water was rationed; the water condenser sprang a leak and its bottom fell out. The crew was on the verge of mutiny. Finally, the tall peaks of Isabela Island were sighted – but only for a day. The next morning, Isabela was out of sight. However, the crew was anxious to abandon ship. Captain Petersen tried to dissuade them, hoping for a change of weather. He explained how foolish it would be to row against the strong current, which moved at a fast rate of thirty-five miles per day.

Nevertheless, the crew insisted on leaving the *Alexandra*. On May 8, 1907, Captain Petersen posted a note on the mainmast stating that the ship had been abandoned, and two whale boats of ten men each would attempt rowing to the Galapagos. All of the bark's running lights were lit; the Norwegian flag was hoisted, and the ship abandoned to her fate.

Each small boat had a small sail, a tank of twenty gallons of water, a compass, sextant, clothing, and food. The men rowed constantly, shifting every hour. After the third day of ceaseless rowing, the Captain sighted a peak of Isabela. A breeze started, sails were made fast, and the small boats sailed twenty-five miles and went ashore.

The utter desolation of the land staggered them: burned-out craters, fumeroles, parched lava clinkers, no vegetation, and not a drop of water. After resting awhile, the Captain decided to make a try for Charles Island, where he knew there was water and tortoises. The two whale boats put out to sea again. A heavy mist obscured the sun; they could not get accurate bearings, nor could they sight Charles Island. The Captain's boat lost sight of the First Mate's, never to meet again.

On May 20, 1907, the Captain and his crew of nine approached Santa Cruz (Indefatigable), and the current carried them to shore. Of all the islands in the Galapagos, they had landed on the one most cruel to cross; on it they would spend six terrible months.

Maddened by thirst, the men rushed ashore and clubbed several seals to death, drinking their blood which gushed from their slashed throats. A huge breaker dashed their anchored boat against the rocks, splintering it to matchsticks. A third calamity struck as some of the men ate some small yellow fruit, the "death apples" of the poisonous manchineel tree. They rolled on the ground with pain as their throats and tongues swelled, almost choking them. Next morning, the pain lessened, and more relief came upon finding some brackish water in a pool which rose and fell with the tide.

They subsisted on seal meat, sea turtle, iguanas, and pelican, all eaten raw. One of the crew, a German, drowned in a turtle lagoon near Tortuga Bay, and his bones were found three days later on the beach, nibbled clean of flesh by fish or sharks. The ship's log refers to him as Martin Schaefer; Christiansen remembered him as Herman Schlesinger. Christiansen also related that the Captain buried his money belt containing 600 pounds in English coin, as too heavy to carry.

Fashioning shoes from seal-skin, they kept on the move, hoping to find water. In a small cove they found the remains of a camp fire, footprints, and upturned rocks, probably the camp of the California Academy of Science Expedition which had been there a year before in October, 1906. There were yellowed magazines dated 1894, empty whiskey bottles, two pairs of ladies' slippers, and a man's shirt, all in rotted condition. By this time the nine men were silent; the skipper brooded over the loss of his ship. There was little hope of rescue.

Christiansen relates that an American died of dysentery and was buried in the sand. Captain Petersen's log states that the man had been in a stupor and refused to leave Tortuga Bay with the others. Despite their entreaties, he absolutely would not move. They left him, bearded and tattered, staring into the empty air, with starvation and death facing him in the utter loneliness.

After tortuous hikes over jagged lava, they finally reached Academy Bay at the southern end of the island. This seemed like Paradise, with water, green grass, and trees. Also, they found some discarded matches, which allowed them to cook their food. The smoke of their fire was seen by the sloop *Isadora Jacinta*, of Guayaquil; its German captain had been searching for the luckless crew of the *Alexandra*. The second whale boat containing the First Mate and his crew had reached Chatham safely, and had reported the loss of the captain and the ship.

The bark *Alexandra* came to a wretched and lonesome end on the rocks of the southern end of Isabela, at Iguana Cove, her bow down, stern up, and flag flying.

The German captain and the sloop had been hired by a relative of Captain Petersen to search for the survivors, and he had gone to several islands before seeing the smoke on Santa Cruz. Christiansen said the survivors were taken to Guayaquil, received full pay, and were shipped to Panama aboard a cattleboat. Christiansen got a job dredging the Panama Canal, caught fever, and returned to the United States, where he later became a taxi driver in New York City.

The unfortunate man who remained at Tortuga Bay perished, and his bones were found in 1936 by naturalist Von Hagen. A copy of Captain Petersen's log was in the possession of a settler at Academy Bay, the Icelander Finsen, who translated it from Norwegian to English for the young naturalist. The story then appeared in Von Hagen's book *Ecuador the Unknown*. The taxi driver's version appeared earlier in Beebe's *Galapagos, World's End*.

Progreso and Puerto Chico

War had not touched the Encantadas, and life continued as monotonously as ever. Perhaps the only real excitement during the First World War was the loss of the Australian steamer *Carawa* on the treacherous submerged Schiavoni reef at Wreck Bay. The masts of the wreck projected as a visible warning for many years. They are gone now, and the reef is unmarked, a peril to all ships.

Meanwhile, young Cobos lorded it over his little domain without much trouble. His entire police force consisted of one man who held the office of "Chief of Police." The peons were orderly; they were paid small wages with which they bought necessities from the Cobos store. Once in a while the schooner was delayed and the islanders ran short of staples like rice, flour, and beans, but subsisted well on the ample produce of the plantations and orchards. Meat and fowl were plentiful.

Wreck Bay always was the port of entry to the Galapagos Islands. However, there was nothing here to attract freighters or liners, and the only craft visiting there were small American and British yachts sailing from Panama to the South Seas. Ordinary travellers without a handy yacht had to go by way of Guayaquil, where sometimes they waited over a month for the dilapidated *Manuel J. Cobos*. It is through the writings of the yachtsmen that we learn much of the local news concerning the islands and their inhabitants.

In 1919, Ralph Stock left the Devonshire Hills of England in his 47-foot *Dream Ship*, a Norwegian-built lifeboat. With his sister and a friend, he was realizing a lifelong ambition to sail to the South Seas in his own ship. Three weeks out of Panama, they arrived at the rickety pier in Puerto Chico just in time to celebrate New Year's Eve with young Manuel Cobos at his hacienda.

Up in the hills, Stock was amazed at the fertile fields. Only a few hundred acres were under cultivation by the 200 farm hands, while 3,500 head of cattle grazed in the immense range. Dogs, chickens, and children were everywhere at Progreso, and all seemed quite content and happy. A few of the islanders were curious concerning "rumors" of a war in Europe; they were unaware that the Armistice had been signed a year before. The peons couldn't care less.

The only water available for replenishing the tanks of the *Dream Ship* was "a doubtful-looking fluid," 300 gallons of which was transferred from the beach reservoir to the ship in kerosene tins. Weeks later, the tanks were transformed into aquariums of "energetic animalculae." While taking on water, a conference was held to decide whether the *Dream Ship* should remain a while longer in the Galapagos to become a treasure ship. Intrigued by stories of pirate treasure, Ralph Stock was almost tempted to stay, but sailed away, leaving a disappointed old man on the beach waiting for a ship to accept his offer of being guide to the treasure.

Mr. Johnson of London

No history of desert islands would be complete without the usual tales of buried treasure, and the Galapagos have a goodly share. The legend that Incas buried gold here, to hide it from the clutches of Pizarro, is highly improbable. It is possible, though, that the pirates who came here to divide their spoils may have buried part of their loot in isolated spots.

It is reported that two caches of treasure, consisting of pieces of eight and silver ingots, were found. One cache enabled the finder to build a handsome hotel in Ecuador; the second furnished its discoverer the means to drink himself to death. In 1923, Beebe reported, "A chest with more than 300,000 dollars worth of gold was buried, and less than a score of years ago was salvaged from one of the cliffs of Tower." Whether this find was one of the two mentioned above is unknown.

When Ralph Stock came to Chatham, he met an old hollow-cheeked man who lived in a split-bamboo shack behind the lighthouse. The patriarch always introduced himself with the words, "I'm Johnson, of London," and was seventy-one years old. He had spent over fifty years in the Galapagos, and had almost all that a man could desire: sunlight, freedom, a house, and an Ecuadorian wife who could cook. His remaining wish was to procure a boat and an honest partner to help him unearth some treasure buried on Isabela Island.

Born in London in 1848, Johnson ran away to sea about 1865, and two years later jumped ship at the Galapagos where he had remained ever since. He had worked as carpenter, trader, skipper of a schooner, and now was in charge of the lighthouse. He recalled how smugglers and pirates came to the Galapagos to hide boatloads of money in silver and gold. He knew the exact spot on Isabela where treasure was buried, and in fact, had once gone there to get it. When he arrived near the treasure, he saw a hairy creature guarding it, and shot it through the heart, mistaking it for a goat. Instead, it was a crazed madman, the owner of the cache. Horrified at his deed of manslaughter, Johnson fled from the island upon which he could no longer endure to stay, especially at night.

Years later, he built a small boat, but wrecked it on a reef during an attempt to sail it to Isabela. While building another boat, he broke his rib while steaming a heavy plank of oak. The injury, coupled with the fact that he despaired of finding a partner who would not murder him after the treasure was revealed, discouraged him from completing the boat. Ralph Stock would have accompanied the old man, but his crew dissuaded him from going because of unfavorable weather conditions and the risk of losing their *Dream Ship*.

In 1923, Johnson was still very much alive, but very deaf, and guided Beebe in the *Noma* to obtain water at Freshwater Bay. He died a few years later, and his widow was reputed to have known the secret location of the treasure. The mestizo widow faithfully tended Johnson's grave on the beach. Once in a while she produced a grimy bank note for odd purchases; neighbors assumed she had a hidden hoard stashed away. Some ghoulish peons were eagerly awaiting her death, hoping to ransack her miserable hut. They had a long wait. She died in 1937, reputedly having imparted her secret to one Goya Rico.

The *Amaryllis*

In September of 1920, another Englishman left England in a sixty-two-foot yawl-rigged yacht, on what ended as a successful journey encircling the globe, covering a distance of 31,000 miles. George Muhlhauser, a navigating officer during World War I, sailed the *Amaryllis* to the West Indies where he hired a mulatto boy and a San Blas Indian as crew. The three proceeded to Panama and ran into a snag at the Ecuadorian consul's office.

It seems that Ralph Stock had published an account of the high probability of locating treasure in the Galapagos, and the consul thought Mulhlhauser was on a treasure hunt. Fearing that the archipelago would become another Cocos Island, with people digging and dynamiting all over the place, the consul was suspicious of all small foreign vessels wishing to stop there. After much argument, the consul finally cleared the ship's papers, reluctantly convinced that the *Amaryllis* would stop only for water and had no aspirations for Spanish gold.

The *Amaryllis* did not attempt to enter Wreck Bay at night because of the hazardous reef. Even during the day, tremendous rollers five or six feet high came crashing on the white beach, especially between July and November. These rollers did not stop the *Amaryllis*, and she arrived safely at the wooden pier. Young Cobos and his bookkeeper came aboard and invited the crew to visit the hacienda at Progreso.

George Muhlhauser was not impressed with the village. He described the awful squalor: miserable huts of assorted materials like boards, corrugated iron, and thatch; filthy ground floors swarming with fowl and dogs; heaps of rubbish and empty bottles lying everywhere. He was even less impressed by the water available for his ship. It was stored in a dirty pit; occasionally a horse or cow would stir it up. It had the color of mud or coffee and seemed quite undrinkable. Nevertheless, they filled their tanks, adding large amounts of chloride of lime to kill the bacteria. Fortunately, their passage to the South Seas was swift, and very little of the water was used. The Encantadas never did have much of a reputation as a watering place.

10

OBSERVERS AND OBSERVATIONS

◦◦◦◦◦◦◦◦◦◦◦◦◦◦

William Beebe

When young Charles Darwin visited the Galapagos in 1835, he was limited in many ways. Lack of auxiliary power prevented him from visiting the whole archipelago; in five weeks he stopped at only six of the islands. He was the only naturalist on board, and the best he could do was to collect everything possible, to be analyzed and classified later by experts at home. Nevertheless, his work and deductions, which had such a tremendous impact on human thought, probably will never be equalled.

Darwin would have envied the wonderful preparations for the Harrison Williams Galapagos Expedition of 1923. The luxurious 250-foot yacht *Noma* left New York for a 9,000 mile round-trip voyage to the Galapagos. Under the generous sponsorship of Harrison Williams, and under the direction of William Beebe of the New York Zoological Society, the *Noma* carried twelve scientific technicians who were to record on paper and film as much as they could of important data, and to preserve, alive and dead, the specimens remarkable for their variety and rarity. A crew of forty-four sailors and stokers handled the ship.

The *Noma* steamed to the northwest corner of the huge unexplored island known as Indefatigable. After dropping anchor at Conway Bay, the scientists scrambled ashore to collect sea shells, birds and their eggs and nests, lava, plants, insects, and lizards. The sharp lava cut their shoes; thorns and spines left bloody fingers; but new and unexpected objects were seen and collected, making all the effort worthwhile.

The little island called Eden, only a half mile from Conway Bay, and only a half mile in diameter, was the visible remains of a third of a volcano rim, and had craterlets scattered on its slopes and shore. Here were sea lions and colorful crabs in abundance. Marine iguanas perched on water-worn cinders and imperturbably ignored the spray from the breakers. Their recurved claws allowed them to maintain such a grip on the lava that heavy waves could not pry the lizards loose. A tame snake, two feet long, had no objection to being handled; butterflies, moths, grasshoppers, and the little tropidurus lizards were everywhere.

Near Eden are the Guy Fawkes Islets – three tall, impressive cliffs of etched stratified rock, painted in grey, olive, pink, and yellow. Landing was tricky in the six to eight-foot surf, especially when burdened with motion picture cameras used to photograph sea lion pups at play.

Back again at Indefatigable, studies were made of the marine lizards and other marine life. The scientists dredged the ocean bottom, towed for plankton, seined along the beaches, trolled from launches, and carried out other operations. Aboard ship, they classified and studied their finds, working late into the night.

While enroute to Academy Bay, the *Noma* passed the wreck of a schooner stranded on a reef. There was no sign of survivors, and the hull was being rammed to pieces by the heavy surf. One broken mast rose disconsolately over the wreckage.

From an Ecuadorian steamer at Academy Bay, it was learned that the schooner had struck the reef only a week before. Two survivors in a small boat had been picked up by a passing ship, far from the wreck. The disaster was reported to Guayaquil, and a search party was sent out to find the other twenty-two people, some of whom were women and children. The search was abandoned after no traces of any castaways were found.

At Tagus Cove, in one hour's collecting, twenty-two species of insects were acquired; of these, ten had previously been wholly unknown. Live cormorants and penguins were taken aboard ship. The three penguins made appealing pets, full of curiosity as they waddled about the ship.

The *Noma* steamed to Wreck Bay, hopeful of obtaining fresh water, not only for drinking, but to satisfy the boilers' needs. During the entire trip, the boilers required forty tons of water and a tremendous amount of coal. The brackish water available at a nearby lagoon would have ruined the boilers and was not clean enough for drinking. However, Mr. Johnson of London guided them to the waterfalls of Freshwater Bay, on the south side of Chatham. With the aid of a 150-foot rubber hose, a funnel, and a small boat, four tons of clear water were transferred to the *Noma* through the perilous breakers.

There were three Americans at Wreck Bay who had arrived six weeks previously as passengers on a sloop from Guayaquil. They were waiting for some ship to take them to Indefatigable where, they claimed, they wished to study agricultural possibilities. Without provisions of food or water, their intention was to live off the island. Their plea to the *Noma* to take them there was refused; the *Noma* did not wish to become part of their committing suicide on a desert island. Besides, their reasons for wanting to be marooned on the island seemed vague and mysterious, especially since one of them introduced himself as Mr. Nemo. There were suspicions that these men were on a treasure hunt; it is not known if they ever succeeded in getting to the island.

The *Noma* returned to Panama to re-coal and re-water, then returned to Seymour Bay to obtain specimens of fairy shrimp, moths, spiders, ant-lions, praying mantises, and grasshoppers. The scientists, armed with guns, nets, jars, paint-boxes, and other paraphernalia also found an extremely primitive insect, the lepismid, which had remained unchanged for thirty-five million years. It was a giant species, three inches in length, had never developed wings, and was found under stones. This creature was appropriate for islands that recalled Tertiary yesteryears.

Five miles north of Indefatigable are two islets which Beebe named Daphne Major and Daphne Minor. The first was three-quarters of a mile in diameter, with a steep slope and an almost perfect crater rim all around, "looking like an open mouth of a submerged bottle." Daphne Minor, with its flat bushy top, looked like a stopper for this bottle.

Seldom visited, the crater held a most delightful surprise for the expedition. Hundreds of feet below the rim, the floor of the center was monopolized by a pure culture of blue-footed boobies, of all ages and sizes from egg to adult. There were over four hundred nests, and the blue feet were prominent against the white sand floor and black lava slopes. An unearthly din made conversation impossible. There were many dead carcasses, victims of starvation and old age. It took a strong, healthy bird to surmount the crater rim to find food in the ocean. Only one tortoise was seen during the entire expedition, at Duncan. On the way to Tower, an enormous school of porpoises, about three thousand individuals, was seen leaping by, ten to fifteen abreast. The floating laboratory left the Galapagos on April 29, 1923, and Beebe remarked that he "hated to leave these no-man's wonderlands."

Only 100 hours were actually spent in the islands themselves, but the expedition returned with more specimens, photographs, sketches, and information than Darwin could have collected in years. Six months after the trip, twenty-two scientific papers were published. Beebe himself published his delightful book, *Galapagos, World's End*, which was translated into many languages. It had a strange effect upon certain Europeans and upon the future history of the Galapagos.

In 1924, the British St. George expedition did some outstanding geological studies in the Galapagos. On a pole at Post Office Bay, they found a weather-beaten cask serving as the current mailbox. The letters "U.S. Mail" were faintly visible. This cask was discarded into the brush, and a freshly painted barrel was substituted in its stead.

Arcturus Expedition

William Beebe returned to the Galapagos in 1925 as director of the eleventh expedition of the New York Zoological Society. The luxurious 2,400-ton steam yacht *Arcturus*, generously loaned by Henry D. Whiton, left Brooklyn on February 11, 1925, and returned six months later with specimens ranging from microscopic creatures to a giant devilfish weighing more than a ton. Several cameramen had filmed this and the previous trip, and the movies were shown all over America.

Like the *Noma*, the *Arcturus* was equipped with laboratories, dark rooms, diving equipment, and a staff and crew totalling fifty-four persons. Studies were made in the Sargasso Sea, Cocos Island, and the Galapagos Archipelago. The entire expedition was described by Beebe in another popular book, *Arcturus Adventure*.

The expedition made a special point of visiting Hood Island, an elliptical and flat desert island lying southeast of Chatham. It has soft contours and no visible cones, and its highest altitude is 910 feet. It is not wooded; there are about fifty species of cactus and other desert plants.

The unique feature of Hood is the albatross rookery on the southern coast of the island. The albatross does not nest anywhere else in the Galapagos and is usually associated with the colder regions of South America. The Galapagos species averages over three feet in body length and has a mighty wingspread of eight to nine feet. Head and neck are pure white, the beak is yellow, the body is gray, and the wings are dark brown. The birds prefer small squids as food, and lay their eggs on the red lava soil without any nest whatsoever. They do not fear man and are master flyers.

A unique and distinctive tortoise is found on Hood; it has a beautiful saddle-shaped shell unlike any tortoise of the other islands. The most colorful of all Galapagos marine iguanas are found here, too, basking on the sun-baked rocks along a shoreline with thousands of caves, coves, pinnacles, and peninsulas. The iguanas are mostly black in color, but the top of their head, crest, and part of the back are emerald green; the flanks have bright red spots.

The most memorable event of the entire expedition was the witnessing of a spectacular volcanic eruption on Isabela Island. As the *Arcturus* steamed around the northern end of Isabela, Beebe was quite impressed by the two 5,000-foot-high craters at this end of the island. He wrote, ''I gave these nameless mountains the titles of Mount Whiton and Mount Williams after the two gentlemen without whose ship and generosity it is probable that this volcanic outburst would never have been recorded.'' These huge craters were quite dead, and perhaps plugged with solid lava, but their slopes and shoulders were active with fumeroles out of which poured grayish-white wisps of gases.

Beebe landed near an older flow, which resembled a river suddenly solidified into glassy jet black, like an obsidian ocean complete with ossified ripples and waves. The transparent wave crests broke into large sheets, and clanged upon each other like steel falling upon steel with a metallic ring. Enclosed gases had caused the cooling lava to form bubbles and pinnacles and gargoyle images in deep jet-black.

The exploring party proceeded up the slope, but the black lava was intensely heated by a towering and merciless sun. Between lava and sun, climbing became unbearable. Invisible gases from the fumeroles made the climbers deathly sick. Severe cramps in legs and feet made the return trip a nightmare, and they returned crawling on all fours, lucky to be alive. The purpose of this somewhat foolhardy climb was not clearly explained.

The *Arcturus* returned to Isabela nine weeks later on June 14, 1925, and by this time, visible in the daylight, lava streams flowed as red as blood, pouring out of nine or ten vents. The lava flowed thirty-four miles per hour. As the temperature of the ocean began to rise, panic-stricken fish headed for cooler water, while birds were attracted by the floating, dying fish.

"The greatest tragedy that we saw was a full-grown sea lion which suddenly leaped high, close to the shore. Five times he sprang, arching over eight or ten feet clear of the seething water and in blind agony headed straight for the scarlet delta of lava. There was no final effort – the last leap apparently carried him straight to death," Beebe sadly commented. At night the spectators feasted upon the sight of the beautifully symmetrical red cone of fire.

The settlement of Villamil on the southern end of Isabela survived the eruption, but how many of the rare flightless cormorants and little penguins perished in the deadly gases is unknown. Unaided by man, Nature, too, has a way of destroying the creations it has preserved for millions of years.

Zane Grey

After a conference with William Beebe, concerning the possibilities of big game fishing around the Galapagos, author Zane Grey approached the Encantadas on February 10, 1925. His 190-foot three-masted schooner, *Fisherman*, built in Nova Scotia only five years before, had left tropical Cocos Island and sailed directly south to "one of the wildest and lonesomest places in all the Seven Seas."

As the schooner came within sight of Marchena Island and its twin cinder-pile, Abingdon, Grey was startled at the contrast between Cocos and these northerly isles of the Encantadas. Marchena he found to be "a desert island, iron-hued and gray, ghastly, stark, barren, yet somehow beautiful. How incredible the change between Cocos and Marchena, only a little over 200 miles apart!" He also had not expected the delightfully cool weather here at the Equator.

Fisherman dropped anchor in Conway Bay behind "Eden Island, a pyramid-like rock that would have been a mountain in less colossal surroundings." Here Grey encountered a huge iguana about four feet long which clung so tenaciously to the lava rocks that Grey could not pry him off. The brush covering of the island was "impenetrable as a wall, and infinitely more cruel," Grey commented. "I never saw a worse place than the jungle of this particular island."

Of James he said, "The solitude of the place seemed terrific. Infinitely more than lonely! Any desert is inhospitable, but a volcanic desert surrounded by a swift sea of salt water is staggering to the consciousness of civilized man."

Fishing off Chatham Island, he remarked, "It was a marvellous sight to peer down into that exquisitely clear water and see fish as thickly laid as fence pickets, and the deeper down, the larger they showed. All kinds of fish lived together down there. We saw yellow-tail and amber-jack swim among the sharks as if they were all friendly. But the instant we hooked a poor luckless fish he was set upon by these voracious monsters and devoured . . . . They appeared from all sides as if by magic . . . . One appeared to be about twelve feet long or more, and as big as a barrel . . . . They were undoubtedly man-eating sharks . . . , a swarm of ravenous wolves."

William Beebe disputed these qualities: "We were diving in helmets, and walking about the bottom with these self-same man-eating sharks swimming around and over us, dashing at and taking our hooked fish, but except for a mild curiosity, paying no attention to ourselves . . . . I will go on record as saying that it is perfectly safe to sit or walk around, or climb up and down ladders and ropes, to leap or twist quickly about, protected only by a copper helmet and a bathing suit, among the sharks of Cocos and the Galapagos."

The *Firecrest*

On July 17, 1925, the *Firecrest* dropped anchor in Wreck Bay. Alain Gerbault, the French tennis champion, was on the first quarter of a voyage in which he single-handedly sailed around the world in four-and-a-half years. A succession of squalls, rain, calms, variable winds, and a northerly drift greeted him after he left Panama, so that it took thirty-seven days to reach the Galapagos with continuous tacking.

Mr. Johnson of London came aboard, and seeing only one solitary crew member on the thirty-nine foot English cutter, expressed his doubts: "You were two, and you have drowned the other!"

At Progreso, Gerbault found the village a mere semicircle of thatched huts. "It was a vision of South America with gauchos, horses roaming about at large, lassos, and many-coloured ponchos, and dirty, ragged but picturesque peons."

Invited to dinner at the Cobos Hacienda, Gerbault was surprised to find fully armed guards stationed at doors and windows. Inside, there were automatic pistols lying about everywhere; the host's bedroom was a veritable arsenal, and the host explained that he anticipated an attack. He cautioned Gerbault to overhaul his weapons on the *Firecrest* and never to walk unarmed.

Several months before, while Cobos was inspecting the sawmill, some convicts had invaded his home, seized the guns, and fired upon Cobos from the windows. He fled on horseback into the mountains where he hid for four days before it was safe to return. Also, at that time, five convicts seized a thirty-foot cutter at Wreck Bay. A month later the small vessel was spotted by a steamer near the coast of Panama with three survivors dying of hunger. They were suspected of cannibalism.

Gerbault spent two weeks at Wreck Bay and found Cobos's fears unwarranted. No attempts were made to seize the *Firecrest*; the peons danced and feasted, and seemed content and peaceful.

Yachtsmen

Combining science with pleasure, many well-known yachtsmen came to the Encantadas in the carefree 1920's – a time when American millionaires vied with each other in building bigger and better yachts. Representing various museums and carrying qualified scientists, many yachts sailed on purposeful, well-planned voyages which were of immeasurable value.

In 1926, William K. Vanderbilt came to the Galapagos in the 211-foot *Ara* to do some oceanographic work and found the volcano on Isabela Island still erupting. On a similar trip in 1928, he obtained five tortoises at Duncan which were given to the New York Zoo. Two years later, when Vincent Astor's 263-foot *Nourmahal* came to Duncan, Dr. Townsend could not find even one specimen of *Testudo ephippium*, even though eight men searched diligently. These tortoises were plentiful in 1906; between 1848 and 1863, four ships recorded having removed 356.

In 1927, Captain G. Allan Hancock led an expedition to the Galapagos aboard the famous mystery ship, *Oaxaca*, which, during World War I, was a camouflaged submarine fighter of unusual power and speed. Captain Hancock rebuilt it as a yacht and conducted scientific expeditions to both the Galapagos and Alaska. At Narborough, the crew of the *Oaxaca* witnessed molten lava flows down the rugged slopes, as white clouds of steam hissed skyward from the water's edge. Thousands of fish were killed by the heat, steam, and sulphurous sedimentation.

In April of 1928, Dr. Charles Haskins Townsend had been in charge of an expedition on the steamer *Albatross*, sponsored by the New York Zoological Society and the United States Bureau of Fisheries. The object of the trip was to procure enough tortoises to stock the tortoise colonies planned in zoological gardens of Florida, New Orleans, Houston, San Antonio, Bermuda, Honolulu, and Sydney. Because the tortoises threatened to become extinct in the Galapagos, and the Ecuadorian government was not protecting them, it was deemed necessary to remove them to places where the curious creatures would be better appreciated, and where, it was hoped, they would multiply. With the help of twenty Ecuadorian colonists from Villamil, 180 tortoises were captured on southern Isabela.

At Charles Island, the expedition had to content itself with twelve skeletons of the special species, *Testudo galapagoensis*, which became extinct in 1848. Logbook records show that twelve whaleships carried off 1,775 of these creatures, leading to a rapid extinction of the species. In 1930, eight specimens were removed by the *Nourmahal* from Indefatigable for a tortoise colony in southern Florida.

On January 5, 1929, the Crane Expedition of the Field Museum of Chicago arrived on the spanking-new brigantine yacht *Illyria*, owned by young Cornelius Crane. The 147-foot yacht, with squaresails on the foremast, and fore and aft sails on the mainmast, presented a remarkable sight as it entered Post Office Bay. Unfortunately, only two hunters – Ecuadorians – were on shore to appreciate the view. They were in the employ of a hide dealer named Olsen, and he had sailed away for medical care. Due to a language barrier, no questions were asked about the spacious house on shore, an unusual sight in this desolate place. After a trek into the hills, several bulls were shot to replenish the larder of the *Illyria*, and Dr. Moss collected the mail from the barrel.

The ship sailed to Academy Bay at Santa Cruz Island, and here found three Norwegian men, a Norwegian family, and three graves. Unable to find wild tortoises, the scientists bought several from the colonists, then sailed away for further exploration in the South Seas. They were unaware that tragedies had occurred in the previous two years at both of these anchorages, and that the Norwegians were remnants of several misguided groups which had become disenchanted with the Enchanted Isles.

In 1929, the motor yacht *Arcadia* did some sports fishing in the Galapagos and even caught a big whale. Numerous other yachts dropped by for a visit, usually as an interlude before the more romantic South Seas.

Some had other ideas in mind. A handful of Englishmen crossed the Atlantic in a small auxiliary ketch on their way to adventure and treasure hunting. After their *Southern Pearl* passed through the Panama Canal, they cruised about the Galapagos Islands during the summer of 1932. Not having any pirate maps handy, and with so many islands to choose from, they finally left for Costa Rica to obtain a permit to dig on Cocos Island. There they found that a Canadian corporation had already received exclusive rights. The ketch was sold and converted to a freighter for coastwise trading.

Sulivan Bay

One of the favorite haunts of yachtsmen is Sulivan Bay on the eastern end of James Island, directly across from Bartholomew Islet. The latter has a spectacular formation called Sentinel Rock at one end of a crescent beach. This rock comes to a sharp point two hundred feet above the turquoise bay. Herds of tame sea lions sun themselves on the yellow sands nearby.

The mountainsides of both James and Bartholomew are barren and reddish-brown in color. Walking is difficult over the jagged crusts, which give way without warning, the fragments bouncing off each other with a metallic ring. In 1707, privateer Woodes Rogers wrote, "They tell me the island is nothing but loose Rocks, like Cynders, very rotten and heavy, and the Earth so parch'd that it will not bear a man, but break into Holes under his Feet, which makes me suppose there has been a Vulcano here." He did indeed suppose correctly.

Gases in the cooling lava formed large bubbles which solidified into rounded blisters, some, several feet high. One of these on Bartholomew resembles a cave with a six-foot high entrance; yachtsmen leave notes in the interior. In 1928, a note was left by the *Svaap*, to be replaced by the *Yankee* in 1933. Later, a sort of guest registry was maintained; visitors added their name to an old list, which is carefully replaced into its hiding place in this curious cave.

A hike to the highest crater rim a few hundred feet high on Bartholomew presents an unsurpassed panorama of the major islands. Closest to it across the narrow strait are the numerous cones of James and Indefatigable Islands. Chatham is seen in the hazy distance; Isabela looms a mile into the clouds and stretches for an interminable distance. Everywhere are craters, whose slopes are pocked with more craters and dotted with cones. Only in the Encantadas is such a weird sight possible.

11

MOSTLY NORSEMEN

In his popular book, *Galapagos, World's End,* William Beebe gave a glowing report of the wonders of the Enchanted Galapagos. However, his account was from the perspective of a naturalist who found the islands a mecca for scientists and fishermen. Nowhere in the book did he recommend permanent settlement; in fact, he often mentioned the absolute scarcity of water and the extreme ruggedness of the wastelands. However, he did tell of salt lakes and the abundance of fish in the deep waters of the archipelago.

It is no wonder, then, that expert fishermen like Norwegians would be attracted to a place that teemed with fish. Furthermore, there was a market for salted and dried fish in Catholic Latin America, especially during Lent and fasting seasons. When the Norwegian translation of Beebe's book appeared on the bookstands of Norway in 1925, it created quite a sensation. At that time, Norway was suffering from the effects of a post-war depression: the economic outlook was gloomy, the value of the krone was fluctuating, businesses were failing, and speculation was rampant. The simple uncomplicated life on a remote island seemed especially inviting.

Henry Randall, an Oslo promoter not averse to making some fast kroner, seized the opportunity of selling the idea of a colonization scheme to his countrymen. Neither he nor his partner, Christensen, had ever been to the Galapagos. To decoy his victims to the verdant paradise, he indulged in some lurid and fraudulent advertising.

The Galapagos Islands, Randall claimed, were a Promised Land, not only for the fishermen but also for the farmer. The fertile soil could support a hundred thousand people, and what's more, the land was free. There was hidden wealth in the hills: gold, silver, coal, oil, and diamonds. Chatham Island boasted of electric lights; its manager drove an automobile.

For a large slice of Paradise, each prospective colonist was asked to contribute 2,000 kroner per family into the organization's coffers. With these funds, agricultural and fish-canning machinery would be purchased, and transportation and a permit from the Ecuadorian government would be included.

Almost simultaneously, three separate colonies left Norway sometime in 1926, with fantasies of future prosperity, and the prospect of living in a far more temperate climâte than cold and vigorous Norway.

Colony at Chatham Island

Late in 1926, an old 100-ton three-masted schooner, formerly a concrete-hauling boat now named *Albemarle*, arrived at Wreck Bay. On board were fifty men, fourteen women, and five children who had left Norway with high hopes and all their wordly possessions to start an agricultural colony on Chatham Island. With them came an elderly Norwegian named Arthur Wurm-Muller, who had been the Norwegian vice-consul from Guayaquil, and who spoke English and Spanish as well as his native tongue. More women and children were to arrive later and would be sent for as soon as the men had established the colony.

The *Albemarle* was heavily laden with furniture, farming implements, fishing materials, diamond-drilling equipment, prefabricated wooden houses cut and ready for assembly, some wagons, and even a Ford tractor.

When the ship docked at the rickety wooden pier, the would-be colonists no doubt felt a twinge of disappointment. The little port of Baquerizo Moreno consisted of a lighthouse, several dilapidated buildings to house the governor and his small garrison, and a huge shed serving as a warehouse. Two streaks of rusty rails ran from the shore across the pier – remnants of the old, narrow-gauge railway that had transported produce in the heyday of the Cobos empire. Several small fishing boats were rotting away on the beach; chickens were pecking around a few thatched huts, where shabbily clad peons watched from the doorways.

Adding to their dismay was the fact that there was very little acreage fit for agriculture. Worse still, almost all of the arable land was owned by the heirs of the slain tyrant, whose convicts had cleared it with their sweat and blood.

The portion of land allotted to the Norwegians was five miles back in the mountains near Progreso. Their equipment was laboriously hauled up the dirt road, and, eventually, fourteen houses were erected from Norwegian lumber, and in typical Norwegian style. Doggedly, they began to clear the land, but the tough unyielding lava conquered most of them. Wurm-Muller claimed that few of the settlers were fit for the game. Within a year, many started to drift back to Norway, sadder, wiser, and poorer. Their equipment was sold to the Ecuadorians at a great loss.

William Robinson stated that the *Albemarle* was sold in Panama to a Colombian, and that the Norwegians were cheated out of a goodly portion of the money received for the ship. Roydon Bristow, in 1931, claimed that the schooner was sold to the Ecuadorian government and became the *Pro Patria*, which, with a tugboat, formed the entire Ecuadorian navy. At any rate, the disillusioned settlers returned to the old country as best they could. Relief funds were solicited in Norway and the United States to aid in sending the victims home.

In November of 1928, young William Albert Robinson and his friend Bill Wright arrived at Wreck Bay in the *Svaap*, a jib-headed Alden ketch only thirty-two-and-a-half feet long. The name of their little yacht meant "Dream" in Sanskrit, and they were on the beginning of their three-and-a-half-year dream voyage around the world. They left New York in June and were leisurely cruising past the Galapagos on their way to the South Pacific.

Robinson found about half a dozen shacks on the beach at Baquerizo Moreno. An enormous flag flew over a little blockhouse. "The smaller the country, the larger the flag," he commented. At Progreso he saw the decrepit sugar mill and its soot-blackened chimney. The garrison headquarters was in a frame shack; Señor Cobos lived in a stone and wood house. The other two hundred peons resided in squalid huts, laid out in three rows in a semicircle surrounded with mud and grass. There were no trees or other vegetation about the village.

Robinson found only fourteen of the original sixty-nine Norwegians left on the island; four of these left on the *Manuel J. Cobos* while the *Svaap* was still in port. It seemed that the colony failed through the lack of leadership, cooperation, and funds to maintain them until their farms were on a paying basis.

Robinson was quite captivated with the heroic Norwegian girl who elected to stay after the rest of the "lotus eaters" had left the island. He wrote, "High in the hills, with only a mysterious hermit nearby, Karin tills the land with a handful of cutthroats and ex-convicts. She rides among them unafraid of their knives and machetes, with a tiny gun in her pocket. They obey her every order." Robinson gave her a little honeybear which he had obtained in South America.

In the summer of 1929, the former governor of Pennsylvania, Gifford Pinchot, and friends arrived at Wreck Bay on the beautiful 148-foot three-masted schooner *Mary Pinchot*. The group found nine Norwegians left: Wurm-Muller; the fishermen, Jenssen and Nuggerud; a very discouraged young couple planning to leave, and four members of the Guldberg family.

The Guldbergs consisted of a father, two daughters, and a son. The eldest daughter, Karin, ran their little plantation; the father puttered around in a garden. The son and other daughter, Snefrid, dreamed of returning to the cities of Norway; eventually these two left the island.

When Pinchot visited the Guldberg home in the hills, the two girls eagerly showed him their treasures: some quartz which they still hoped might be diamonds, and pyrites which they hoped were gold. He also saw a "full-fledged telephone instrument on the wall, unconnected and useless, a symbol of suppressed longing for civilization which they gallantly refused to acknowledge.''

Several years later, Karin married young Manuel Cobos. On the site of the previous Cobos hacienda, they built a new home with Norwegian pine taken from the dozen deserted houses of the disenchanted colonists.

The Russian Hermit

The elderly Mr. Guldberg, in strange contrast to his aggressive and energetic daughter, was a rather phlegmatic individual. The monotonous life at Progreso appealed to him, and after Karin's marriage, he set up housekeeping in a small wooden shack abandoned by a previous colonist. However, he did not live alone; he found companionship with a mysterious ''hermit'' who had been on Chatham for some years before the Norwegians arrived.

Arthur Zeen was not really a hermit; he only looked like one. With long red hair falling to his shoulders, a full red beard, and deep blue eyes, the tall man presented a striking appearance. Though wearing a ragged shirt and shabby pair of trousers patched with sackcloth, he still managed to look dignified but of undetermined age.

Zeen claimed he had been a railroad construction engineer in that part of Russia which at times has been the nation of Estonia. When the Bolsheviks came to power, he left Russia and somehow found himself working in the gold mines of South America. Here some of his enemies traced him, and he found refuge in the Galapagos.

At first, Zeen worked as a humble peon on the Cobos plantation. Soon he was given a piece of land, upon which he built a shack and raised his own food. However, he did not live or act like a lowly peon. Rough bookcases containing hundreds of books lined the walls of his hut. He spoke five languages: English, French, Spanish, German, and Russian. He spoke of prewar days in London, Paris, and Berlin. He spurned all magazines except the Literary Digest.

Surely, this intellectual personage could not have been a mere construction engineer! Speculation was rife as to the identity of this philosopher and linguist. Many believed he was an exiled nobleman with hidden wealth, and there were some who claimed Zeen was none other than the terrible Rasputin who escaped from Russia to this forgotten World's End. And if he was in fact Estonian, why was Estonian not given as one of the languages he spoke? It's certainly very different from the other five.

Whatever may have been an exciting and mysterious past was certainly disguised by the hermit's rather innocent life at Progreso. He and Mr. Guldberg raised peanuts, maize, coffee, sugar, eucre, and other vegetables; oranges, limes, avocados, and bananas were plucked as needed from orchards gone wild; pigs, ducks, and chickens supplied their protein needs. Farming and fishing left no time for political plots.

Years later in 1937, when Arthur Zeen and Christian Estampa visited later immigrants, the Conways, at James Island, Frances Conway found the reputed Estonian intelligent and literate. But she did not question him too closely, because in the Galapagos she learned that "strangers are handled with courteous caution," having on several occasions been introduced to convicts and other people who preferred to keep secret their reasons for coming to the islands. Little did she know that this man, who reminded her of St. Nick in faded trousers and patched shirt, may have been hiding a rather famous, or perhaps infamous, personage behind that almost white beard.

Colony at Charles Island

Unlike the colony at Chatham, another attempt at colonization consisted of twenty-two men; no women or children arrived with them at Post Office Bay, Charles Island, in 1927. Each man had invested $900 in the venture, and this entitled him to one-way fare, a share in the jointly owned equipment, and title to 100 acres of land. Christensen and Randall arrived with this group. They did not have their own ship, but came on a commercial freighter which stopped at the Canary Islands, Panama, and Guayaquil. Perhaps it was the schooner *Manuel J. Cobos* which brought them to Post Office Bay.

This colony lasted only one year, but a great deal was accomplished during that time. A large two-story house was set on four-feet high concrete piers. The wooden structure, built in Norwegian style, was painted brown with white trimming. A flight of steps led up from a concrete base to a broad veranda, onto which opened the three rooms of the main floor. The second story was a large, roomy attic. Apparently, this building served as a dormitory and living quarters for the whole group.

The house was wired for electricity; a small dynamo was located in another building behind the main house. There was also an aerial stretched between two poles outside. A large water tank stood beside the house, and a three-foot high wall encircled the residence. A flagpole stood in a cleared circle in front of the house; a neat, graveled path, bordered with lava, stones, and shells, led from the circle to the house.

A hundred yards of rail were laid for a narrow-gauge railway; it consisted of one car, with which to haul heavy materials from the beach to the house; a crane lifted them into and from the car. A pier made of angle irons jutted out from the beach.

Near the beach was a blacksmith shop, and several large tubs for salting fish. Rock salt was obtained from salt flats about three miles north of Post Office Bay, and piled near the tubs. One of the chief occupations of this colony was the catching of bacalao (gray grouper) and rock cod; these were rubbed with salt, then dried flat for export to the mainland. Drying racks were constructed on the beach, and nearby was another huge water tank, three-sided, and evidently from some ship. Pipes led to a gully which, during the rainy season, was a small brook.

Canning equipment had been brought, but there seems to be no record that it was ever used there. With confidence for a prosperous future, the men laid out streets; street signs were placed on poles. Some farming equipment, such as plows and a harrow, were brought inland near the caves, but this was mainly a fishing, not an agricultural, community.

Despite all the careful preparation and plans, this colony collapsed in about one year's time. The men had displayed great enthusiasm and diligence, as shown by their work, but they, too, became discouraged. The company had gone bankrupt; it was said they'd had trouble shipping and marketing their fish. Perhaps too, the abject monotony and isolation had undermined their original intentions. And hardship, privation, and loneliness may have helped turn their dream into a nightmare.

Whatever the causes, eighteen of the original twenty-two men left for the mainland, disappointed and destitute. Twelve of them died in Ecuador shortly afterwards. The last four remained on the island for a while, then eventually left. Randall and Christensen were said to have fled to California to evade a twenty-year sentence which awaited them in Norway; their misrepresentations came to the attention of the Norwegian government as complaints were filed by those who returned. Before the government had time to intervene, a third group set out for the Galapagos and arrived there in the summer of 1927.

Colony at Santa Cruz Island

Forty-five Norwegians left Larvik, Norway, to start a new life at Academy Bay. The intelligent planning, careful preparation, and excellent equipment seemed to guarantee success. Contracts were made with the Ecuadorian government which promised them a schoolhouse, a pier, and a factory to house the canning machinery.

Very quickly, seven fine houses of Norwegian pine were erected close to the beach; another building was constructed of cement and the canning machinery installed in it; a stone pier projected from the beach; streets were laid out and named. A Ford tractor was brought, not for farming, but to drive a dynamo to generate power for the canning factory.

Since this was to be mainly a fishing community, two fishing boats were brought and put into use immediately. Unfortunately, after three months, one of the boats was caught by a huge roller and dashed against the rocks on the southwestern shore of the island. Two brothers, both good swimmers, were drowned; their bodies were buried near the settlement. The second boat,

Falcon, was twenty-six feet long but had no engine. It was fully employed, and soon the canning business began in earnest. Machinery stamped out cans which were filled with tuna or lobster, sealed, put into a high-pressure boiler, and cooked. They were then packed in crates for shipment to Guayaquil. Rock cod, obtained from small Barrington Island southeast of Academy Bay, was boned and salted, dried on racks, and packed into 100-pound bales.

Meanwhile, a trail was cut to the top of one of the central craters where, Randall had advertised, there was a freshwater lake. The crater was dry. However, on higher slopes were found fertile fields suitable for farming; in fact, several abandoned farms were already in existence there.

The colonists had erected a huge tank to collect and store rainwater at their settlement, but had trouble keeping it filled. Having heard that water was available at Conway Bay on the other side of the island, an exploring party was landed there. The boat was to return for them in several weeks.

The scouts searched in vain for water; their peon guides failed them. Intending to walk back to Academy Bay, the group climbed the hills inland. Not too far from Conway Bay they found an old plantation that had been deserted many years before. There they found an abundance of orange trees, bananas, and guavas. Also growing wild were Spanish crops such as yuca (a kind of sweet potato), sugar cane, and corn. Perhaps this plantation dated back to the days of the pirates or whalers, when Spanish prisoners were put ashore, or to some colony begun by Ecuadorians in the distant past. The plantation was cleared, and provided the Norwegians with an abundant supply of fruit and vegetables.

Another large, neglected plantation contained a species of agave resembling the century plant; tradition claims that the swashbucklers used the fiber from these plants for making rope.

Another problem which the colonists had not anticipated was the host of rapacious black mosquitos which made life miserable. The settlers should have been forewarned by Beebe's report: "Galapagos mosquitos work on a strict schedule, and precisely at sunset they appear in innumerable swarms taking over the night shift from the biting flies that are very industrious during daylight hours."

Sharks were a plague to fishing; they were extremely numerous around Santa Cruz Island. It was not uncommon to haul in half a fish; sometimes half the catch in the nets consisted of sharks.

It was not long before the Norwegians realized that their Promised Land was full of empty promises. There was no coal, oil, or precious minerals as advertised, only an abundance of hard work.

Fish were plentiful, and the industrious colonists soon had bales of dried bacalao stacked on the beach. That was as far as the fish went for a while. There was no ship available to haul the bales to the mainland. The schooner

Cobos, privately owned, was usually too deeply laden with sugar, coffee, hides, cattle, and passengers to carry the Norwegian cargo. The accumulated bales did not approach a full load for chartering a separate schooner. Unable to sell their fish, the Norwegians could not afford to buy supplies and fuel.

Finally, when the colonists did manage to send their dried and canned fish to the mainland, another problem arose. They had no agent to store and sell the fish. The fish buyers of Guayaquil formed a ring, and forcing the Norwegians to sell their load at a ridiculously low price, reaped a huge profit in inland towns.

Things went from bad to worse at the end of the first year. Machine parts wore out and broke down; spare parts were ordered from Norway, but none were available for the obsolete canning machine. The boiler blew up, and later a man burned to death when kerosene on his clothing caught fire in the canning factory; soon, even the toughest and the most obstinate colonists succumbed to abject and incurable despair.

Some of the less hardy immigrants had left at the very beginning of the settlement, unable or unwilling to cope with the brutal realities that presented themselves; now everyone was anxious to leave; the homes were sold to any buyer who wanted them. Those not sold were confiscated by the Ecuadorian government. The machinery and tractor were abandoned to become rusty monuments to failure.

Besides financial knavery and lack of transport, there were other reasons for the failure of this enterprise. With no authoritative leadership, arguments arose as to the distribution of labor; decisions voted upon were rarely followed through. In any cooperative plan where money, resources, and labor are pooled together, there is bound to be trouble. Inequalities crop up and cause arguments among people already irritated by the primitive conditions.

Petty grievances, jealousy, and mistrust were exaggerated out of proportion. There were too many bachelors mixed with married people. There was no school as promised, and parents found no time available to educate their children.

The inhospitable Galapagos had again scored a partial victory over the intruders. Three of the colonists took to the hills to start plantations; and two young men, owners of the *Falcon*, remained on shore as fishermen, determined to hold out to the bitter end.

Captain Paul Bruun

A colorful personality who came to the Galapagos as a result of the Norwegian colonies was the genial Captain Paul Bruun, "with a quiet manner and a charming smile." Like all other Europeans who came to the Galapagos – "that region of earth which offers such kindly anonymity to many strange existences'' – he was regarded with suspicion. Many claimed his reputation was as sinister as the "notorious bark" of which he was master.

Dore Strauch Koerwin wrote that the tall, elderly, blond Norseman arrived in Ecuador shortly after World War I to escape pursuit by Norwegian law: "During the war he had misused his flag's neutrality to act as a spy in Germany's pay, and had surrendered secrets of the British Naval campaign to the German government. Many British ships cruising the North Sea had been sunk as the result of these data.'' She claimed that he arrived in Ecuador without papers and with an amazing yarn of having lost them in a typhoon.

Of Frau Koerwin, more later. She was not a notoriously careful reporter. The facts of the matter are that Paul Bruun did not arrive in the Pacific until about 1927. Coming from a family of sea captains, he had gone to sea at the age of twelve, and at sixteen was mate of a schooner which crossed from Newfoundland to Liverpool in a record twelve days. Later he became skipper of a passenger boat which travelled between Bergen and Newcastle. While on this route during World War I, he saved the British Government a fortune in gold by refusing to stop when intercepted by a German submarine.

After the war, Bruun owned two steamers, but lost them in the post-war slump, then commanded a luxury tourist liner. When he learned that a ten-ton boat was being sent to the Norwegian colonies in the Galapagos, he asked for the job as captain. With a crew of three, he sailed the tiny thirty-eight foot *Isabella* from Norway to Panama, and finally arrived at Guayaquil. By this time the colonies had disintegrated, and the *Isabella* became involved in a legal dispute.

The Ecuadorian government hired Captain Bruun to make a voyage around the islands to search for the crew of a vessel that had caught fire. Then he entered the service of Señor Alvarado and shuttled the schooner *Manuel J. Cobos* between the islands and Guayaquil. Being an enterprising person, he started various side projects involving salt, hides, and salted fish. His profits were sent to his wife and daughters in Norway.

At one time, Captain Bruun helped to quell a mutiny on James Island. An Ecuadorian had received a contract to extract salt from the lake near James Bay, and arrived there with an oil engine and about seventy laborers. A track was constructed, and a steel cable hauled the bags of salt down the hillside. However, the salt had first to be dug out of the lake and rafted to a platform, where it was dried and packed in bags, then hauled by means of a winch to the rim of the crater. The work was difficult, the sun was hot, and water rations were running short. When Bruun arrived, he found the contractor and several men defending themselves and their huts with pistols against machete-armed mutineers. Order was restored, and soon afterwards the enterprise collapsed. The track and cable were left to rust away.

Meanwhile, the Cobos Empire, too, had begun to crumble. Sugar cane rotted away at the plantation for lack of cutters – there was no more free convict labor available since the penal colony was abolished. The sugar factory rusted away, and the jungle was slowly creeping over the cleared land. The plantation, factory, and schooner were seized by creditors, and young Señor Cobos and his bride Karin were forced to leave the island. Later, they succeeded in recouping a small part of their land, and Cobos was hired as manager of the plantation he once owned.

For a while, Captian Bruun operated the *Manuel J. Cobos* for the German trading company which had control of the Cobos assets. When the ship was returned to Cobos and Alvarado, the Norseman resigned his captaincy and settled in the abandoned Norwegian house – "the Casa" – at Post Office Bay in May of 1930.

Post Office Bay, 1929

At the end of 1928, when Bill Robinson placed the *Svaap's* mail in the famous barrel, he found only one resident on Floreana – a Norwegian fisherman named Urholt. A month later, the *Illyria* encountered two Ecuadorian hunters there, who said they were in the employ of a man named Olsen. However, when the *Mary Pinchot* anchored at Post Office Bay in the summer of 1929, the island was deserted.

Believing that Floreana was wholly uninhabited, Governor Pinchot was amazed to find a solid two-story house at Post Office Bay. Receiving no answer to his knock, the Governor and his party entered and looked around.

The living room contained clocks, whale harpoons, two stands of shotguns and rifles, and a large "talking machine." Two bookshelves were filled with English and Norwegian books and magazines. A great pile of Swedish newspapers, dated 1927 and 1928, lay in a corner. A table was set with tablecloth, cutlery, a well-filled sugar bowl, a bottle of pickles, and plates with some fragments of food on them. A log book, with a last entry made on June 3rd of 1929, contained notes of a man named Christensen, and bore signatures of guests with the Vanderbilt expedition of 1928.

Other rooms contained bunks with mattresses, whaling cannon, knick-knacks, watches, diaries, ink, old clothes, and soiled linen. There was no sign of women's things anywhere. The attic contained a stand of pegs for Lyle gun lines, two home-made rawhide saddles, a complete bridle and bit, and small harpoons.

Evidences of recent occupation were found in the kitchen: a dried head of cabbage, a bag of sweet potatoes, potted meat in a large crock, dried beef hung across a pole, a paper bag of spoiled eggs, and a pot of soup covered with mildew.

Outside the house, the crew found salted groupers in four large tubs beside a pile of salt; a railroad car stood empty on the tracks; new halyards hung from a staff; and a net was drying on the smooth rocks. Several half-starved dogs greeted them.

To ascertain whether or not the previous occupants of the mystery house needed help, one of the *Mary Pinchot's* crewmen slowly read through the diaries. It was possible that the vanished owners had been blown to sea while fishing, or were lost in a crevasse inland.

The log book revealed that the residents had been two young Norwegians and an Ecuadorian. The last of the ill-fated Norwegian colony that had built the house, they owned a fishing sloop and presumably had gone on a fishing trip. The entire story of the fraudulent promoter and defunct colony thus became known to Governor Pinchot. In the frequent references to friends at home in Norway and the detailed accounts of trivial events, he detected the men's loneliness.

Later, the *Mary Pinchot* sailed to Academy Bay, where the Governor was relieved to find the Post Office Bay settlers unharmed. They had gone fishing and were blown off course towards Academy Bay. One of them was ill and later left for Guayaquil for treatment; the Indio lad Hugo alone returned to Post Office Bay.

On September 19, 1929, the schooner *Manuel J. Cobos* brought a strange couple to Floreana. The man and woman saw the desolation of the abandoned house, and the sad remnants of the disillusioned colonists, but they were not discouraged. "I forgot the wasted hope and toil it bore witness to, and thought only, full of my own hope and assurance, that we had come to make an Eden here and that we could not fail," wrote the woman. The couple believed there was a mystical sanction for their coming to Floreana.

12

PARADISE ON FLOREANA

Adam and Eve of Floreana

Doctor Ritter is important to the history of the Galapagos Islands because he was mainly responsible for the influx of European escapists and neurotics who were to drift to the islands after 1930.

So much nonsense has been written about the "free-love, back-to-nature" colony of Dr. Ritter on Floreana that an attempt will be made in this chapter to present facts as accurately as possible, using information given by the doctor himself, by his companion Dore, and by people intimately acquainted with both.

The story of Doctor Friedrich Ritter began in Berlin in 1927. At the age of thirty-nine, he was well established in a successful dental practice and was conducting some medical research in dietetics. His eighteen-year, childless marriage to an opera singer was on the verge of dissolution; the doctor had found a new soul-mate more amenable to his unconventional ideas.

It seems that the doctor was quite a fanatic regarding nutrition, believing that half of all human illnesses were the result of improper diet. Not only was he a strict vegetarian, but he also advocated the prolonged mastication of food. In fact, he chewed his vegetables so well that his own teeth were ground down to useless stubs.

The good doctor also objected to modern clothing, which he thought hindered freedom of movement and was uncomfortable. He designed a special shoe of soft leather, without heels, to replace the civilized shoe. Nudism was a popular fad in post-war Europe, and Dr. Ritter endorsed it wholeheartedly.

The complexities of modern life had interfered with the doctor's intellectual pursuits, giving him very little time for contemplation and philosophical studies; he dreamed of the day when he could leave the crowded cities. "Organized society," he said, "appeared to me a huge impersonal monster forging ever-new chains with which to shackle the free development of its members.'' He needed open spaces where he could think and act freely. Meanwhile, he conducted his medical researches at a Berlin clinic. One day while visiting patients, he met Dore Strauch Koerwin, a woman about fifteen years younger than himself. After a few discussions and an exchange of books and ideas, they discovered a bond of sympathy in their mutual dislike of modern life. Ten days after their first meeting, Dore left the hospital, attributing her complete cure to following the doctor's advice about conquering her illness with willpower.

Years before, Dore had received training as a teacher, but took a position in a bank when no teaching appointment was available. She supported socialistic movements, read a great deal of Nietzsche and Schopenhauer, and enrolled in night school courses preparatory to entering medical school. For a year-and-a-half she subsisted on a diet exclusively of figs.

At the age of twenty-three, Dore found herself married to an elderly, penurious schoolmaster who insisted that she retain her position at the bank. Disappointed with her marriage, and rebellious at being a hausfrau subject to her husband's ''paltry opinions,'' Dore suffered mental stresses which resulted in a breakdown of her health.

While in the hospital, she was immediately attracted to the doctor with the ''astonishing blond mane, his youthful bearing, and his steel-blue eyes that looked out from under his forehead so compellingly.'' Dore became an avid disciple of this ''John the Baptist who sought the wilderness.''

For two years, Ritter and Dore made their plans for their great experiment. They were going to prove that a man can double his life span by living a simple, uncomplicated life in the open air, untrammeled by clothing and luxuries, eating vegetables raised by his own hand, and cultivating his mental powers. Through self-denial, self-knowledge, and by stifling the animal within them, they hoped to achieve happiness and mental peace on a higher plane.

After an intense study of all remote archipelagos and islands, Dr. Ritter selected the Galapagos as the site for his forthcoming nirvana. ''I needed uniformity of day and season, a climate as unchangeable as possible; no confusion, but eternal regularity,'' he wrote. Darwin's description convinced the doctor that the islands were made more livable by the cooling effect of the Humboldt Current. William Beebe's book added finality to their decision. In this ideal solitude, they would depend entirely upon nature, and by not wasting their energy in fighting inclement weather, they would have more energy and time for the ''higher struggle.''

The summer of 1929 found Ritter and Dore busily preparing for their migration to the Encantadas. Gardening implements, carpentry tools, mattresses, linens, kitchen equipment, calico, a limited amount of medical supplies and instruments, clothing, mosquito netting, and other goods were carefully packed into wooden crates which themselves would later serve as cupboards and tables.

Anticipating trouble with his stubby teeth, Dr. Ritter had all of them extracted and replaced by a stainless steel denture coated with porcelain enamel. These teeth were to become quite famous, and were remembered long after Dr. Ritter's philosophies were forgotten. Contrary to many reports, Dore retained her own teeth and was to suffer future agonies from extractions without anesthetics. The doctor refused to take any morphia to the islands; pain was to be overcome by power of the will.

A very practical arrangement was made regarding the spouses left behind; Mrs. Ritter agreed to become housekeeper for Mr. Koerwin. To avoid scandal and embarrassment to all parties, the entire experiment was kept secret. Without any publicity or fanfare, Dr. Ritter and Dore Koerwin (disguised as a man) turned their backs upon European civilization and sailed from Amsterdam aboard a Dutch merchantman on July 3, 1929.

Four weeks later, they arrived at Guayaquil, only to learn that the *Manuel J. Cobos* would not return from the islands for another month. The German consul told them that land was not available for purchase in the islands, but that the Ecuadorian government had no objections to settlers squatting anywhere they wished. Hearing that herds of livestock roamed the island of Floreana, Ritter bought a good stock of barbed wire at Guayaquil, in addition to rice, beans, peas, vegetable seeds, and tins of crackers. Dore's desire for a flatiron was met with a frown of disappointment; Dr. Ritter would not allow such fripperies in his Eden where clothing would not be worn. Also, firmly believing that human hair is the best protection for the head, the couple strolled hatless in the fierce Ecuadorian sun, while straw-hatted Indios considered them "mucho loco."

On September 29, 1929, after a complete tour of the islands, Ritter and Dore were put ashore at Floreana with their cargo. Captain Bruun had tried in vain to persuade them to become his partners in the hide and dried-fish business; the last Norwegian on Floreana was leaving the island. His assistant, the Indio lad named Hugo, agreed to work for Dr. Ritter for a short time.

Undismayed by the rusty relics representing the blasted dreams of the previous settlers, Ritter and Dore began their Rousseauistic life, subsisting on canned goods while preparing their garden. They refused to live in the Norwegian house at Post Office Bay, even though Captain Bruun told them they were welcome to the place. Instead, they selected a remote spot inside the rim of a horseshoe crater, about a twenty minute climb from Black Beach. Here was a good spring, fertile soil, fruit trees growing wild, and a picturesque view of the sea and beach. Taking formal possession of their garden, Dr. Ritter sprinkled the ground with a few drops of spring water, while Dore did a ceremonial dance "to the music of nature's silent melodies."

Their first dwelling was a "pirate" cave, and with the help of Hugo and a captured horse, some of their equipment was hauled up from Post Office Bay. Later, with sheets of corrugated iron purchased from Captain Bruun, they built a shelter under a plum tree, consisting merely of a roof laid on the horizontal branches. In the mild, windless climate of Floreana, this flimsy dwelling was sufficient. It was called "Friedo," a combination of the first syllables of the names Friedrich and Dore, and the German word for peace, thus embracing "our oneness and our common dream," they said.

With superhuman effort, the determined couple began the formidable task of clearing their land. Being of short stature and slender build, and unaccustomed to heavy labor, both worked to a point of exhaustion in moving huge boulders. However, the initial hardships were accepted quite philosophically by Dr. Ritter: "Heaven and Hell are states of mind. How could we even imagine a heaven if we have not experienced a hell to give it meaning?" This is reminiscent of a man who keeps banging his head against the wall "because it feels so good when I stop."

While toiling at Friedo, Dr. Ritter wrote that their conventional garb was to go about "naked, except for high hip boots to protect the feet and legs against rocks and thorns." Their bodies were beet-red from the sun, and at times "swarms of plaguish flies fall upon our naked bodies and sting us until the blood flows." Years later Dore wrote, "If we did sometimes play Eve and Adam in our little Eden, then it was only when we knew ourselves completely alone." Newspaper accounts had described the couple as promenading in the nude in full sight of everybody. They did have a sign posted at the entrance to their little estate saying, "Knock strongly, and enter when three minutes have passed." Most visitors fired a warning shot as they approached, to spare the sunbathers any embarrassment.

For the first few months they were strenuously occupied from morning until night, transporting their goods and rebuilding fences which the marauding cattle trampled down. Sleep was impossible at night as "wild asses brayed, cows lowed and bellowed, pigs grunted and squealed, hounds bayed at the moon in pursuit of cats who made savage love and fought each other – a devil's chorus."

Bruised and scratched, the pioneers gratefully accepted a supply of bandages and medicine from a British warship that arrived at Post Office Bay on October 28. Shortly afterwards, the Indio boy Hugo left on the schooner, having been trampled by a furious bull which also gored him in the armpit.

In November, the *Mary Pinchot* stopped at Post Office Bay on its return trip from the South Seas, leaving food and a trim little rowboat as a gift; the boat was twelve feet long and three feet wide at the stern. It was to play an important role in future events.

In December, Ritter's arm was seriously injured by a falling tree, and Dore had burned her knee quite badly on some hot ashes. To add to their troubles, in January their rowboat and a large supply of their stores were stolen from the house at Post Office Bay. Without any weapons whatsoever, they were frightened at the prospect of marauding bandits in the vicinity, and left a note for Captain Bruun in the barrel, reporting the theft and their injuries.

On January 17, 1929, two yachts arrived simultaneously at Post Office Bay. The white *Mizpah* belonged to Commander Eugene F. Macdonald who had been treasure hunting at Cocos; the huge 225-foot black yacht *Camargo* was owned by Mr. Julius Fleishman. Macdonald found a melodramatic note in the barrel, and immediately began a search for the distressed islanders who reported they were short of food and injured.

Adam and Eve presented quite a savage appearance. Ritter, with unkempt hair and beard, wore tattered work-stained clothing. Dore, sunburnt and with calloused hands, looked rather pathetic in her faded cotton dress. The islanders were given generous supplies of food, clothing, medicinals, and a gun.

After leaving the island, Commander Macdonald sent a radiogram from the yacht to the Associated Press, relating his experience in the Galapagos, not realizing what a storm of publicity he would create for the Ritters. Newspapers and magazines all over the world printed the story of the dramatic ''rescue'' of Adam and Eve, and worldwide attention was focused on this lonely spot in the Pacific. Strangely enough, two years later, the *Camargo* also was to rescue three American castaways on Cocos Island, who spent six months there after a shipwreck.

Meanwhile, unaware of the journalistic furor they had caused, Ritter and Dore returned to battling the hostile elements of the Encantadas. No longer bothered with a food shortage, they were able to devote more time to planning their garden.

New problems arose with the rainy season; better shelters had to be constructed for their supplies. Then hordes of insects plagued them – roaches, beetles, caterpillars, plant lice, and ants. Boiling water was poured down anthills; no chemicals were available to kill the bugs which invaded the bedclothes or the moths which drilled holes in the fruit. ''The sordid and unnatural struggle between man and man that marks so-called civilization'' was replaced by ''the state of war between man and the wilder forces of nature.''

Dr. Ritter did not mention the struggle between man and woman in his little Eden – Dore was quite eloquent in her book about their bitter quarrels.

It was not long before Dore realized that her superman had banished all love and tenderness from his new life. Feeling cheated, disappointed, and rejected, Dore resented this cold and impersonal attitude which he assumed toward her the very moment they left Germany. His argument was that abstract happiness can only be achieved by freeing oneself from attachments to worldly things. He forbade Dore to lavish affection on her chickens, cats, and burro, but she fought back and continued to pamper her pets. She also planted flowers against his express command, and he pulled them out by the roots, because "it conflicted with his theory of the conservation of energy to . . . spend time, thought, and care upon quite outward, unimportant things." Apparently, there was no place for love of beauty or love of anything else in Dr. Ritter's special world.

Many arguments arose over Ritter's insistence upon eating the beef from Hugo's indiscriminate slaughter of cattle for their hides. Dore maintained that it was against their sacred vegetarian principles, but Ritter said it was a sin to waste food. He consumed large quantities of beef and potted pork, although in his writings, and in talking to visitors, he claimed he was a strict vegetarian.

Another source of friction was the doctor's frequent nagging over Dore's domestic inefficiency. Poor Dore had left Berlin to escape household drudgery; here at Friedo, the "ceaseless and excessive manual toil dulled the edge of our whole spiritual life for me," she complained. Also, in his extreme masculine conceit, Ritter believed in complete wifely subjugation to the husband, and this resulted in a constant battle of wills. Eventually, realizing she could never really become the superwoman he desired, Dore gave up the struggle and became indifferent to his criticisms and reproaches. "And so I lived beside him in a solitude too bitter to be described. I had forgotten that he had ever talked of love to me," she wrote, resigning herself to a loveless future.

It is a curious fact that in drawings of their dwelling and in references to their living accommodations, Dore mentioned two bedsteads. However, many visitors to Friedo reported how greatly impressed they were with the huge, bulky double bed which dominated the interior of the house. Perhaps Adam and Eve had not entirely stifled the animal in them, that interfered with intellectual harmony, as much as Dore would have her readers believe.

When the *Nourmahal* anchored at Post Office Bay early in 1930, one of the guests aboard brought a supply of sea biscuits and vegetable seeds for the Ritters. Suydam Cutting saw the rainproof shack and a garden laid out with signs of the zodiac. After he realized how much labor had been required to "transform this hostile land to a decent habitation," he commented that the Galapagos are truly a paradise for the scientific collector, "but for human beings seeking a home they are a living hell."

Paradise Gets Crowded

While Dr. Ritter was "grappling every hour of the day with a primitive dynamic reality which civilized man in his cities and towns has all but forgotten," the news of his experiment was circulated widely in Europe and America. The sensation-hungry public gobbled up exaggerated accounts of the doctor's flight from civilization with another man's wife. From Ritter's former landlady, Berlin reporters learned the name of the lady involved, and soon were harassing Mr. Koerwin with questions. The stainless steel denture and nudism were choice items that received full discussion. The island was romantically described as a tropical paradise of fruit trees and tame beasts.

On May 5, 1930, a special courier from the Ecuadorian post office disembarked from the *Manuel J. Cobos*, bearing a parcel of mail for the Ritters. Newspapers, and forty-six letters from complete strangers, revealed to the Ritters that their secret was exposed. The lurid headlines and garbled accounts upset Dore especially because the scandal would affect her husband, who had been pretty decent about her affair with the doctor. A deluge of letters was to keep coming, mostly from Germany.

Ignoring the letters obviously written by cranks, Dr. Ritter did send replies to the "like-minded souls" who wanted to join his settlement. He urged most of them not to follow, stressing the hardships and his desire for privacy. He was "rather appalled by the prospect of having our retreat become a haven of refuge for all the misfits of the world." Two misfits on Floreana were enough.

By the end of the year, five young Germans arrived separately; four joined forces and moved into the caves, while the fifth, a schoolteacher named Schmidt, built himself a hut apart from the others. Discreetly, they visited the Ritters only upon invitation, after being told in no uncertain terms that they were considered intruders. They were given plants and advice, but none stayed very long. Even the solitary hermit found his voluntary exile "cold and unnatural," but he remained long after the others had left. Several admitted that their prime reason for coming was to stake a claim for some of the land, since they were quite certain that either the United States or Japan was about to purchase the islands. Of the six burros they had brought with them, only one survived the mistreatment and overwork. Dore adopted "Burro," and it became a source of pleasure to her.

Then there was the aristocratic lady from Berlin who arrived with three monkeys, a parrot, a dog, a rabbit, an Indio cook, and a tubercular husband. Her plan was to have Dr. Ritter cure her husband as good advertising for his "coming health resort." The monkeys were brought as "tasters" to test the toxic qualities of the wild plants on the island. When told that she and her zoo could not pitch their tent on Ritter's cleared land, she angrily left on the next boat, abandoning the monkeys to shift for themselves. Dore wrote that one monkey, "mad with hunger, broke into another settler's kitchen and began flinging pots and pans furiously about, behaving in such a manner that the only thing to do was to put an end to it." Of this incident the doctor wrote, "We shot one that attacked us."

A German named Schimmf was one of the residents of the caves. It is surprising that neither Ritter nor Dore mentioned anything about him, since he was quite an intellectual and had once been a medical student. He had bought a small plantation in Tahiti and started working his way there aboard ship. In 1920, he had gotten as far as British Samoa, only to be deported as an alien, and ended up in South America. The writings of Dr. Ritter attracted him to Floreana; Ritter and Dore ignored him.

Another German arrived with his Ecuadorian wife and immediately proceeded shooting cattle and curing hides. His project had not been influenced by the Ritters; he had been working for a German firm in Ecuador and heard about the wild cattle in the Galapagos. His enterprise was quickly stopped by the Governor from Chatham, who confiscated the hides because the German had neglected to obtain a permit. No doubt it was Captain Bruun who brought news of the hide business to the Governor; the German was poaching on the Captain's private concession.

Next came the reporters from Germany, the United States, and South America. The Ritters were photographed and questioned, and themselves wrote articles for magazines defending their experiment and trying to clear up some of the distortions about themselves. A German editor had criticized Ritter as having taken ''a philosopher's way out'' by escaping from everyday dilemmas which he could not solve: ''This Dr. Ritter is just another example of a restless thinker who, not content with life and lacking the strength of will to adjust himself to it, is helpless to face the battle of reality and gives up the struggle. But in this case he seems to have found a new one.''

In rebuttal, Ritter answered, ''We toil and moil against greater odds and bear daily a far heavier burden of labor than is required of most men and women in society. Still, we regard our lot as the preferable one for us. We are the absolute masters of our destiny. . . . We have not at all withdrawn from life; we have merely withdrawn from a certain kind of life – the too highly mechanized existence of modern society.''

Perhaps the Ritters were pleased with an article which appeared in a Guayaquil newspaper written by an Ecuadorian naval officer who visited them shortly after their arrival at Floreana: ''A German couple are living as man and wife on Floreana in a very primitive fashion, distinguished from that of our early ancestors by the fact that both of them are highly educated and have moved in cultured European circles. They are living on a vegetable diet, shunning the use of meats, and they appear to thrive on it. Their thoughts are free from prejudices of the civilized world. As for myself, I was surprised at such novelty and self-possession. They seem to possess a supernatural ability to stand the silence which is disturbed only by . . . wild things . . . . Their dwelling is decidely original in construction, built of branches to give it security and covered with corrugated plates . . . . They sleep on the floor like Adam and Eve in their earthly Paradise.''

Even Captain Bruun decided to settle on Floreana. He had taken advantage of the sudden boom on the island, selling distilled water and renting rooms at the Casa for the would-be settlers and reporters who came and went. The Ritters were quite angry with him, especially Dore, when they discovered that the captain's crew had stolen all their property and rowboat in January. The captain offered the excuse that his men thought Ritter and Dore had been slain by wild beasts – that the crew had come to dismantle all the derelict machinery at Post Office Bay and found the Casa unoccupied, and so assumed the Ritters were dead. Captain Bruun did not return the rowboat, but claimed that the *Mary Pinchot* had intended it for his own use, and he christened it *Sigfrid*.

A handsome young Dane named Knud Arends had gone into partnership with the captain, after Bruun had resigned his command of the schooner *Cobos*. With borrowed capital they bought a 35-foot boat and started a fishing camp at Post Office Bay. Ten Indios were hired to clean, slice, salt, and dry the rock cod on long benches near the Casa. There also was a workshop, drying sheds, salt receptacles, and a condenser for distilling sea water. The place buzzed with activity; the captain and Arends were hard workers, and the project had a good chance of success. Later, they were joined by Wurm-Muller, the elderly Norwegian ex-consul who was one of the leftovers from the defunct colony at Chatham. He visited the Ritters often and was quite welcome at Friedo. He lived at the Casa with Bruun; his chickens, pigs, dogs, and goat lived underneath the house. The leisurely life at Floreana was quite a change of pace for this man who had spent most of his life travelling through the United States, South Africa, and Ecuador as broker, businessman, coal-miner, engineer, and, finally, as Norwegian consul.

Arends and Bruun were quite proud of their motorboat, *Norge*, built in Guayaquil. Thirty-five feet long, with an eleven foot beam, almost flat-bottomed and with a diesel engine, she was able to cruise at seven to eight knots. Captain Bruun converted her into a motor-sailer by adding some homemade spars and sails.

Except for the Indio boy, Hugo, the Ritters found Floreana uninhabited when they first arrived in September of 1929. In the spring of 1931 there were twenty-one people on the island: Ritter, Dore, Arends, Bruun, Wurm-Muller, ten Indios, five Germans, and one Ecuadorian woman. By the end of 1931, Ritter and Dore would again have the island all to themselves.

Doctor Temple Utley

In May of 1931, the 51-foot yawl *Inyala* arrived at Post Office Bay. Aboard was a tubercular English physician who, at the age of thirty-five, was fulfilling a boyhood dream of sailing the South Seas. Dr. Temple Utley had left England with a friend who sailed as far as Panama. At Barbados, the doctor was joined by a West Indian quadroon with the colorful name of Winston Cheeseman, nicknamed Mobile.

Dr. Utley had not planned on stopping at the Galapagos, but his "interest had been piqued by the description in a Panama paper of an eccentric German physician who lived, with his wife, a hermit's life on one of the islands . . . . I gathered it was another case of the present desire to flee from European civilization which I feel myself. To the Panama paper the most interesting fact about the Ritters seemed to be that they went about naked."

After sixteen days out of Panama, Dr. Utley and Mobile arrived at Chatham on May 6, 1931, and were entertained at the Cobos Hacienda, where they gorged themselves on fresh fruit. They deplored the sight of the rotting sugar cane and derelict machinery, and the evidence of the decay of the plantation.

"The climate of the Galapagos Islands is the finest in the world," wrote Utley. "The atmosphere is dry and very definitely bracing; the nights have just a pleasant chill about them . . . . It is completely a white man's country. There are no endemic diseases, no dangerous animals, no poisonous insects . . . I have found the sort of thing I have been looking for. Beauty, isolation, remoteness, and with it all, fertility and kindliness of environment."

Captain Bruun greeted the doctor at Post Office Bay, and "seven bottles of rum went west" the first night. These two became inseparable companions for the next two months. The nervous, chain-smoking, fragile doctor and the sturdy Viking went sailing about the islands; they fished, played two-handed cutthroat, dined, drank guarapo (distillation of sugar cane), and reminisced about Europe.

Doctor Utley screwed up enough courage to visit the Ritters on May 24, 1931. He stated, "I was very shy about calling on Dr. Ritter, as I gathered from the Panama paper that he was a fierce ogre, who detested visitors, resenting bitterly any intrusion on his privacy." But he was hospitably greeted by the Ritters, who soon discovered that he and they had philosophical interests in common, and discussed Lao Tse, Schopenhauer, Nietzsche, and Freud.

Of the garden, Utley wrote, "Altogether this strange oasis will be a rare puzzle to anthropologists about 10,000 A.D. They will find the temple of a sun-worshipping race with an advanced knowledge of mathematics. For with a German love of harmony the garden boundaries form a parabola, the path bisecting it runs true north and south, the trees are planted in harmonical series. These are just a few of the mathematical propositions embodied; there were many more."

The Ritters were now in the process of building a new house with a stone foundation. Of the old plum-tree house, Utley commented, "The most prominent object was an immense double bed of massive construction." He was impressed by all the homemade furniture and the strictly vegetarian dinner he was served, and that Ritter was an absolute teetotaler.

Noticing the uncontrollable nervousness of Doctor Utley, Dore wrote, "He seemed to be pursued by something . . . . It gradually came out that he had been a medical officer in an insane asylum. He talked a great deal of the various patients he had, and it was not difficult . . . to see that his own mind had suffered in contact with these unfortunates."

The Death of Captain Bruun

On June 20, 1931, a merry group left Post Office Bay to get supplies from Villamil. Aboard the *Norge* were Captain Bruun, Dr. Utley, the school-teacher Schmidt, the Governor from Chatham, and eight Indio peons. They caught sixty cod along the way, and finally arrived at the worst harbor to approach in all of the archipelago.

After zigzagging between reefs and huge breakers, they finally an-chored at Villamil. Señor Gil entertained them and sold some supplies. At this time there were about eighty residents there, some living in houses on piles along the beach.

On June 22, the *Norge* left Villamil with a dozen tortoises, 5,000 cigars, an adequate supply of rum, two cheeses, a bag of sweet potatoes, and five chickens. Besides Captain Bruun, the Governor, Utley, Schmidt, and three peons, there was a new hand: a cheerful double-murderer named Ovendo. The distance to Post Office Bay was only forty miles, but they were not destined to reach it. Bucking heavy seas and a strong current, they began drifting too far south and west. The next day was a dead calm, and their fuel was almost gone. Captain Bruun decided to return to Villamil, but the *Norge* was driven to the southwestern tip of Isabela Island, and anchored at San Pedro Cove, twenty-three miles west of Villamil.

On June 25, it was decided after a conference that Dr. Utley and two peons would remain on the *Norge*. The Governor and Ovendo would reach Villamil on foot, while Captain Bruun, Schmidt, and the peon Alberto would sail to Villamil and Floreana in their dinghy to get fuel. It took the Governor and the murderer five days to walk the inhospitable twenty miles to Villamil over loose lava rock covered with dense cactus and thorny shrubs. They arrived half dead from thirst and exhaustion, with their clothing and shoes in tatters.

Captain Bruun improvised a sail on the twelve-foot *Sigfrid*, a boat which was in a bad, rotten state of disrepair. Because it needed constant bailing it was nicknamed "The Submarine." The three men, having arrived safely at Villamil, caulked the boat and set sail for Floreana. After three days in that "leaky tea tray," rowing against wind and current, they were driven back to Villamil. The schooner *Cobos* arrived also at Villamil and gave Bruun the needed fuel. The schooner towed them to San Pedro, and the Sigfrid, with five men aboard, tried to enter the cove despite the tremendous sea and enormous breakers.

Dr. Utley had spent the week on the *Norge* waiting for the return of the skipper with the fuel. He amused himself by reading novels, hunting tortoises, watching seals and birds, and writing in his journal. On July 2, he was washing his clothing on the beach when he saw the *Sigfrid* approaching. A huge breaker crashed over it, spilling four rowers into the sea, while Captain Bruun alone tried to paddle it with one oar. A series of breakers dashed the boat against the rocks. Dr. Utley and his men managed to recover the body, but all attempts at artificial respiration failed. The Viking had been conquered by the sea, and was buried on the beach by his heart-broken friend, the doctor. A simple cross made from the wreckage of his own boat was planted over the sailor's grave.

More hardships were to follow. Now seven men were stranded at San Pedro, and the anchor line of the *Norge* was in bad shape. Dr. Utley moored her to the rocks, hoping the increasing swells would not shove her aground. Two of the men successfully reached Villamil by foot in several days, while the *Norge* was being prepared for rowing. Oars, rowing benches, and rowlocks were constructed. A rescue party arrived from Villamil with food, and two men joined the *Norge* group while the others returned on foot to Villamil.

On the ninth of July, the anchor line of the *Norge* parted, and Dr. Utley and six men began rowing. They lost ground, and the *Norge* drifted to the west. A wind arose, and they rounded the western end of Isabela, anchoring in Webb Cove. The anchor was a homemade affair clinging to rusty wire. Southeast of the cove was the diabolic Cerro Azul, completely devoid of vegetation. The men decided to cross the waterless waste which no one, to their knowledge, had ever traversed before. On the far side of Cerro Azul was a hut containing water and food, in a camp called Alemania.

On July 13, with sixteen bottles of water and some iguana meat, the group left the *Norge*. Dr. Utley was a little unsure whether he would survive the trip on his one lung. It was Schmidt who cracked up first, and begged the others to shoot him. They managed to urge him to stagger onwards over the coke-like cinders.

Three days later, they were chewing cactus to slake their thirst and stave their hunger, while Schmidt moaned and raved. Luckily, Ovendo went ahead and located a waterhole, bringing back about five quarts of water. The men continued to climb over hellish cinders which slithered and collapsed underfoot. With improvised sandals, they managed to cross the summit of the mountain and found themselves on the moist green slope with many puddles of water. At Alemania, they received beef, eggs, milk, fruit, and boots for their lacerated feet. It had taken them five days from the *Norge* to Alemania. They rode to Villamil on horseback.

On Floreana at Post Office Bay, Bruun's partner Arends had arrived from Guayaquil with a new outboard motor. The ship which brought him removed the four Germans and the Ecuadorian woman, as well as the Indio fishermen, from Floreana. Except for Mobile, who was still there on the *Inyala* waiting for Dr. Utley, only Wurm-Muller and the Ritters remained. On July 12, Arends and Mobile fitted the outboard motor on a whaleboat named *Pinta*, and they motored to Isabela, accompanied by a cook, a blacksmith, and an old man. Unable to find the *Norge*, they anchored near shore west of San Pedro Cove and went to sleep. None of them being seamen, they had made the mistake of anchoring close to shore, in the open, on one of the most savage coasts in the world. In the morning, they were awakened when the *Pinta* was shattered against the rocks. They salvaged the motor, some water, and a few matches.

In hiking back towards Villamil three days later, they found the mound of lava blocks, and read Captain Bruun's name on the rude cross over the grave. Upset and exhausted, Arends could not continue any farther, and Mobile proceeded to Villamil alone. Earlier, the cook and the old man had taken a different route. The blacksmith had fallen behind.

On the sixth day, Mobile arrived at Villamil, having endured the heat, lava, thirst, and hunger. Later he admitted he would have taken his life had he had the means. A rescue party set out and found Arends and the blacksmith. Arends, with a badly infected foot, was helped back to Villamil, having spent twelve days on the lava. The cook arrived alone at Villamil, fat and in good condition; he was suspected of having eaten his companion, the old man whose corpse was never found.

The two Norwegians from Academy Bay, Estampa and Wold, arrived at Villamil in their fishing boat, *Falcon*. They took Arends and Dr. Utley to Webb Cove, where they found the *Norge* had swamped, her stern down in the water. All returned to Floreana, where they broke the news of Captain Bruun's death to his old crony, Wurm-Muller.

Two more Norwegians, Jensen and Nuggerud, arrived from Chatham in their boat *Dinamita*. The *Falcon*, *Dinamita* and *Inyala* all proceeded to Webb Cove to salvage the *Norge*. Dr. Utley had taken ample provisions aboard, and planned to sail from Webb Cove to the Marquesas with Mobile. The Norwegians entreated him to remain with them and join their fishing enterprise, hauling salt cod to Guayaquil on the *Inyala*. The lure of the South Seas proved too strong, and Dr. Utley left the Galapagos on August 11, 1931. After many leisurely stops in various islands, his last port was Suva, Fiji, in 1933. There he accepted a position as general practitioner, but died in 1935. In letters to England, he had written before his death, "I often regret I did not stay in the Galapagos . . . . The Galapagos were the high water mark of my adventures . . . . The life I lived there was the new life I had been looking for, and if Bruun had not been drowned, I would probably be there still . . . ."

Schmidt, the schoolteacher, decided to remain at Villamil, where he planned to operate a chicken farm. Wurm-Muller, too, left Post Office Bay after his wife arrived from Guayaquil. Against his wishes, she prevailed upon him to settle at Academy Bay, where she thought she would find more congenial neighbors.

At the end of 1931, Dr. Ritter and Dore were alone on Floreana. With the corrugated sheet iron abandoned by other settlers, they enlarged the roof of their dwelling. Awnings of sailcloth formed the walls. Their sleeping quarters, about ten feet in diameter, were enclosed in a large cage of insect-proof wire netting. Adam and Eve were now keeping house in a circular cage with a tin roof.

Velero III

On the third day of January, 1932, the 195-foot cruiser, *Velero III*, anchored in Post Office Bay; Captain George Allan Hancock was making his yearly visit to Pacific Islands. A firm believer in "travel with a purpose," Captain Hancock had equipped his yacht with scientific parapher-nalia. Representatives of the San Diego Zoological Society and California Academy of Sciences added a serious and academic atmosphere to the cruise. They interrupted their studies for a visit with the Ritters.

Professor Schmitt of the National Museum wrote about Dr. Ritter: "When I first met him in 1933 he seemed to have turned his energies more to writing his scheme of philosophy and of life as it should be untrammeled by the conventions of modern civilization than to improving his place."

Dore was delighted with Captain Hancock's gift of a light cast iron cookstove and a supply of flour, and she baked bread four times a month. A year before, Ritter had written, "Man is not a grain-eating chicken. I am glad we got entirely rid of flour dabbling." After a year of bananas and vegeta-bles, no doubt bread was most welcome.

In articles appearing in the *Atlantic Monthly*, Ritter described his vege-tarian diet. Two meals a day were eaten, with breakfast consisting of fruit. Noon lunch was a combination of "a sweet food and a salt food." The sweet food was a mixture of beaten raw eggs, bananas or other fruit, and sugar cane syrup. The salt food was a salad of raw or cooked greens and vegetables, with peanut butter or coconut oil. It is obvious why Ritter was quite happy to accept steaks from hunters who visited Floreana. The vegetarian Methuselah tortoises lived to be 300 years old; Dr. Ritter hoped to reach the age of 140 with his rigorous diet. Perhaps the bleak prospect of a hundred more years as a misanthrope induced him to relax his rules a little.

Arrival of the Wittmers

A reporter from a Cologne newspaper had visited the Ritters at Floreana, and of course all Germans took a keen interest in every little detail of his story. One Cologne resident, disregarding all the sensationalism, took a serious interest in the island. Heinz Wittmer, a war veteran who held an important municipal position, was dissatisfied with the trend in Germany. He (according to Dennis Puleston) wrote to Dr. Ritter, and in return received an enthusiastic report. With careful preparation, Wittmer invested his savings in equipment and supplies, and left for Floreana with wife Margret and his son by a previous marriage. Twelve-year-old Harry had very poor eyesight, and the parents hoped life on the island would benefit his equally poor health.

At Wreck Bay, the little family purchased seeds and plants, and chartered a fishing vessel to take them to Black Beach, arriving there on August 28, 1932. They spent their first night in a tent on the beach, then moved to the caves. Mrs. Wittmer was an expectant mother, and Dore was somewhat miffed that the family had selected this island because there was a resident doctor available. She also was reluctant to loan her burro, and was a little disappointed because Frau Wittmer did not spout Nietzsche and Schopenhauer with every breath.

With true German industry, the Wittmers immediately set to work clearing their land and planting the seeds and shoots. In a very short time, they had erected a substantial log house with a thatched roof. Located on the site of the former convict settlement, Asilo de la Paz, it was further inland and south of Ritter's place, and contained possibly the best spring on the island. Here they kept to themselves, and Dore was surprised that the Wittmers were no trouble at all.

Heinz and Margret Wittmer were sensible, practical people. They had no special theories to test and only wanted a peaceful, quiet life for their growing family. It was quite obvious that Margret was a far better housekeeper than Dore. Her little home boasted of extreme neatness, curtains, and table linens. The Wittmers had not left civilization behind; they had brought it with them.

Besides being a fastidious housewife, Mrs. Wittmer insisted on keeping up appearances. Heinz and Harry were always shaven and shorn, attired in clean garments and boots. Dr. Ritter went about with a long beard, his long hair tied with a string (like the Vikings, he said); Dore dressed in a careless and barefoot manner. After three years on the island, the Ritters had forsaken their nudist ways; Dr. Ritter also cheerfully exchanged his ample supply of fruit and vegetables for pork and beef from the Wittmers.

Toward the end of September, the Wittmers and Ritters watched the reddish glow in the sky as flames rose above Narborough Island. It was not an eruption, but sulphur which had caught fire in the immense crater, and poisonous gases filled the air. Fortunately, they were a hundred miles away.

Three other persons watched the fiery sky from their sixty-foot yawl *Cockatoo*. Captain Charley Pease had sailed from Miami, Florida, with an elderly black sailor named Zachary (who had once skippered large square-riggers), and a young college drop-out named Charley Otterman who found life at sea more interesting than classes. The trio had spent a month sportfishing in the Galapagos and were enroute to the Marquesas. Having heard that there were settlers on Floreana, they hiked from Post Office Bay into the hills, where they found the Wittmers living in a cave in early October of 1932. After a brief visit cut short by language barriers, the mariners returned to the *Cockatoo* unaware that the Ritters were also living on Floreana, but closer to Black Beach.

13

MOSTLY ARRIVALS

c.o.o.o.o.o.o.o.o.o.o.o.o

Academy Bay Goes International

While five Germans were struggling on Floreana, six Norwegians were quite well established on one of the immense volcanoes of Santa Cruz Island (Indefatigable). Clouds and mists drape the summit of this extinct crater, once filled with fire, but now a waterless pit. Only wild burros and hogs climb the long uniform slopes of the 2,835-foot flat cone. The lava, which had bubbled out of the crater in a ten-mile radius, is difficult to cross. It is covered by dense jungles on the upper slopes and parched cactus-country below.

On the southern coast, at the base of a snowless Galapagos Fujiyama, is a reef-encumbered bay whose southeastern end is sheltered from huge breakers by tiny Jensen Island. When the brigantine yacht *Illyria* dropped anchor near this point on January 11, 1929, Mr. Crane and his guests could see four or five houses on the beach. Going ashore, they found an abandoned canning factory, a derelict Ford tractor, three graves, three dogs, and some chickens. With one of the crew acting as interpreter, they learned from the Norwegian fishermen on shore the sad fate of the defunct colony.

After a four-hour hike along the slope behind Academy Bay, past cacti over twelve feet tall and enormous prickly-pears, the explorers came to a thousand-foot elevation where the air was damp and the vegetation luxuriant in the rich red soil. In a clearing planted with banana and plantain trees, pineapple, and papayas, stood a little house on stilts, whose occupants were surprised to see their first visitors in over six months.

Blonde-bearded and bespectacled Mr. Horneman, about forty years old, had brought his pretty German bride to the Galapagos with the Norwegian expedition. Their son, now eight months old, was the first native of Santa Cruz, and the parents did express some anxiety over the lack of medical care should the baby become ill.

Their little three-room house was neat and clean; photographs of snowy Norway hung on the walls. A bookcase full of Norwegian scientific books, and the couple's ability to speak several languages, attested to their excellent education. They had started their plantation after the other settlers had left, and were experiencing trouble in getting supplies and tools from the mainland. Their closest neighbor was a single Norwegian, who had a shack about one-half mile away.

There was another plantation nearby which belonged to two fishermen, Estampa and Wold. However, it was running wild from neglect, as the fishermen spent most of their time on the shore. This plantation, called Las Fortunas, had been started by the colony to supply the needs of the group. Now Estampa and Wold, sometimes with hired peons, occasionally cut back the jungle which tried to engulf the clearing.

These two fishermen eked out a living with their salted fish, which they sold at Wreck Bay. In exchange, they received coffee, tea, salt, and staples. Their fruit and vegetables came from the plantation; goat meat and beef were obtained from Floreana and Barrington. They used turtle oil for cooking, and kept a turtle farm, made of an enclosed rock basin for keeping the yellow-green sea turtles in stock; these were caught at Tortuga Beach on the southwestern side of Santa Cruz.

Christian Edwardson Estampa and his friend Wold were blonde, blue-eyed Scandinavians about thirty years old. Emaciated, burned by sun and wind, teeth gone, skin erupting in salt-water boils, with clothing in tatters, they did appear like a pair of castaways on a desert isle. However, they were well content with their lot and had only two desires. First of all, they needed a motorboat. The twenty-six foot *Falcon* was an excellent craft, but sometimes it would lie becalmed for days, and at other times was almost wrecked on the rocky reefs by strong breakers. Their second wish was to sail to Norway and return to the Galapagos with brides.

When the *Mary Pinchot* arrived in Academy Bay in July of 1929, the Hornemans were gone. They had sailed to Chile where Mr. Horneman, a geologist, hoped to work a few years to raise enough capital for the purchase of more equipment for his plantation in the Galapagos. Estampa, Wold, and another Norwegian were still there. The third man may have been Arne Graffer, who, with two sons, is pictured in DeWitt's Meredith's *Voyages of the Velero III*.

Not too long afterwards they were joined by an intrepid German whose intention was to explore the interior of this indefatigable Santa Cruz. Like the Ritters, this Nordic had a theory; his was that man should revert to the primitive life, using only the weapons of primitive man. This modern Neanderthal intended to traipse into the jungle with a bow and arrows, despite the protestations of the fishermen that primitive man, having a herd instinct against danger, never hunted alone. They suggested he carry a compass, but the German claimed he had a compass in his head. One day he set off by himself and never returned. The Norwegians searched for days and found the bow and arrows; the body was never found. The hunter presumably lost his way and perished of hunger and thirst.

Early in 1930, the white-hulled motor yacht, *Nourmahal* came to Academy Bay with a whole complement of botanists, ornithologists, archeologists, photographers, and artists. Estampa and Wold were entertained with cocktails amidst a distinguished company of Kermit Roosevelt, Vincent Astor, Dr. Townsend, and Suydam Cutting dressed in evening clothes. The fishermen were quite overcome when Vincent Astor and Kermit Roosevelt arranged to deposit money in Quito for the purchase of a motor for the *Falcon.* In due time, a small, single-cylinder, semi-diesel (gasoline starter) engine was installed, giving the *Falcon* a speed of five knots.

It is not too surprising that visitors showered gifts upon the fishermen. Estampa and Wold were congenial, helpful fellows who found a useful niche in the Encantadas. With the *Falcon,* they toured the islands hauling produce and sharing their excesses of fruit. They welcomed newcomers and guided visitors, and were extremely well-liked for what Von Hagen called "their homespun pleasantness." Life can be beautiful, even in the Galapagos.

Wold was destined to remain a bachelor, but Estampa soon found a bride in Norway who agreed to share his pioneering life in the Encantadas. However, years later Estampa once more visited Norway, and this time was returning to the Galapagos with fourteen couples. Unfortunately, their ship was wrecked off the coast of Spain and only a thirteen-year-old girl survived; Estampa's body was never found.

The Raders and Finsen

When the *Manuel J. Cobos* arrived at Academy Bay in the summer of 1931, it deposited on shore a Danish couple, one Icelander, and three Ecuadorians. In addition, it unloaded a vast amount of lumber and building equipment, a rowboat, and a twenty-eight-foot motor launch which it towed along.

The Raders and Finsen, all elderly people in their late fifties, came to this desert island to spend their last years in peace and comfort. They had no intention of starting out as struggling pioneers; they had sufficient money and resources to build a large house with a modern kitchen and bathrooms, a three-room guesthouse, and another dwelling for their servants.

Mr. Rader was a tall Danish architect who migrated to the United States to build bridges and harbors. In Mexico, he married a Danish artist who was visiting relatives there. During an oil boom, the Raders travelled back and forth between the United States and Mexico, designing mining and oil camps. During this time he met Mr. Finsen.

Finsen came from Iceland and worked as a rigger for a trawl-making firm. Later, he rigged boats for salmon fisheries on the Pacific Coast of the

United States. Because he was an expert at splicing steel wire, he was hired as a rigger in an oil-drilling crew and worked in Mexico and South America. He was a small man with a broken nose, full gray beard, and was extremely quick and energetic.

While in Chile, Mr. Rader decided he would like to try a new life in the dry climate of the Galapagos. His wife and Finsen liked the idea. Rader then purchased land in the islands from the Ecuadorian government, and all three sailed for Academy Bay. Rader and Finsen had worked together in the oil fields, fought bandits in Mexico, roamed all over Central and South America, and had built 150 petroleum tanks in Venezuela. With all their experience in adapting to new surroundings and persons, living in the bleak Galapagos presented no insurmountable problems.

Immediately after their arrival at Academy Bay, they dug a well whose brackish water would be used in the bathroom of their house. A foundation was laid, and soon the framework of the house was completed. Rainwater was collected from 630 square feet of roof. The place was called Rocas Negros (Black Rocks), and this name was painted on the porch entrance, which faced a magnificent view of the Bay with Barrington Island in sight ten miles southeast. Building was stopped when the first shipment of materials was exhausted. Rader left for Guayaquil for more supplies, while Danish Mrs. Rader, Icelander Finsen, their three Ecuadorian workers, and Norwegians Estampa and Wold were left as the sole occupants of the cosmopolitan community. They were soon joined by a young Englishman.

Roydon Bristow

When the Raders started building their house, a fifty-two foot double-ended ketch left England on its way to the gold fields of New Guinea. Aboard the Cornish fishing smack *Gold Digger* were three adventurers ready to "load up with gold" in the Pacific. Their navigator was 25-year-old Roydon Bristow, who was a little skeptical as to their ultimate success. Having crossed the Atlantic and sailed through Panama, they arrived at the Galapagos in September of 1931. There, Bristow parted company with his shipmates after some disagreements. He was quite delighted with Academy Bay and decided to stay awhile until he could arrange passage on some other ship. Eventually, he stayed about nine months.

Mrs. Rader and Finsen adopted the agreeable young man into their household, and soon he was busily employed in the construction of 160 feet of stone wall around the premises. He visited the other islands with the fishermen, learned to make rawhide rope, battled the mosquitos, and became a typical islander. "I lived an elementary life in the sunshine," he wrote, "hunting, gardening, fishing, a woodsman and a pioneer; at sunset I sat in a well-kept home and enjoyed the delights of civilized society."

Bristow enjoyed the freedom from governmental interference: "The islands are one of the few spots in an overgoverned world where one can arrive, live or starve, with no notice taken or objections raised. There are no immigration laws and no laws at all in reality; the sole authority is the governor on Chatham Island with his ten soldiers, and unless a vessel happens to be in Wreck Bay he is as much marooned as anyone else. News travels slowly. Nobody bothers about the Galapagos."

There was no radio anywhere in the islands and so: "Our news was always well-matured when it reached us by schooner. News was discussed with extreme interest – as though we were living on another planet – gold standard, Indian affairs, disarmament and politics – it was amusing to look down from a great height and see what the ants were worrying about."

The *Nourmahal* came again in 1931, bringing clothing, boots, cigarettes, and tobacco for the fishermen. In return, Mr. Astor received two giant tortoises which Estampa and Wold had captured. He was also delighted with the two extremely rare baby tortoises which Mrs. Rader donated. Surprised to find an Englishman at Academy Bay, Mr. Astor parted with forty novels from the yacht's library and presented them to Bristow along with cigarettes and liquor.

New Arrivals

At the end of 1931, the three-masted schooner *Pro Patria* arrived at Academy Bay. Formerly owned by the Norwegian colony at Chatham, it was the pride of the Ecuadorian navy. The *Pro Patria* had brought a new governor and troops to relieve the incumbents, then made a few stops at the various islands. At Academy Bay it deposited nine persons and all their chattels on the stone pier – seven Norwegians, one German, and one Dutchman.

Standing disconsolate on the quay was Wurm-Muller, "the uprooted Crusoe of Floreana, with his wife, his goat, chickens and dogs, and all his worldly possessions" including a gramophone. He had been extremely content living in the Casa at Post Office Bay, and had sent for his wife living in Guayaquil. She arrived at the Casa, but her only neighbors, the philosophic Ritters, were not to her liking. When the *Pro Patria* arrived at the Bay, Mrs. Wurm-Muller persuaded her husband to move to Academy Bay, into one of the Norwegian houses confiscated by the Ecuadorian government.

Wurm-Muller, still grieving over the loss of Captain Bruun, was also worried about Arends who had gone to Isabela to salvage the *Norge*. He was greatly relieved to see Arends, Nuggerud, and Jensen arrive in the *Dinamita*, towing the *Norge* behind.

The *Pro Patria* had also brought Mr. Horneman, his wife, and son (now three years old). They had returned to their little plantation after discovering that economic conditions on the mainland were in bad shape. He was an avid botanist, besides being a geologist, and looked more like a scientist than pioneer; he worked hard to establish a happy home and became a permanent resident.

The Hornemans were a good example proving that a closely-knit family can succeed far better than a communal group. Perhaps the greatest factor contributing to their success was that wealth and profit were not their main considerations. Later, the Wittmers and the Lundhs would prove the same point. Another arrival with the Hornemans was their Norwegian neighbor, who returned to his little shack a half mile from the Hornemans.

Mr. Lundh, a retired sea captain, had heard of the Galapagos in Norway and came to Academy Bay to look things over. He liked what he saw, and later returned to Guayaquil to send for his wife and child and to procure materials for a home. Thirty years later his widow and son were still living happily at Academy Bay.

The Dutchman and German had heard about the Galapagos in Guayaquil. After arriving at Academy Bay, they moved into the cottage at Las Fortunas, having made an agreement to tend the plantation for fishermen Estampa and Wold. The Dutchman immediately made the house habitable, corraled some horses and pigs, started a vegetable garden, and soon was bringing fruit and vegetables to the fishermen at the beach, returning with fish and meat for himself and the Hornemans.

The German did not stay long. He had left his druggist's shop in Santiago, Chile, to his wife and children when business was slack, hoping to return to Germany. Instead, he somehow got sidetracked and arrived in the Galapagos. Roydon Bristow wrote, "When the German landed with a bag of beans and a bag of lentils, he said he had found Paradise; when I saw him in the hills he was not quite so sure. After the schooner arrived he came down the hill and sailed away in her. Asked why he was leaving, he said, 'The food! The work! Ach! It vos Hell!' And that was the last of him."

When the schooner *Cobos* took on board the disgruntled German, it also dropped off Mr. Rader with his building materials, along with an Austrian, a Spaniard, and three Ecuadorians to add to the mixture of nationalities.

The Ecuadorians consisted of a man, with his wife and child, in the employ of Mr. Rader. José was a good fisherman, and formerly had been mate on the schooner *Cobos* until it was seized for debt. He was intelligent and industrious, and of great help to the Raders. He was one of the few people who knew where to find oysters, a rarity in the Galapagos.

Joe Hager, the Viennese Austrian, had been a field engineer for an oil company in Colombia and lost his position during the oil slump. With a spade, pick, axe, hammock, and other supplies, he arrived to homestead in the Galapagos. He was making a preliminary survey of all the islands to determine which was most suited for cattle raising and farming. Santa Cruz did not please him, nor did Isabela; he finally settled on Chatham.

The tall, elderly Spaniard was an aristocratic soldier of fortune who had fought and roamed through every republic in South America. His large Stetson hat sported badges of the various regiments in which he had served. His manners and speech were those of a gentleman, but his appearance, especially the bushy black beard, was reminiscent of the buccaneers who caroused in these islands 150 years earlier. In khaki shirt and breeches, the barefoot hero wore a Sam Browne belt to which was strapped a holster containing an enormous Colt revolver fastened to a heavy chain passing over his shoulder.

The revolver seemed to be superfluous protection, as the Spaniard was accompanied by three huge and ferocious hounds wearing fancy leather collars. One of the dogs had a monkey riding his back. The dogs fed themselves on wild game; though savage, they obeyed the slightest command of their master.

The Spaniard planned to spend a few months in the Galapagos, because this was the remaining outpost of South America which he had not visited. Finding Academy Bay too peaceful and tame, he and the Austrian, dogs, and monkey, left for the wilds of Isabela in the *Norge.*

Three years later, Robinson found the small community a hot-bed of social rivalry, envy, and jealousy, with families not on speaking terms with their neighbors. However, at least their petty quarrels did not terminate in murder, as happened later in the explosive situation which developed on Floreana. Whether mosquitos or monotony or both were to blame for this irascible human behavior at Academy Bay is not known.

Adam and Eve Revisited

Roydon Bristow went calling on the Ritters at Floreana and was greeted by a barefooted Dore in a blue frock, and a bearded, toothless Dr. Ritter with the hair of a prophet. He shared their meal of minced onions, turnips, carrots, and fried egg-plant, followed by dessert – a foamy meringue of beaten egg whites, chocolate, and sugar. He sampled their bananas, papayas, watermelon, and oranges, finding them superior to any fruit on the other islands.

The doctor had acquired a mincing machine to save the wear and tear on his stainless steel denture, which he preferred not to wear while eating, because it was supposed to last another hundred years. He only wore his teeth to aid conversation, and they did improve his appearance. (In time, Dore lost her teeth, and a visitor, the Danish deep-sea explorer, Hakon Mielche, wrote several years later, "His disciple, Miss Dore, smiled a toothless welcome, for the couple had at their disposal only one pair of false teeth, and when I visited them, it was Ritter's day . . . .") Bristow had been served some fried minced meat, but Dore and the doctor partook of none, still claiming to be vegetarians, a pose which seemed to impress visitors.

In their two years on the island, the doctor had developed a well-irrigated garden, supplying food all year round. He trapped animals with snares and pits, thus obtaining hides which he tanned. The leather was used for rawhide ropes and chairs, and for hinges on lockers. He had ingenious contrivances like the sugar cane press made from a stump of an ironwood tree. A gun named Little Bertha – a thirty-inch grooved piece of wood equipped with a trigger and spring – shot pebbles at birds that plagued the garden. Shelves were suspended from tree boughs to keep rats from the larder. Plum-tree House boasted of a wooden floor, but there seemed to be no wardrobe in sight. Two nails were knocked into a tree trunk; apparently the nudists had little use for clothing.

Bristow was quite amazed at Dore's prewar attitude as to the position of the German woman in the home. He wondered why she was so emphatic and so detailed about the subservience of woman. Her view was that woman is the lesser being, whose duty it was in life to help her husband fulfill his mission, and the man is justified in beating his wife for any disobedience. The doctor seemed to be extremely pleased with his disciple's outlook.

Bristow wrote, "The doctor does not smoke and drinks nothing but water; I don't think he finds occasion to beat his wife; apparently he has no vices," and finally concluded, "The Ritters are one of the most interesting couples in the world. Call them cranks, but they had the courage to put their theories to the test and to make a practical experiment."

Mr. Rader, whose age and experience rendered him somewhat more perspicacious and less impressionable than young Bristow, had a far less charitable opinion of the Ritters. On his frequent hunting trips to Floreana, he got to know "the conceited little gnome" quite well. He disapproved of the Ritter's tin-roofed cage, which he took as a sign of indolence. Even the Wittmers, who were not rich like Mr. Rader, had built themselves a fine stone house to replace their original log cabin.

As they watched Ritter's stainless steel fangs attack huge beef steaks, Rader's hunting dogs developed an inferiority complex; the doctor's claims to vegetarianism were an obvious fraud. Ritter's acceptance of handouts from the yachts, even going so far as writing for the items he needed, seemed quite a racket to Rader, who also frowned upon the nudism.

Rader also claimed that Ritter "kicked hell out of Dore and made her work like a mule," while he took life easy, writing his insignificant philosophies and answering his fan mail. Ritter also wrote copious letters to the Ecuadorian authorities with complaints about the islanders, especially Baroness Wehrborn when she arrived. The Baroness turned out to be a particular thorn in his sun-tanned hide. Publicity appealed to the selfstyled Buddha's vanity, and he became quite perturbed when the Baroness stole his limelight.

Roydon Bristow left the Raders in the summer of 1932, struck with wanderlust and unable to resist the invitation of a beautiful yacht sailing to the

South Seas. The total population of the islands at this time numbered about two hundred: twenty-two were Europeans, and the remainder were Ecuadorians at Progreso and Villamil. The Wittmers had arrived in 1932. The notorious Baroness, with her masculine entourage, was to make her dramatic entry about October 15, 1932.

Fall of the Cobos Empire

Meanwhile, on the island of Chatham (San Cristobal), conditions were going from bad to worse. The vast Cobos plantation was experiencing labor problems; ever since the penal colony was abolished, cheap labor was no longer available. Sugar cane lay rotting in the fields for want of cutters, and coffee beans remained unpicked. The sugar factory rusted away, and weeds grew over tracks and derelict machinery. The decaying plantation, hewn and blasted from the wilderness by the tyrant Cobos, was reverting to the jungle.

The estate of young Cobos and his brother-in-law, Alvarado, was passing into the hands of a German company in Guayaquil, to whom Alvarado was indebted for over $100,000. When the creditors seized the plantation, Cobos and his wife Karin were forced to leave the island. They returned after Cobos managed to salvage a small portion of the estate for himself. He also retained the position of manager of the rest of the rancho, which later became more or less a government operation. The three hundred inhabitants of the island were completely dependent upon this organization, which now owned the wild cattle, horses, sugar cane, coffee, machinery, and local store.

In 1936, the Comandante at Chatham told Von Hagen that the Europeans at Academy Bay lived "como puercos," but Von Hagen saw for himself that "the Scandinavian peasant lived regally in comparison to an Ecuadorian one." Of the settlers on Chatham, he said, "For the most part the inhabitants lead a wretched existence, owing their livelihood to an organization which controls the food supply and the only ship – the schooner *San Cristobal*."

The schooner *Manuel J. Cobos*, repainted and renamed *San Cristobal* continued its faithful service between Guayaquil and the islands, and was again renamed *Montecristi*. Even as recently as 1951, Crealock was surprised to find the indestructible tired old schooner still afloat: "A pile of lumber leaned against the jetty – we looked again . . . . Good God! The lumber had a name painted on it – *Montecristi* – it was the ship herself, the steamer.

"No one knows just how old the *Montecristi* is, for no one can remember farther back than sixty years. She was once a stubby schooner, but a patch of sail and an asthmatic old engine have replaced her original rig, and her planking has been renewed so often that no solid places remain in her frames for new fastenings. Yet once a month she staggers from her home port in Ecuador, and totters into Wreck Bay to lean wearily against the jetty."

Since 1880, the "notorious bark" had shuttled back and forth without accident between the mainland and the islands; with its curious cargoes and even more curious passengers.

As for the rickety wooden pier at Wreck Bay, it, too, had defied the ages. Remarkably free of barnacles and algae, the wood pilings and rough-hewn planks withstood the ravages of time and salt water. Natives say the extremely hard wood comes from the matazarno tree, found on Santa Cruz Island. The impervious wood, the durable schooner, the Methuselah tortoises – all are in keeping with the ageless lava heaps of the Galapagos where time stands still.

> "Time goes, you say? Ah, no!
> Time stays. We go."
>
> Austin Dobson

14
FEUDS, MURDERS, AND MYSTERIES

A remote corner of World's End would be the ideal setting for a perfect crime. Many sinister deeds, no doubt, had passed undetected in secret nooks in the unexplored, uninhabited vastnesses of the Galapagos. The discovery of bleached bones occasioned no surprise; many unfortunates had died here, lost in the impenetrable interior or cast ashore by angry seas. Victims of violence by the hand of their fellow man could be concealed in crevices, burned to ashes, or tossed to the sharks, while the murderer escaped punishment.

The disappearance in 1934 of a publicity-mad Baroness and her lover from the island of Floreana stirred up some interest, but the affair would soon have been forgotten had not an ironic twist of Fate cast her second lover upon the shore of another island. When the crew of an American tuna clipper discovered two mummified bodies on the parched sand of Marchena Island, the eyes of the world once more focused upon Floreana as a sordid drama unfolded.

Stranger than the bizarre drama itself is the fact that Hollywood never seized the opportunity of filming this unique mystery. It had all the ingredients of a real thriller: a weird setting, a gun-toting self-styled Empress with an assortment of lovers, an eccentric doctor who stole another man's wife, six deaths, yachting millionaires, shipwrecks, bloodshed, sex, nudism, silk panties, and stainless steel teeth. There was love, hate, jealousy, sadism, and death. In due time, the inevitably distorted accounts of the double murder were smeared in the Sunday supplements of newspapers, with all sorts of speculation as to what became of the Baroness and if the murderer had any accomplices. Because of conflicting stories and contradictions by the few principals involved, the mystery has never been solved; the bodies of the Baroness and her lover were never found.

The tragedy began on the island of Floreana; the cast of major characters consisted of the Ritters, the Wittmers, and the amorous eccentric who set up court with three men.

The Baroness

On the fifteenth of October, 1932, the schooner *Cobos* dropped anchor in Post Office Bay, and its crew immediately began to unload twenty-four pieces of luggage, over one hundred packing cases, and ninety bags of cement. In addition, there was enough livestock to fill a barnyard: two cows, a calf, several donkeys, ducks, hens, turkeys, pigeons, and rabbits. The ship had been chartered by a woman of "dubious antecedents, uncertain age, and still more ambiguous behavior." She had amused herself during the six-day voyage from Guayaquil to Floreana with reading the mail intended for the Ritters and Wittmers, removing photographs which struck her fancy.

Baroness Eloise Bousquet de Wagner Wehrborn, an Austrian by birth, was not a beauty. Of medium height, platinum blonde hair, about age forty, and with very prominent protruding yellow buck-teeth, she relied upon her vivacity and girlish antics to charm her lovers. It was rumored that she had served as a "Mata Hari" in Constantinople during the war, and as a dancer there, met and married a French baron, an airman. She later operated a dress shop in Paris and met Alfred Rudolph Lorenz, a German architect who had Robert Philippson in his employ as engineer.

An Ecuadorian named Valdivieso had arrived in Europe as a stowaway, and while working for a railroad in France, met the Baroness. Intrigued by the stories of Doctor Ritter in European newspapers, the Baroness questioned Valdivieso about the Galapagos. Somehow she enticed Lorenz to finance an expedition to the islands, and arrived with the three men in Guayaquil.

Soon, Ecuadorian newspapers were printing stories about the fabulous plans for Floreana. The Baroness, with her architect and engineer, was planning to build a handsome hotel to accommodate the yachting millionaires and the tourists who would soon be arriving on Grace Line ships to this upcoming Miami of the Pacific.

The Baroness spent her first night on Floreana at the Ritter house, where she and Dore quickly appraised each other – a case of mutual hate at first sight. Doctor Ritter remained philosophically aloof. The Wittmers became quite agitated when the Baroness announced she would settle near their spring. Meanwhile, she ensconced herself at the Casa at Post Office Bay, while her consorts hauled all the equipment to the caves near the spring. For several weeks, all was peaceful, but the Ritters and Wittmers shared the hope that the unwelcome neighbors would depart in due time.

Unaware of newcomers at Floreana, fisherman Estampa, a writer named Franke, and two peons came ashore to procure some wild beef. They were confronted by three men and a woman, who ordered the hunters off the island. With dramatic gestures, the woman informed them that she lay claim to the whole island and everything on it, and only the Ritters and Wittmers were "permitted" to remain. The hunters returned to their *Falcon* overnight, but went ashore the following morning. They shot and skinned two calves and carried the meat to their rowboat. Once again they were confronted by the unholy four, this time brandishing rifles. At gunpoint, Estampa was ordered to get the hides. Instead, he escaped and found refuge at the Ritter place. With the use of the Wittmer's dinghy, he eventually returned to the *Falcon*. Meanwhile, the Baroness had freed the other three men when she discovered her own two cows and calf were unharmed. On behalf of Estampa, Ritter mailed a complaint to the Governor of the Galapagos at Chatham.

Another complaint was issued by Pablo and Rosa Rolando, a honeymooning couple who were shipwrecked on Floreana. The Baroness ordered them off the island, casting them adrift in a small boat. A fishing vessel rescued them and the incident was reported to the authorities. The Baroness herself told the story to European newspapers to build up publicity and notoriety for the self-proclaimed "Empress of the Galapagos."

The Ritters diligently avoided the Baroness. However, the birth of Rolf Wittmer, in January of 1933, created an atmosphere of cheer and friendliness. Doctor Ritter had rendered medical aid after post-natal complications arose, and hostilities were forgotten. The Baroness oozed sweetness and invited the Ritters to her newly-erected "Hacienda Paradiso." Spanish for paradise is "paraiso"; the quartet was not too scholarly.

The men had constructed a large one-room shanty of boulders and timbers, roofed with corrugated iron and walled with canvas. Carpets and draperies decorated the walls; brightly-colored cushions were heaped onto two large divans which served as beds at night. A separate storeroom was relegated for the Ecuadorian. Outside, a space was cleared for a garden, with a careful arrangement of stones marking off future flower beds amidst the vegetables.

Luncheon was served outdoors, where Dore carefully examined the silverware, quite convinced that the coat-of-arms was a fake and the Baroness an impostor. She observed the femme-fatale, fashionably dressed in a black and white frock, pouring her charms upon the philosophic Doctor Ritter. The Baroness confided to Dore that no man could resist her, and though her title lured them at first, "it's something else that keeps them." Dore diagnosed the Baroness as "completely sex-mad."

Indeed, the Baroness did have some strange hold over her admirers. With Valdivieso it may have been fear, because he was extremely anxious to leave the island. The tall, slender, boyish-looking, blond Lorenz seemed a willing slave at first, but soon was degraded into a menial, performing servile tasks. Philippson, now top favorite with the Baroness, bullied the weaker

Lorenz, and the two rivals abhorred each other. The fickle Baroness, whose ardor blew hot and cold, didn't hesitate to use her horsewhip on both during her frequent outbursts of bad temper.

Early in February of 1933, the huge motor yacht, *Velero III*, dropped anchor in Post Office Bay, and the Baroness met her first millionaire. Captain G. Allan Hancock came to bestow his largess of clothing and tools upon the Ritters, whom he had met the year before. With him came Professor Schmitt of the National Museum, and both were surprised at finding the Wittmer family on the island. They had read about the Baroness and were eager to meet her.

The Baroness did not bedazzle Hancock enough to make him a partner in her hotel venture, but he did promise to return with camera equipment to film a pirate movie, *The Empress of Floreana*. He entertained her on the yacht and presented her with gifts. The Baroness appropriated for herself the blankets and case of tinned milk intended for the Wittmer baby. Valdivieso left the island on board the *Velero III*, having included the Wittmers' collapsible dinghy with his belongings. Righteously indignant, Herr Wittmer penned a letter of complaint to the Governor concerning the theft of the boat, the milk, and a previous incident of rice stolen by the Baroness.

Shortly afterwards, Vincent Astor's *Nourmahal* arrived at Black Beach with a wheelbarrow and supplies for Doctor Ritter. The Baroness sent Philippson to the yacht with a letter of invitation which was ignored. After wining and dining the Ritters aboard ship, the *Nourmahal* left without having called upon the Baroness. The scorned queen furiously stormed into Friedo as the Ritters were opening their gifts, and demanded a share. Ritter tossed her and Philippson out.

The next batch of mail received by the Wittmers and Ritters contained newspaper clippings of "The Revolution on Floreana." They related how Doctor Ritter, who had opposed the tyrannical rule of the new Empress, was now in chains. These wild reports, carried by major European papers, were accompanied by pictures of the Baroness dressed as a pirate. The American Weekly Sunday supplement featured luridly illustrated reports showing the Empress dressed in abbreviated silk shorts, bare-shouldered in a halter bra, and wearing two pearl-handled revolvers suspended from a cartridge belt at her waist.

Obviously, the Baroness was cleverly drawing attention to her "luxury hotel" by sending false reports to the press. She was soon deluged with letters from adventurers and riff-raff who wished to join her freebooter army and would support her cause, provided, of course, that she paid their passage. Yachts appeared at Post Office Bay, and the owners had themselves photographed with the notorious Empress, hoping some of the dubious fame would rub off on them as they got their name in print associated with hers. Bright red arrows directed visitors to "Hacienda Paradiso." A welcoming message posted at Post Office Bay urged tired travellers to seek refreshment and solace at this desert oasis. The new celebrity eclipsed Doctor Ritter; nobody bothered about him anymore.

Intrigued by newspaper reports and by friend Estampa's experience, Mr. Rader of Academy Bay sailed to Floreana to participate in the interesting social events. Having tangled with Mexican bandits, Rader had no qualms about being ordered off the island. He was greeted by a charming aristocrat who quickly surmised that Rader was no fool. The Baroness showed him her fan mail and clippings, gloated about her ability to hoodwink people, and admitted her intention of snagging some infatuated millionaire to build a fancy hotel on what she called "The Island of Love."

In the summer of 1933, the Governor and his entire army of seven soldiers arrived at Floreana to investigate the numerous complaints about the curious behavior of the Baroness. Utterly smitten by her charms, he invited her to Chatham as his guest. She returned after a week with title to four square miles of land; the Ritters and Wittmers got a mere fifty acres apiece. More-over, she brought a new lover, the handsome Knud Arends, partner of the late Captain Bruun. Presumably, he had been hired for about ninety sucres a month to work for the Baroness. Lorenz continued to do all the drudgery, while the Baroness and Arends set out daily on "hunting expeditions."

The Island of Love quickly became the Island of Hate as the deposed lover Philippson, tormented by jealousy, became quarrelsome and vented his spleen upon the weaker Lorenz. After only one year on the island, Lorenz now looked thin, pale, and extremely ill. Dore Koerwin attributed his tubercular appearance to arsenic poisoning, but it seems hardly likely that the Baroness would poison her chief cook and household drudge. The defense-less Lorenz often sought refuge with the Wittmers or Ritters after savage beatings at the hand of Philippson.

Busy with her new lover, the Baroness had her men screen visitors who called at Paradise; unimportant boatmen were shown the way out. More affluent yachtsmen bearing gifts were granted a royal audience. Usually dressed in a riding outfit, complete with breeches, high boots, horsewhip, and the highly publicized revolver, she reclined upon a divan and chatted with her dazzled guests. The honor of serving tea was conferred to Philippson, whose manners were quite polished; Lorenz and Arends stayed in the background. The splendid actress then awed her visitors with tales of the royal court in Vienna, and gossiped about previous millionaire guests. Sometimes she wore short green silk pants and an embroidered peasant blouse or brief halter bra.

The strange doings on Floreana attracted journalists and a German named Boeckman, who came twice. On his second visit, in September of 1933, he brought his brother-in-law, Linde, and an Ecuadorian soldier acting as courier for the mail to the islands. The trio stayed overnight with the Ritters, and on the following day went hunting with the Baroness and Arends.

Late that evening, the agitated journalist summoned Doctor Ritter, because Arends had been shot in the abdomen. It seemed that several hours earlier, the Baroness, smitten with love for the handsome Linde, intended to wound him slightly to prolong his stay on the island. Arends inadvertently knelt in the line of fire and was seriously wounded. On previous occasions, the Baroness had tamed wild dogs by shooting them in the leg and nursing them afterwards. Linde had openly rejected her wiles and blandishments all day, so the Baroness had resorted to a desperate measure to make her conquest.

The schooner *Cobos* took Arends on a stretcher to Guayaquil, and Ritter wrote another letter to the Governor requesting the removal of the insane Baroness from Floreana. Dore claimed that the Baroness later paid a heavy financial settlement to Arends as an aftermath of the accident, and as a result was almost without funds.

It was in December of 1933 that three ships arrived at Post Office Bay almost simultaneously. The author, Hakon Mielche, and five other young Danes, came in the forty-year old fishing boat, *Monsoon*, which was circling the globe collecting curios for sale to museums. Captain Hancock came once more to film a short movie of the Baroness. The *Velero III* then departed to explore the islands.

The Baroness had predicted correctly that tourists would flock to her fabled summer resort; a whole boatload of them arrived on the Norwegian liner, *Stella Polaris*, to photograph the queer assortment of inmates of the Galapagoan zoo at Floreana. Their visit to Post Office Bay was a special treat on their expensive round-the-world cruise. During their one-day stay, many hiked over to Hacienda Paradiso where they were treated to cups of tepid water, despite the fact that the Baroness's lengthy invitation promised they would share in the bounty which generous yachtmen had showered upon this Eden. Mielche had seen cases of Johnny Walker and Cliquot being transferred from the *Velero III* to this desert oasis.

Many postcards were mailed in the famous barrel, with all tourists convinced that they had seen the Galapagos in this brief visit. The Baroness and Ritters were invited to a party on board the *Stella Polaris*. According to Dore, the Baroness was a neglected wall-flower and left early. It was the last time Dore ever saw her again.

When the *Monsoon* had arrived earlier at Wreck Bay, Mielche received a batch of letters from the Governor to deliver to the settlers on Floreana. After visiting Karin Cobos, now the mother of two children, Mielche was piloted by the Norwegian Nuggerud to Post Office Bay on the *Dinamita*.

After reading the long notice posted by the Baroness near the barrel, Mielche trudged up the path to Paradise, whose entrance was through a curiously out-of-place Japanese gate with large red letters spelling out "Welcome." Heaven turned out to be a wooden hut in the center of a vegetable garden where a tubercular cook and curly-haired gigolo served tea. Pale

Lorenz already had one foot in the grave; "Baby" Philippson wore a smile much too sweet, like that of a gigolo in a cheap Berlin restaurant. The goddess herself was by no means beautiful: swollen lids, strong spectacles, long yellow rabbit-teeth, and hanks of hair held by a ribbon. She "cantered about" in a sort of "baby's rompers."

Next, Mielche visited the small philosopher Ritter, of the long, pointed nose and watery, protruding eyes. His toes pointed inwards as if his "legs were screwed on wrong." His toothless companion Dore wore beach "pyjamas," but no shoes on her large black feet. "Her neck had not been washed for a month and had been given a marbled effect by the passage of drops of sweat."

Ritter boasted that his wife in Germany, a veritable Brunhilde, was longing for him, and some day would arrive on Floreana to demand him back. He also admired his own works, bound in Floreana leather – a private edition in "oasis morocco" – and kept it near his brand-new typewriter. To Mielche, Ritter's philosophy was a "comprehensive cocktail of the strangest ingredients, a curious mixture of foreign words, faded theories and well-chewed phrases." Just before his departure, Mielche was asked if Ritter did not indeed resemble Faust.

It was with some trepidation that Mielche then left for the Wittmer household, fearing he would encounter more odd misfits. Instead, he found the only sane family on the island, living in a beautiful stone house. The Wittmers were ordinary people who knew nothing of Kant or the cartography of the human brain. Frau Wittmer was charming and the children were well-behaved. After a pleasant visit, Mielche sailed away from "this place of queer animals and their strange population of human jetsam," only to be wrecked later on a coral reef in the South Pacific.

Captain Hancock cruised extensively in the Galapagos archipelago on a scientific mission and returned again to Floreana. This time he visited only the Ritters, a little irked, perhaps, at the Baroness, who insisted he take her to Hollywood.

On December 29, 1933, Captain Irving Johnson and his wife Electa arrived at Post Office Bay in the schooner *Yankee* on its first voyage around the world with a group of schoolboys. They were greeted by Philippson, who invited them to Hacienda Paradiso, where the Johnsons saw nothing but domestic harmony. Of the Baroness they wrote, "Though she was not pretty, she had a personal charm and a keen interest in life." Philippson looked "marvelously well" and Lorenz was "probably tubercular," and rather meek, and stated he was leaving in a few weeks. The Johnsons admired the artistic touches which made the residence attractive: a window box of flowers, a well-kept garden, bright paint on fences and beehives, and the decorative gate at the entrance. The Baroness told them not to visit the Wittmers, as the trip was not worth the bother.

A flashing mirror from the hillside at Black Beach was an invitation to the *Yankee* from Doctor Ritter. The Johnsons saw all the ingenious contraptions at Friedo and reported that both occupants were toothless. They noticed the special enmity between the Baroness and the Ritters, each group having accused the other of theft of animals and equipment. Johnson wrote, "The night that Dore and Ritter came down to the Yankee for supper, they met the Baroness on her way home from the ship, so Ritter had to rush back and guard his house till she should have passed."

A severe drought struck Floreana at the beginning of 1934 and many wild animals died of thirst. The springs gave scant supplies of water. Tempers grew short. Doctor Ritter refused to give medical aid to Wittmer, who was suffering from a bad tooth abcess, and Arthur Eichler claims that Ritter and the Baroness almost came to blows when Ritter found the Baroness bathing in his spring – she called him an "insane Buddha." The Wittmers were busy putting finishing touches on their new stone house and did not visit their neighbors, but Lorenz often came to them in bad shape from unmerciful beatings.

Mrs. Wittmer stated that, towards the end of March, 1934, the Baroness came to the Wittmer house and announced that she and Philippson were leaving at once for Tahiti. A boat had arrived at Post Office Bay and invited the two to sail with them, they were leaving immediately, and would Mrs. Wittmer please tell Lorenz to look after Hacienda Paradiso. The Baroness left, and she and Philippson were never seen again. During this time, Lorenz and the boy, Harry Wittmer, were reputedly gathering firewood in the jungle.

Dore Koerwin's version of the disappearance of the Baroness was that, in March, Lorenz had some violent arguments with the Baroness after which he was beaten unconscious by Philippson and the woman. He fled to the Wittmers, also instructing Ritter to post a note in the barrel requesting the next ship to remove Lorenz from the island. At noon of March 19, 1934, Ritter and Dore heard a horrible shriek of panic followed by silence. The next day Lorenz appeared at the Ritter place, in good spirits, announcing that he had caught two baby burros for the Ritters. The Ritters did not ask Lorenz whether he had heard the shriek of terror. A few days later, Herr Wittmer arrived and delivered a tirade against the Baroness, then Frau Wittmer gave them a detailed account of the Baroness's hasty departure, and how she left her shack in complete disorder from packing. Ritter agreed to buy some of the supplies which the Baroness had abandoned from Lorenz. Ritter cautiously recorded all the statements in case anyone should question them later.

When the Ritters arrived at Paradise, they found the place perfectly tidy and saw that the Baroness had not taken anything except the clothing she wore, not even items of sentimental value: family photographs, a copy of *Dorian Grey*, her favorite long-stemmed Russian cigarettes. Philippson, too, had not taken his mother's photo. A layer of dust lay on everything, indicating that no cleaning had been done since the disappearance of the pair. When asked if there was any chance the Baroness would return, Lorenz replied, "There's no danger of that – not any more." Lorenz and Wittmer then proceeded to tear down the house.

The Wittmer version of this incident was that the Wittmers were shocked at finding Ritter opening the crates and buying things from Lorenz. When the Wittmers questioned him about the summary disposal of the property of the Baroness, who might return, Ritter said, "She won't be back. Take my word for it."

About July 10, Trygve Nuggerud arrived at Post Office Bay in the *Dinamita*, a 40-foot open boat, accompanied by a Danish reporter named Rolf Blomberg. They left soon afterwards with Lorenz aboard, and a packet of Wittmer letters to be mailed. The *Dinamita* arrived safely at Academy Bay, where Blomberg disembarked. Lorenz, Nuggerud, and an Ecuadorian named José Pasmino sailed for Wreck Bay on July 13, 1934.

Strange Saga of the *Cimba*

On July 23, 1934, the small thirty-five-foot schooner *Cimba* anchored at Post Office Bay after sixteen days of calm and squalls out of Panama. Young Richard Maury and Russell (Dombey) Dickinson had sailed from Nova Scotia and were proceeding to the South Seas. They rowed ashore. "On the beach we came upon the wreck of a small boat, two skeletons and the wind-worn footprints of a man," Richard wrote. They found the post office barrel empty, found tracings of streets that led to nowhere, a solitary building in partial ruin, and a crude arrow pointing to a path leading to Hacienda Paradiso. They spent the night on the beach by a roaring fire and ate pancakes.

At sunrise, they heard a rifle shot, fired in reply and marched inland. Soon they were met by a boy "whose hair fell almost to his shoulders, whose sunburned body was almost bare except for a loincloth supporting a long knife in a skin sheath . . . . A bearded man, his hair reaching well down a coarse shirt, was suddenly shaking us by the hand." They followed him up the incline, and at what Richard called "House of Paradise" they met a pleasant matron who treated them to melons and a salad of greens. With the help of an English-German dictionary, the conversation proceeding haltingly. "They explained to us, their first visitors in over two years, that they asked only ammunition and matches from the outside world," said Richard. The old man could not explain the rifle shot the boys heard at sunrise. A small, eighteen-month-old baby was shown to them, also the neat house and bountiful garden.

Richard and Dombey then left. "Some distance on, there was a crude obelisk of stones marking the beginning of a trail to Black Beach where the widow of a Doctor Ritter lived in seclusion. Too late to think of deviating, we held south under large ashen craters to Post Office Bay.''

Back in the *Cimba* they sailed away, and Richard wrote: ''To our regret we were leaving something unsolved, footprints, unexplained gun shots . . . . We opened the volume – *Galapagos, World's End* – to the fly leaf where our friend, the lady at Paradise, had written an inscription. As far as we knew on going ashore, there were but two camps on the island, one belonging to the widow at Black Beach, the other to the notorious Baroness Wagner whom we thought we had visited that day. But the signature beneath the inscription was not hers at all, but that of someone else.''

It is obvious that the young men had mistaken Frau Wittmer for the Baroness. Richard Maury's book was published in 1939, five years after his visit to Post Office Bay. He was endowed with either a poor memory or a vivid imagination, because his story had so many glaring discrepancies that they should be pointed out. The language barrier may have given him a distorted story.

It is curious that reporter Rolf Blomberg, being very observant, as most reporters are, failed to notice any wrecked boats or loose skeletons lying about Post Office Bay when he arrived there less than two weeks before the *Cimba*. Maury did not specify that the skeletons were human, but we assume that is what he meant. He apparently did not question the Wittmers about them. His description of Harry and Herr Wittmer is incorrect. Harry usually wore seal-skin shorts and had his dark hair cut short; the fastidious Frau Wittmer was fussy about appearances. Herr Wittmer was almost bald; his few remaining hairs were clipped short. As to visitors, Blomberg and Nuggerud had been there two weeks before the *Cimba*. And what about Hakon Mielche who arrived six months before in December? Or Mr. Hancock?

The Wittmers were well aware that Ritter fired rifle shots when he saw boats approach the Bay. He had a good view of the sea at the Friedo elevation, and may have seen the beach fire also. Why did Maury call Dore a widow, when Doctor Ritter was very much alive and did not die until four months after the *Cimba* sailed away? After leaving the Wittmers, Maury said he headed south for Post Office Bay. It is a wonder he found the *Cimba* because he was headed in the wrong direction; Post Office Bay is north of the Wittmers.

In view of all these inaccuracies, the story of the skeletons and wreck seems quite a fabrication, especially since these bones mysteriously had disappeared when the *Cobos* arrived at the same bay less than a month later, on August 20, 1934.

Svaap

Another foreign yacht in Galapagos waters in the spring and summer of 1934 was the little thirty-two foot ketch, *Svaap*. William Albert Robinson was making his second trip to the Galapagos, accompanied by his wife Florence and friend Daniel West. Strangely enough, it was the barrel at Post Office Bay which led to the romance between Robinson and Florence Crane. Cornelius Crane's *Illyria* had picked up the mail from the barrel, which included letters deposited by Robinson in 1928. This subsequently led to a friendship between the two men, and to a meeting of Robinson and Crane's sister, Florence.

From the coast of South America, the *Svaap* sailed to Hood Island at the end of March 1934, about the same time that the Baroness disappeared. At Chatham, Robinson renewed his acquaintance with Karin Cobos, who still had the honey bear he had given her in 1928. On April 5 the *Svaap* left for Academy Bay, where Robinson visited his old friend, Wurm-Muller, and from him learned of the death of Captain Bruun, with whom he had once shared a Thanksgiving dinner. Nuggerud, too, was living at Academy Bay, and was very proud of his *Dinamita*. Estampa was busy making a baby cradle from a huge tortoise shell for the new heir expected in a few days; Rader and Finsen were still there. Robinson didn't stay long, because he found the place gloomy and depressing, full of mosquitos and personal quarrels among the few people there.

Svaap then proceeded to Isabela Island, where, near Elizabeth Bay, it anchored at a secluded spot which the crew named Pelican Cove. Here they remained to study the bird and animal life, photographing penguins and iguanas. One day, in the middle of April, the yacht *Stranger* was a welcome visitor at Penguin Cove, and Robinson helped the owner, Fred Lewis, capture a wild dog pup. A few days later, Robinson was attacked by the pup's angry family and forced to shoot the wild pack.

At Tagus Cove on May 20, Robinson suffered an acute attack of appendicitis. The Galapagos was a bad place to get sick – the only doctor available was Doctor Ritter at Floreana, a perilous trip for a sick man. Fortunately, the tuna boat *Santa Cruz* arrived and radioed for medical instructions. There was plenty of ice on board, but though the patient had his midsection frozen numb, the appendix ruptured the next day. On May 23, two navy seaplanes arrived with surgeons, and later, an American destroyer took the patient and his crew to Panama.

Little *Svaap* was left alone in gloomy Tagus Cove. It had been stripped of valuables before Robinson's departure and left riding to its two anchors. In gratitude for the extraordinary effort made by the U.S. Navy, Robinson offered the *Svaap*, the smallest craft that had ever circled the globe, as a gift to the Naval Academy at Annapolis.

President Roosevelt accepted the gift with pleasure, but *Svaap* never returned to the United States. Andrew Mellon's huge 170-foot diesel cruiser *Vagabondia* arrived at Tagus Cove and found the *Svaap* pirated and in bad condition. The crew salvaged the engine for Robinson and took the hull to the Norwegians at Academy Bay. The Governor at Chatham confiscated the *Svaap*, and a flood of letters passed between Panama, Chatham, and Tahiti, where Robinson was recuperating. The *Svaap* was hauled back and forth between Academy and Wreck Bays. On February 9, 1936, anchored at Wreck Bay, the *Svaap* was wrecked by a northerly blow and was a total loss. The reefs of the Encantadas had claimed another victim.

Death of Doctor Ritter

The schooner *Manuel J. Cobos* arrived with mail for Floreana on August 20, 1934, and the islanders received newspaper clippings concerning the disappearance of the Baroness. Reporter Blomberg had not swallowed the tale of her departure to Tahiti; no ship had arrived at any port with the Baroness and Philippson, and for certain not at Tahiti. Also, the *Dinamita* with Lorenz, Nuggerud, and Pasmino was missing.

Was the Baroness lost at sea? Were she and Philippson murdered? Why had the agitated Lorenz begged so desperately to be taken to Wreck Bay, from which the *Cobos* was soon to leave for the mainland? These were questions asked by the press, and all sorts of solutions to the mystery were offered.

No one knew the name of the yacht on which the Baroness left, nor even the exact date. Dore Koerwin said it was March 19; others said it was March 24 or 28. Time and dates are easily lost track of on lonely islands. Neither the Wittmers nor the Ritters saw the boat, nor made any attempt whatsoever to see it leave; maybe they knew it did not exist.

There were rumors that the Baroness was seen as a dancer in a third-rate night club in Tahiti, also in Panama. Why had the publicity-mad Empress suddenly become silent about her activities? After everyone solved the mystery to his own satisfaction, the Baroness was forgotten – for a while.

Meanwhile, Dore Koerwin wrote that after the Baroness was gone, a marvelous peace had settled upon Friedo; she and the Doctor lived in perfect harmony, having reached an "infinite understanding of each other." Mrs. Wittmer, on the other hand, reported that Doctor Ritter often came to their home complaining that Dore's constant quarreling was getting on his nerves, and that Dore was planning to leave the island. Reporter Blomberg came again, quite concerned over the missing *Dinamita.*

On November 6, 1934, the well-known American broadcaster, Phillips Lord, arrived at Post Office Bay in his beautiful four-masted schooner, *Seth Parker.* While at Friedo, he watched Ritter open a jar of potted pork for feeding the chickens. Within a few days, the chickens were dying of the spoiled meat, and this information was relayed to Mr. Lord by his crew. Upon a visit to the Ritters, Frau Wittmer was quite shocked to find the doctor busily potting these same chickens which had died of food poisoning. A long drought had ruined the Ritter crops, and he was preparing for the hungry season ahead. Dore claimed the poultry had been carefully "neutralized" of poison.

Several weeks later, after a three-hour hike made tortuous by a lame leg, Dore arrived at the Wittmer house seeking help for the doctor, who was dying. She claimed that both she and the doctor had eaten some of the potted chicken, but only Ritter became ill. After administering charcoal and chalk antidotes, Dore watched the doctor become progressively worse. When the Wittmers arrived, Ritter could only write messages, as his tongue had swelled. Paralysis set in, and the so-called vegetarian, who did not practice what he preached, died of meat poisoning. However, since meat is plentiful year-round on Floreana, while fruits are seasonal, and vegetables uncertain because of drought; it may not have been possible for the Ritters to adhere to strict vegetarianism, and so there may be some excuse for his apostasy.

The Wittmers reported that the doctor's dying moments were filled with hate towards Dore, and he made repeated feeble attempts to punch and kick her. His last written message to Dore was, "I curse you with my dying breath." Dore states that he died with his arms stretched towards her, and his face was "transfigured with a look so lucid, so triumphant, so calm, so tender."

Doctor Friedrich Ritter was buried in a corner of his garden, under the palm trees he planted. Herr Wittmer placed a rough cross over the grave with the inscription "Fr. Ritter, 21. XI, 34." Three years before his death, the doctor had written, "Paradise is not impossible of attainment. It is only a state of soul within one's self, and it consists of love, patience, and contentment. These are truly the entrance gates of heaven; since we possess all three, we do not ask for anything more." Perhaps in their earlier years on the island, Doctor Ritter and Dore had found what they had been searching for. At least, they had the determination and courage to stick to their chosen life at Floreana for five years, under conditions which had driven off countless others.

On the verge of a nervous breakdown, Dore remained with the Wittmers, waiting for a ship to remove her from the island. On December 6, 1934, the *Velero III* arrived. Dore was soon back in Germany. *The Life and Letters* of Doctor Ritter were published, and Dore wrote *Satan Came to Eden*, a book colored by jealousy and hate. Haunted by the memories of her strange adventures in a place called Friedo at World's End, Dore died in Germany in 1942.

Death of Lorenz and Nuggerud

Captain Hancock had made the special trip to the Galapagos at the end of 1934 for several reasons. First of all, he had received an urgent message from Doctor Ritter, stating that the doctor had secrets to impart whose nature was so dreadful that he could not set them down on paper. Secondly, two bodies had been found on Marchena Island, and a passport identified one of them as Lorenz.

On November 14, 1934, the American tuna clipper, *Santa Amaro*, was attracted by a white rag of distress fluttering from a pole on the beach of lonely Marchena Island, 160 miles north of Floreana. Near an overturned skiff lay two bodies, mummified by the scorching heat. The hacked-up remains of a seal and iguana bore mute evidence of their last meal. Near a bundle of baby clothing was a packet of letters from Floreana and Academy Bay. A radio message was sent to Los Angeles reporting the discovery. At a later date, the faded letters and notes were delivered to the German consular authorities; their contents were never divulged. Rumors were widespread that the letters contained accusations of murder. To confuse the issue, Dore claimed she did not know what terrible news Doctor Ritter wished to divulge to Captain Hancock.

Immediately, the press got to work; old files on the Baroness were re-examined, and soon, theories as to the identity of the bodies were printed. Some said it was Lorenz and Wittmer, others said it was the Baroness and Philippson, or perhaps the Ritters or Wittmers searching for a new Eden. Captain Hancock positively identified them as Lorenz and Nuggerud; he had met them both before, and their features were still recognizable.

Doctor Ritter had sent disturbing letters hinting of murder to friends in America, and a letter implicating Herr Wittmer to the Ecuadorian authorities. Mail travels slowly from the Galapagos, and Doctor Ritter died before some of these letters arrived at their intended destination. The islanders at Academy Bay, too, had written of their suspicions. No one believed the story of the mysterious yacht that sailed away with the Baroness; the only foreign yacht in the Galapagos waters at the end of March was *Svaap*, which now was anchored in Tagus Cove, abandoned. The *Stranger* did not arrive until the middle of April.

Mrs. Wittmer clung to her story of the departure of the Baroness by yacht; her statements had been recorded by Ritter in April. Understandably, she may have been shielding her husband or son Harry, both of whom may have had some knowledge of the truth of the affair. Their sympathies certainly were with the abused Lorenz, who often came to them for shelter. The concensus was that the Ritters were innocent; though they hated the Baroness, they lived rather far from Hacienda Paradiso – a two-hour walk – to have been involved. That distance, too, casts doubt upon Dore's story of a woman's scream of terror – unless the crime was committed, not on the beach or at the Baroness's dwelling, but on the path closer to Friedo. In that case they would have heard gunshots if she had been shot, and Lorenz was too weak to have committed the murder by other means, except poison. Herr Wittmer stated that he believed Lorenz may have shot his victims on the beach and thrown them to the sharks.

Captain Hancock later sent a letter to Hakon Mielche concerning his suspicions about the strange doings on Floreana. Hancock believed that Lorenz had murdered the pair in their sleep, buried their bodies, and invented the story of the yacht. Another story circulated that Lorenz had learned the secret of pirate treasure from the Baroness, murdered the pair, then set out treasure-hunting among the islands with Nuggerud. At any rate, it seemed quite certain now that Lorenz was the murderer, with or without accomplices, and had fled with a bad conscience from the scene of his crime. In his nervous flight, he caused the death of Nuggerud and the Ecuadorian, José Pasmino. Mrs. Nuggerud and her baby, too, became the "innocent victims of a frontier life beset by mysterious dangers."

At first, Nuggerud had refused to take Lorenz to Wreck Bay. The currents were extremely strong in July, and the *Dinamita* had no sail. In case of engine failure or fuel shortage, the 40-foot open boat would drift helplessly northwest, driven by the Humboldt Current. However, Nuggerud's wife was ill, and the extra payment offered by Lorenz would pay for her medical attention. The trio left on July 13, 1934. What happened to the *Dinamita* is not known; it was never found. Perhaps José elected to stay with the larger boat while the other two took a chance in the smaller, home-made skiff. More likely is the possibility that the *Dinamita* sank or was wrecked, and only two survivors managed to escape a watery grave, only to die a lingering death of thirst on desolate Marchena Island.

The Ecuadorian authorities made a cursory investigation in January of 1935; they really were not too concerned with the affairs of aliens squatting on Ecuadorian soil. Ritter had written to them that he had heard stories and a woman's scream in the night, and that Wittmer had fired the shots. Dore had set the time as noon. Anyway, the military police doubted Ritter's statement, because he lived three miles from Paradiso, with an 1,800-foot mountain in between. To their knowledge, he did not possess superhuman hearing abilities. The Wittmers said Ritter was throwing suspicion off himself by the accusation. There were vague rumors, too, that Dore had deliberately poisoned Doctor Ritter. Reporters invaded the island for a while, but soon stopped as the wearied public tired of the case repeated ad nauseam.

With the Baroness, Philippson, Lorenz, and Ritter dead, and Dore gone, the Wittmers were to have Floreana to themselves for two more years. On February 17, 1935, Frau Wittmer and three-year-old Rolf left Floreana for a visit to Rolf's grandparents in Germany. A Cologne newspaper also had offered Frau Wittmer a large fee for an article refuting some of the charges Dore was openly making against the Wittmers in Germany. After many delays and an absence of eleven months, Frau Wittmer and Rolf resumed their quiet life at their "Asilo de la Paz" with Harry and his father.

It was not until May 31, 1937, that new settlers arrived at Floreana: Don Ezekiel Zavala, wife Maria, daughter Marta, and an Indian servant boy named José. The Zavalas had lived on Isabela Island for fifteen years; now Zavala had been put on a military payroll to shoot the excess cattle. He spurned the title to Friedo, preferring to live at Black Beach where he declared himself Port Captain.

Meanwhile, Post Office Bay was deserted; weeds and thorn bushes began to cover what vestiges were left of the ill-fated Norwegian colony. The frame house was collapsing. Ships' names and dates were scrawled on the rusting water tanks; one tank still bore the white letters, painted in the Baroness's own hand, inviting the world to Paradise. The white barrel faithfully remained at its station.

One trail, now called "El Camino de la Muerte," reflected the sinister history of the island. The Irving Johnsons heard an observer remark of Floreana: "When a man falls out of a tree, everyone wants to know who pushed him."

15

MOSTLY ABOUT BOATS

Like Spenser's *Wand'ring Isles*, the Encantadas have often been considered places to be shunned by boatmen,

> For they have oft drawn many a wand'ring wight
> Into most deadly daunger and distressed plight.

However, because of the islands' convenient location between the Panama Canal and the South Seas, boats of all sizes – from Robinson's little 32-foot *Svaap* to J.P. Morgan's huge 343-foot steam yacht *Corsair* – stop by for a short interlude, and many a traveller wishes he had time to linger longer. By studying the unique "guest list" on the walls of Darwin Bay and Tagus Cove, or the placards at Post Office Bay, the wanderer gets a pretty good idea of the large number of yachting visitors who came here.

Many of these callers were impressed enough by the Galapagos to write about them; for this we owe the yachting authors a vote of thanks. There is no Galapagos Historical Society to record the strange, much less the ordinary, events that occur.

After all the hullabaloo about the Baroness died down, the Galapagos reverted to their normal forgotten and neglected condition, but sailboats and cruisers continued visiting.

In 1934, after the *Svaap*, *Stranger*, *Seth Parker*, *Vagabondia*, and *Velero III*, perhaps the last ship to arrive was one whose name confused port captains all over the world.

Igdrasil

Igdrasil was the Tree of Life in Norse mythology, with roots running down into Hell and branches reaching into Heaven. The ship was named by a couple who later discovered the ship was well named, for it did prove that "Life on a small ship is just like that, sometimes pleasant, sometimes not."

Professor R.S. Strout resigned his position at the Georgia School of

Technology in Atlanta, and with his wife Edith's help, constructed a thirty-seven-foot craft suitable for ocean voyages. They left Jacksonville, Florida, in June of 1934, and arrived in the Galapagos the following December.

The *Igdrasil* stopped at Marchena Island, where the bodies of Lorenz and Nuggerud still lay unburied, but the Strouts did not chance to see them. They stopped at James Bay, Sulivan Bay, and Seymour Bay, and spent Christmas Day with the settlers at Academy Bay. Mrs. Strout was the first woman to reach the crater's rim at Indefatigable.

At Post Office Bay, they visited Mrs. Wittmer, who chose to be silent about recent events, and no mention was made of the bodies at Marchena or the disappearance of the Baroness. The *Igdrasil* then proceeded to Tagus Cove and Penguin Cove, and with only thirty gallons of water to last three thousand miles, it sailed to the Marquesas. The Strouts travelled 38,000 miles around the world in a leisurely voyage of three years.

Seth Parker

The beautiful four-masted schooner *Seth Parker* had taken sixty days to sail from the Panama Canal to the Galapagos; this time may have included a stop at Cocos Island. At Post Office Bay, the owner, Phillips Lord, had been with Dr. Ritter when the fatal jar of pork had been opened in November of 1934.

The ship proceeded to the South Seas, and at Tahiti signed on as crew a Marquesan named Tehate. Off the coast of the Samoan islands, the *Seth Parker* was buffeted by a hurricane and wrecked, badly damaged in hull and spars. The cruiser *Australia* answered the S O S call and removed some of the crew. Phillips Lord, the captain, and several men remained aboard to await the arrival of a tug from Pago Pago to tow the schooner to port.

The cruiser *Australia*, with Tehate aboard, proceeded to Panama, where it disembarked the castaways at Balboa. Tehate was stranded without funds. Not knowing what to do with him, the authorities locked him up in quarantine until some ship would agree to take him home to the South Seas.

Director

In February of 1935, the fifty-nine-foot pilot schooner, *Director*, having served twenty-three years in the North Atlantic, arrived at Balboa. The owners, Bruce and Sheridan Fahnestock; their navigator, Dennis Puleston; George Harris; and a powerful black nicknamed Hey-Hey were on their way to the South Seas, collecting specimens for museums, taking motion and still pictures, and exploring the interiors of many islands. They took pity on stranded Tehate and invited him to sail with them.

The distance from Panama to the Galapagos is roughly nine hundred miles by steamship, but over fifteen hundred for sailing with tacking. The vessel must strive continuously against the equatorial counter-current which sets toward the east just north of the equator. Most sailing vessels make the trip in anywhere from sixteen to fifty days. It is on record that one whaling vessel was becalmed for so long that she ran out of food and water, and after her bottom began to rot out, the crew was forced to take to their small whaleboats, subsisting on fish and rainwater. The *Cimba* took sixteen days; *Marpatcha* made it in sixteen out of Salina Cruz. The *Arthur Rogers* once made the trip in ten days; the *Gloria Dalton* also took ten days out of Buenaventura. Alain Gerbault singlehandedly crossed from Panama to Wreck Bay in thirty-seven days on the *Firecrest*; the second time around the world he covered the same distance in forty-five days on a ship modestly named *Alain Gerbault*.

Le Toumelin told of a vessel becalmed in the doldrums for three months in 1923. Captain Desdemaines-Hugon left Rouen, France, in the fore-and-aft rigged three-masted ship *Suzaky*. Aboard was a group of people, including two women, who planned to settle permanently in Tahiti. The woodenhulled sailing vessel, with no auxiliary engine, had crossed the Atlantic without incident. After leaving Panama, the ship became trapped in the windless doldrums. Despite thundershowers and squalls, no wind arose sufficient to move the heavy vessel. The heat and humidity made life miserable, and slowly, food rations grew low. Then the teredo worms began to chew up the hull, so that the pumps were manned day and night to keep the ship afloat. Sharks were caught and harnessed in a futile attempt to tow the ship. Finally, after ninety-three days of misery, the *Suzaky* was rescued by an American vessel which towed it to Costa Rica. The *Suzaky* was beached and condemned as unseaworthy. By contrast, the *Director*, in an unbeaten record, sailed from Panama to Tower Island in exactly seven days. The wind held, the current stayed off duty, and they averaged 160 miles per day.

The moment the *Director* anchored on the edge of the old crater wall of Darwin Bay (Isla Genovesa), the crew immediately sensed the natural hostility of these "fifteen lava bubbles of land in a remote bit of sea that invite no visitors." They spent an eerie night there, as the wailing shriek of a sea lions echoed and re-echoed against the sheer lava cliffs, and huge mantas slapped the water with deafening impact. A light was lowered into the sea to view the strange bulbous creatures with trailing arms which swarmed about. A shark was shot, and it immediately turned its long body and "gulped with his razor teeth at his own wounded stomach!" It was soon attacked by other sharks, and, needless to say, the crew of the *Director* did not go swimming for weeks. To them, this was "the land that God had forgotten. We were in hell and we knew it."

The next morning was no less spooky than the preceding night. An exploring party hiked to the crater lake, brushing aside huge spider webs that "tangled one like a Sargasso Sea." Ankles were cut by crumbling rock bubbles. Along the way, the hikers passed a nameless grave whose huge cross was imbedded in a heap of lava.

Soon afterwards, the men encountered an unusual sight. In a clearing full of decaying bones, they saw about one hundred adult frigate birds awaiting death in this graveyard. There were no young birds or nests to be seen, only the ancient dying birds who could no longer fly to feed themselves; they were dying of old age and starvation.

Another mishap marred the visit of the *Director* to the circular Bahia de Darwin. Sheridan Fahnestock was lowered in a bosun chair to a ledge, in an attempt to paint the name of the ship on one of the cliff walls. Before he could finish, he slipped and fell to the rocks below. His companions found him unconscious, and suffering from a twisted ankle. Future visitors no doubt thought *"Direc"* was a strange name for a ship.

The *Director* sailed to Wreck Bay and anchored near little *Svaap*, "alone, forlorn, deserted, seized by the Ecuadorian government – a ship that had fought her way around the world, had been captured by Red Sea pirates, and had sailed into New York with all the world behind it," now held for some slight technicality.

Out of a house flying an enormous flag and bearing a sign with the huge letters "Capitan du Port," came several officials who boarded the *Director*. They were warmly greeted with rum and cigarettes – for a good reason. At Panama, the *Director* had not gotten clearance from the Ecuadorian consul because the crew lacked the necessary sum of sixty dollars. As the rum flowed freely and generously, the young port captain forgot all about the ship's papers. The crew disembarked and purchased bananas, limes, papayas, a dozen hens, and five tortoises. The latter were kept alive as specimens for zoos.

At Post Office Bay, the six young men repaired the old barrel and placed their mail inside. A copper sheet was tacked onto the barrel; upon it was hammered the name of the vessel and the date: June, 1935. One month later, the mail was picked up by the U.S.S. *Trenton* on a training cruise.

A crude sign at the head of the bay informed the visitors that Hacienda Paradise was seven miles away, and an arrow pointed to an overgrown trail. Soon they were greeted warmly by Herr Wittmer and Harry – Frau Wittmer and Rolf were in Germany.

George Harris spoke German and learned that Wittmer came to Floreana after receiving glowing reports of the island from Dr. Ritter. George received the impression that Herr Wittmer knew far more about the Baroness's disappearance than he cared to admit. The old man related how the Baroness had settled in a corner of his banana garden, how she had angered the Ritters by finding "the two free-thinkers nude in their taro patch" after failing to give warning as she approached. He told how Lorenz tore down the woman's shack and burned its remains the day after the Baroness disappeared. George, too, felt that the secrets were better left undisclosed; "It isn't a pretty story, the tale of Floreana . . . a witch's tale of the Encantadas."

In a wastebasket at Ritter's deserted house, George found six carbon copies of Dore's diary, dated on his dying day. They stated, "My dear husband would not let me leave his side until he died," and told of the doctor's last moments and burial in the garden. Wittmer declared this statement to be untrue, and that the doctor begged Wittmer to keep Dore away because she was trying to kill him.

On the beach, Tehate prepared a Polynesian "himaa" filled with a wild pig donated by Wittmer, yams, bananas, crawfish, and rock cod. In two hours, the food in the pit was deliciously browned and cooked.

Before departing from Floreana, the crew added a sixth tortoise aboard ship. This was Charley, so named because he was found on Floreana, or Charles Island. Since tortoises were reported extinct on Floreana as far back as 1904, it is unlikely that Charley was indigenous to Floreana, but was brought to the island by some settler. The six tortoises which sailed to Tahiti aboard the *Director* were eventually shipped to the United States. Unfortunately, five of them died of cold weather on a Long Island railroad platform as the result of a careless railroad agent.

Hurricane

The forty-five-foot ketch *Hurricane* arrived at Post Office Bay during this year, having left Pascagoula, Mississippi, on a voyage around the world. Ray Kauffman and two companions described Mr. Wittmer as a powerfully-built, unforgettable character, "a free soul in the misty Galapagos highlands," who had found peace and contentment in creative physical work, and who had no intention of ever returning to regimented Germany.

The trio went pig hunting with Wittmer and also gathered a sack of oranges and bananas. Their stay in the Galapagos was well remembered for such gourmet delights as lobster cocktails, broiled Galapagos duck, orange marmalade, fresh vegetable soup, and barbecued ham.

M/S Stranger

A large vessel that made a yearly trip to the Galapagos was the 220-foot double-ended cruiser *Stranger*, with a speed of fifteen knots. Captain Fred Lewis, a Los Angeles millionaire, had purchased it from a Chicago millionaire named Armour, who had used it for collecting plants all over the world. It was constructed along the lines of a freighter, with a great hold for storing plants and animals.

When the *Stranger* arrived in the Galapagos in November of 1935, it carried thirty sea scouts in addition to a professional crew of seventeen men. The scouts had been invited by Captain Lewis to gain practical experience aboard a large ship. The boys were of great help to naturalist Von Hagen in searching for tortoises.

Four years later, this ship was to carry the best equipped and best financed treasure-hunting expedition of its time to Cocos Island. It had the most modern electrical detecting devices, plus digging tools from hand shovels to power-lifting machinery. After ten days of steady digging, the discouraged party quit. Their "doodle-bug" located every deposit of metal ore on the island, but no treasure.

Velero III

Captain G. Allan Hancock, a devoted patron of science, was a frequent visitor to the Galapagos aboard his 195-foot *Velero III*, a very fast power cruiser of exceptionally beautiful design, like a miniature destroyer. Built in 1931, the ship was designed specifically as a medium for scientists. Dedicated to the advancement of marine science and related branches of biology, it made five trips to the Galapagos, besides various expeditions throughout the Gulf of California, the Caribbean, and coasts of Central and South America.

During its visits to the Galapagos in the years 1931 to 1938, the *Velero III* engaged in many rescue operations while cruising about these dangerous waters. Adventurous fishermen from the Ecuadorian mainland often ventured too far west and became stranded in the islands without water. The *Velero III* often had opened its lockers to supply provisions and water for these men. On one occasion, four men had wrecked their hardly seaworthy craft on Gordon Rocks and were forced to walk four miles to Academy Bay, a tortuous trip through thorny brush and rough lava. Luckily, the *Velero III* happened to be in port, and volunteered to salvage their craft. It was towed to Wreck Bay, and the fishermen were furnished with food and clothing from the ship's stores.

The settlers themselves benefited by the cruiser's visits. Workmen from the *Velero III* helped install a new American motor on one of the fishing sloops, because the settlers lacked the proper tools. The Wittmers and Ritters were grateful for the mail and supplies carried aboard the ship. It was the *Velero III* which took Dore to Guayaquil after Ritter's death. And it was Captain Hancock who identified the mummified bodies found on Marchena. Thus, the *Velero III* played an integral part in the dramas of the early 1930's, and in his book about the ship's voyages, De Witt Meredith commented about these tragic events:

> Isolationists of Floreana sought happiness and release from civilization. They could count on the climate and processes of Nature to keep them alive, but human frailty brought tragedy to live among them. Jealousies and thievery promoted hateful strife. None were bound by rules of conduct to which they

were accustomed in communal life. Each tried to create his own world in a space too small for any such experiment, even though there is a vast expanse of land.

George Banning, a guest aboard the *Velero III*, had remarked about the tortoise: "The creature owed his downfall to ships in days gone by – now it is to ships he owes his salvation." The Ecuadorians in the Galapagos were responsible for the continued extermination of the tortoise, and the *Velero III* was trying to secure as many as possible for American zoos and to rescue them from the stew pot. The last tortoise from Chatham was being boiled for oil just as Vincent Astor's *Nourmahal* arrived there in 1934. The *Velero III* was more fortunate; it found eighteen tortoises on Hood Island. These had been tethered and destined for the pot, but ended up in the San Diego Zoo. This particular species was thought extinct because eighty years before, a New Bedford whaler could find only seven creatures left on the island. The youngest and smallest tortoises ever found were located by the Hancock Expedition in 1934 – tiny mites only six days old. This expedition was also happy to report the finding of fur seals on Tower. None had been reported since 1905.

In 1934, the Hancock Expedition conducted an experiment in transporting iguanas from one island to another. They knew this was tampering with nature, but the land iguanas on South Seymour seemed to be dying of starvation. Not all, but only forty land iguanas were captured and placed in wooden cages, then released on North Seymour, where there were none before. Two years later, the 1936 expedition found fat iguanas and their eggs thriving on North Seymour. This transplant was a huge success, but it earned a scolding from naturalist Von Hagen, who wrote in 1936, "The philanthropic Captain Hancock of Los Angeles, who makes the Galapagos his exclusive domain, decided that the iguanas on South Seymour were starving (they had been there only some 10 million years), and moved them to North Seymour. Now there is a reason why certain species occur on certain islands in the Galapagos, and until we can find out the distributional pattern for the fauna, we shall not be aided by kindly gentlemen who redistribute the animals on the Galapagos. They make the puzzle more puzzling . . ."

In 1939, the *Velero III* was presented to the University of Southern California as a research vessel. Years later, it was sold to the Standard Oil Company, which spent two million dollars to refurbish the interior with gold-plated doorknobs and other such luxuries.

The *Velero III* was later given to the Sultan of Kuwait by a consortium of oil companies and has been photographed in the Arabian Gulf with a one-pound cannon on its bow for royal salutes! Perhaps today it is hauling such interesting cargo as harems and sheiks, instead of tortoises and iguanas.

Zaca

The beautiful black-hulled 150-foot diesel schooner *Zaca* made expeditions to the Galapagos in 1932 and 1935, sponsored by the San Francisco banker, Templeton Crocker. After World War II, she was purchased by movie actor Errol Flynn, a great admirer of Darwin and Huxley.

Flynn invited his biologist father to accompany him to the Galapagos. "It would be a sentimental journey," he wrote, " recalling us our times in Tasmania and the days when I went into the field with him as he quested for strange items of marine biology." With Professor Carl Hubbs of the Scripps Institute of Oceanography, they sailed towards Acapulco and collected specimens on Mexican islands. The scientists returned to Los Angeles with their biological finds, but Flynn sailed south, where "instead of sailing to the Galapagos, I . . . set course for Cocos Island and spent a week on a strange, haunted sea mountain." Proceeding to Panama, then to the Caribbean, the adventurer never did reach the Galapagos.

Dar Pomorza and Others

The British Cruiser *Apollo* arrived in the Galapagos in 1936; also the 92-foot *Yankee*, with Captain Irving Johnson and his wife Electa making their second voyage to the Galapagos. Aboard the Dutch pilot schooner built in 1897 were twenty-four young people serving as crew on an eighteen-month cruise around the world.

When the huge square-rigged Polish training ship, *Dar Pomorza*, anchored at Post Office Bay, the ship's doctor gave pre-natal care to Mrs. Wittmer, who was expecting her second child. Meanwhile, the young cadets aboard the ship decided the post office at Floreana needed overhauling. They mounted a new white barrel on a new pole, complete with slant roof, side door, and a brass plate giving the name of their ship and date of arrival. A cairn of lava stones surrounded the base of the pole and was artistically decorated with horned cattle skulls.

Seeteufel and Others

In 1937, a tall, distinguished German in naval uniform arrived at Post Office Bay aboard the sailing yacht *Seeteufel* (Seadevil), which was on a round-the-world voyage. To the Governor and the Wittmers, he presented a beautifully illustrated booklet in Spanish, loaded with propaganda concerning the glories of the Nazi government. This was the gallant Count Felix von Luckner, the buccaneering raider of World War I.

During that war, the Count had roved the oceans in the *Seeadler* (Sea Eagle), an old square-rigged steel ship converted into a camouflaged floating arsenal; it sank about 100,000 tons of Allied ships. In addition to his daring raids, the Count had gained fame for his chivalry at sea. He had taken great pains to save the lives of the men whose ships he sank, and landed them in neutral ports. The *Seeadler* was subsequently wrecked on a reef at the beautiful South Sea paradise of Mopelia.

The 110-foot *Seeteufel* made a less traditional exit. Sold in 1943 to Hans Hass, the underwater photographer, it was seized by the Russians at the end of World War II, and nothing has been heard of it since.

The year 1937 also brought the *Nourmahal*, the 277-foot *Viking*, and the huge 350-ton yacht *Meta Nelson*. The latter ship's doctor gave medical advice to Mrs. Wittmer on April 12; Ingeborg Floreanita Wittmer was born five days later.

A small boat arrived in March of 1937 at Post Office Bay. The three men aboard said they came to hunt and fish, but soon admitted that one of them, Charles Hubbard, had been sent by *Liberty Magazine* to secure a story from Mrs. Wittmer concerning the Baroness. He was willing to pay a good fee if the Wittmers could help solve some of the contradictions in Dore Strauch's *Satan Came to Eden*. Hubbard stayed on Floreana for many weeks, and the article was published in the fall of 1937.

The Wittmers received some bad news when Dr. Holcomb and his wife arrived from California on a small yacht. They brought a letter from Governor Puente, at Chatham, requesting the Wittmers to relocate to Wreck Bay, Villamil, Ecuador, or Germany. With the intercession of Count von Luckner, they were finally permitted to stay on Floreana.

Many yachts arrived in 1938: *Stella Polaris, Philante, Haida, Sans Peur, Velero III, Nourmahal, Jockey,* and *Carola*. The little 29-foot *Ahto* brought hardware for some settlers. This little ship, named for the Estonian god of the sea, had been sailed across the Atlantic by Ahto Walter from Estonia and was engaged in fishing between the Galapagos and Costa Rica.

Cap Pilar

In March of 1938, the British barquentine *Cap Pilar* sailed from Australia to the Galapagos as part of its world cruise. Aboard the 130-foot training ship were seventeen young men and their skipper, Adrian Seligman. At Wreck Bay, several "dissipated-looking officials," nursing a hangover from being entertained by a tuna clipper the night before, boarded the ship and demanded the usual high fee. The skipper refused to pay it, but had to sign a declaration that he had not known "that dues in this harbourless ocean desert would be four times as high as those of the largest port in the world."

The officials were disappointed that there was no rum aboard the *Cap Pilar*, but accepted aspirin for their aching heads. The crew was allowed ashore despite non-payment of the fee. Peter Roach, a teen-aged sailor, was not too impressed with Wreck Bay. The first person to approach him on the beach was a Canadian beachcomber in "pyjamas," who asked for rum. Fish and coffee beans were drying on concrete slabs, a dilapidated sugar refinery was being occupied as a dwelling, and an old barracks with a roof and three walls had its fourth side opening onto the beach. The soldiers had rifles which had not been cleaned for years.

Peter declared Progreso to be the filthiest and most slothful village he had ever seen. Near the town was the wreckage of a factory and huge rusted boilers. There was a church with a skeleton of a tower; the villagers lived in hovels with walls of sticks and thatched roofs. A few houses, built by Norwegians over ten years before, were in poor repair and seemed incongruous in their surroundings. Karin and Señor Cobos were still here, parents of four fine children.

There was one store at Progreso, fairly large, which seemed to be the meeting place or club of the village. In the barn-like interior of this Palace of Entertainment, cats and dogs also "live, love, and fulfill every function of their existence." The sailors refused to pay the exorbitant prices asked for items of Japanese and European manufacture, but did receive sacks of oranges, gratis.

The *Cap Pilar* anchored three days at Santa Cruz Island (Conway Bay), which was full of ferocious mosquitos and with "bush so thick one could hardly penetrate inland at all." They dined on ducks and oranges, and did not stop at Floreana where once, they heard, "an Amazon lived with five husbands . . . and ruled her harem with whip, gun, and powerful forearm."

President Roosevelt

The walls of Tagus Cove and Darwin Bay contain the names of many United States naval vessels which visited the Galapagos. In December of 1937, three doctors from the U.S. Naval vessels *Charleston* and *Babbitt* had kindly examined Harry Wittmer and diagnosed his illness as rheumatic fever.

Late in July of 1938, the naval cruisers *Houston* and *Portland* were bound from San Diego to the Panama Canal to Pensacola, Florida, in a roundabout sort of way. When the *Houston* crossed the Equator, President Franklin Delano Roosevelt acted as Senior Shellback (veteran crosser), who initiated the polywogs crossing the Line for their first time. He was relaxing from political cares by fishing, smoking, and resting.

The presidential hook caught roosterfish, wahoos, broomtail groupers, yellowtail, and other large fish. Smaller fish he caught from a shore boat off the beaches of Isabela Island. He also spent some time reading Captain Porter's Journal, and ordered a search party to look for the grave of Lieutenant Cowan on James Island. However, the crew could not locate the grave of this man shot in a duel in 1813. The President's ancestor, Amasa Delano, had also written accounts of the Galapagos in the early 1800's.

At Floreana, Commander Callaghan left a crate full of goodies for the Wittmers: tinned milk, sugar, butter, whisky, Rhine wine, and medical supplies. Perhaps the most thoughtful gift of all was a supply of typewriter ribbons. Professor Waldo Schmitt of the National Museum, who had made three trips to the Galapagos before on the *Velero III*, was aboard the *Houston*, and mindful of the needs of the Wittmers, had helped in making the list of supplies to be packed.

The new residents of Floreana, the American Conways, also received books, magazines, cigarettes, candy, tea, and chocolate. Other gifts of food were made to the five Ecuadorian residents, and American newspapers were soon full of headlines relating that ''Roosevelt feeds starving Galapagans'' and ''President Brings Relief to Hungry Islanders.''

The biggest publicity, however, was given to the late Baroness. *Time Magazine* printed a toothy picture with the caption: ''She brightened the President's log,'' and added ''Landing parties tried to pump the settlers about the Baroness – the queer German woman who, wearing silk panties and a pearl-handled revolver, sought to rule the island several years ago, until she and her retinue of young males came to mysterious ends. The settlers would not talk, and the whereabouts of the Baroness have been unknown for years.''

The *Houston* did not stop at Cocos Island, even though the President, an avid fan of Cocos, had made trips there in 1935 and 1937, and would again in 1940. He had his own ideas about where the treasure was buried, and hoped someday to test his clues.

1940 and 1941

The *Norseman*, *Odyssey*, and *Atlantic* came to the Galapagos in 1940, as did the *Inca*, which had spent some time at Cocos Island. Captain Baverstock, the chief pilot of the Panama Canal and a keen yachtsman, had invited Count von Luckner for a treasure hunt, and after a fruitless search, they departed for the Galapagos. It is quite obvious that Cocos is a treasure island indeed, not to the hunters, but to the government of Costa Rica, which reaps a small fortune issuing permits to dig.

Three ships came in he earlier part of 1941: Dwight Long's 32-foot ketch *Idle Hour*, Vanderbilt's huge two-masted 190-foot schooner *Pioneer*, and the 121-foot cruiser *Carola*.

Leon Mandel of Chicago had sponsored and led the Field Museum Expedition in 1941 aboard the *Carola*, collecting over two thousand specimens of fishes, birds, and reptiles for the Museum and Brookfield Zoo. Most of these were collected at Panama, Cocos, and the Peruvian coast. Sensibly, considerable restraint was used in collecting the scarce Galapagos species needed by the Field Museum for a special exhibit illustrating the processes of evolution.

For the next four years, no private yachts came to the Galapagos; most of the large pleasure yachts had been loaned to the United States Government to act as patrol ships guarding both Atlantic and Pacific shores. Some, like the huge *Corsair*, saw action in the Pacific war theater.

Visits by Ecuadorian vessels, too, like the *Pinta*, the warship *El Calderon,* and the old schooner *San Cristobal* became infrequent, and mail was delayed for months at a time. Only American warships and planes patrolled the Galapagos area, protecting the newly-built American air base on South Seymour Island.

16
MOSTLY ABOUT
PEOPLE

ᴐᴑᴐᴑᴐᴑᴐᴑᴐᴑᴐᴑᴐᴑᴐᴑᴐᴑᴐᴑᴐᴑᴐᴑᴐ

The Katsdalens

There was a great deal of unrest in Europe in the middle thirties; another war seemed inevitable. A young Norwegian carpenter decided to take his wife and 10-year-old son, Alf, to a place where war could not reach them. The Galapagos Islands were well known in Norway, and despite the failure of the three colonies seven years before, the islands seemed like the lesser of two evils.

The Katsdalens arrived at Academy Bay on Santa Cruz in 1935, quite aware of the fact that they were in surroundings hostile to man, and that life would be difficult. However, the incredible hardships of the first year were like a nightmare, and totally unexpected.

With three donkeys to carry their supplies, the new pioneers trudged up the trail to the fertile uplands, where there was good red soil, rich in humus. They pitched a tent and began clearing a small patch of land. The hot summer sun baked them as they hauled away boulders and stumps. Then came the chilly rainy season and they shuddered in the cold dampness. Two of their donkeys died.

It seemed like ages before their seeds began to sprout; then wild pigs uprooted the young crops, and the garden had to be re-planted. Meanwhile, having eaten all their staple provisions and canned foods, the Katsdalens subsisted on wild bananas, three meals a day. The nearest banana grove was seven hours away over arduous terrain, and one round trip took a whole day. Finally, their first crop of cabbage broke the monotony of a diet of bananas and wild pork.

With dogs to keep the pigs out of their garden, the Katsdalens slowly made headway against the terrible odds and soon started building a substantial house of concrete and timber. All of the materials had to be laboriously hauled up from Academy Bay into the hills. Their home, named Miramar, was solid and comfortable and raised above the ground, boasting the only basement in the Galapagos. A formal flower garden was planted around the house.

A few wild cows were captured, and soon there was a good supply of milk and cheese. Three crops of vegetables were harvested per year, and more land was continuously being cleared and planted. In seven years, 160 acres had been cleared, and a weekly tug from the American base at Baltra Island came to haul away onions, potatoes, corn, cabbage, parsley, and carrots. Of course, there were the usual problems of blight, bugs, worms, and an occasional cloudburst that turned everything into mud. The soil was porous and dried fast. Coffee was planted and became the best income producer.

Except for Alf's visits to the base at Baltra, the Katsdalens never went to the outside world. Visitors to Miramar were charmed with the atmosphere of carefree joy and cheerfulness which prevailed in the Katsdalen Garden of Eden.

Darwin Centennial

Exactly 100 years after the youthful Charles Darwin set foot on the clinkered Encantadas, another young naturalist was making a sentimental pilgrimage to the Galapagos to commemorate the one-hundredth anniversary of Darwin's visit.

Victor Wolfgang von Hagen, an American naturalist, and his wife, Christine, disembarked from the decrepit schooner *San Cristobal* at Wreck Bay in September of 1935. With them were several stone masons, who were to build a tall pedestal for the large bust of Darwin donated by the American Museum of Natural History. Von Hagen planned to erect this monument as part of a campaign to arouse the attention of all naturalists "to help save the fauna of the most fascinating theater of living evolution in the world." Earlier pleas by scientists John S. Garth, Waldo L. Schmitt, Robert T. Moore, and Harry S. Swarth had received some recognition but no genuine action by the Ecuadorian government.

While the masons were building the pedestal, the young couple toured the islands aboard the *Stranger* as guests of Captain Fred Lewis. After several weeks, they returned to Wreck Bay, and from a distance could see the Darwin monument near the shore, at an elevated spot overlooking the harbor and facing the heart of the Galapagos Archipelago.

On the day of inauguration, the bust was ceremoniously unveiled and accepted by the commander of the port in the name of Science and the Republic of Ecuador. The granite bust rested upon a tall, quadrilateral pyramid, about two feet on a side at the base, tapering to about one foot wide at the platform for the bust, which was about ten feet above the ground. There was a plaque bearing the portrait of Darwin as a young man, and an inscription written by Major Leonard Darwin, his sole surviving son.

Von Hagen was a little chagrined. "The masons had done a good job, but they found a heart-shaped stone which they put in the center of the monument and wrote thereon, in large conspicuous letters – Aurelio Borrero, Mason. This legend completely dwarfed the name of Charles Darwin." No doubt the masons felt this was a reward for their tough labor. The hard basaltic lava had broken most of their chisels, and they had to search out stones of the correct size and shape to be fitted together, a painstaking task. A similar monument was erected at the University of Guayaquil.

Back in Ecuador, at Von Hagen's persuasion, legislation was begun to declare the Galapagos Archipelago a National Reserve Park. On May 14, 1936, President Paez of Ecuador signed the following decree:

> As the fauna of the Archipelago was nearing the danger line of extinction – an irreparable loss to science – whereas in the Galapagos Islands certain conditions exist that make the area unique in the world – the Government decrees that the islands of Hood, James, Duncan, Barrington, Jervis, Seymour, Tower, Bindloe, Abingdon, Wenman, Culpepper, Indefatigable, and the part of Albemarle north of Perry Isthmus, are to be National Parks – no hunting or capture of animals would be permitted without a permit from the Board of Directors . . . .

To avoid friction with Señor Gil at Villamil, and the Sociedad National at Progreso, Chatham and part of Albemarle were excluded in the decree. The decree authorized the establishment of research stations to deal with scientific institutions desirous of making expeditions, and to prevent tourists and yachtsmen from removing any of the species.

American institutions were not interested at this time in the proposals that Von Hagen had made concerning the Galapagos sanctuary. However, Dr. Julian Huxley persuaded Von Hagen to address the Galapagos Committee of the British Association of Science. Plans were made to purchase the Rader house at Academy Bay for headquarters for a warden; signs were to be posted at all landings against removal or killing of species; wild dogs and cats were to be eliminated by controlled, systematic hunting. Unfortunately, none of these excellent suggestions were followed through, nor did Ecuador enforce its new decree, even though everyone agreed that "there must be a joint guardianship of a heritage that Nature has preserved intact for millions of years, and that man has brought close to extinction in only three hundred years. It is a unique legacy; it may provide some means of finding out what we are and why."

The Angermeyers

In Hitler's Germany, the elderly Angermeyers disliked the warlike trend of their fatherland. They scraped up every pfennig they could find, purchased a boat, and shipped their five sons from Hamburg to the Galapagos. The parents were killed during the war.

After two years of wandering, three of the Angermeyer boys, Gus, Karl, and Fritz, arrived at Academy Bay in 1937 with only strong backs, strong arms, and a determination to start a new life. They went into the hills of Santa Cruz Island and cut trees for a shanty; each plank was hewn by hand. They made nails out of copper wire, and roofing out of sea charts covered with tar. A fishing boat was constructed, using copper wire for rivets and coins for washers. In lieu of paint, shark-liver oil protected the planking.

For three happy years the brothers earned their livelihood by fishing in open boats, employed by the large foreign fishing boats which carry their catches in refrigerated holds to North America. The Angermeyers acted as guides for scientific expeditions and came to know the islands better than anyone had ever known them before.

The Angermeyers purchased their fruit and vegetables from the Katsdalen farm and learned to make bread from a mixture of ripe and fermented bananas. They hunted goats and shot their own beef. Life was idyllic, but their stay in the Galapagos was interrupted.

In October of 1941, the Angermeyer brothers had taken a load of salted fish to Guayaquil, where they also hoped to negotiate the purchase of a boat. Meanwhile, Japan attacked Pearl Harbor, and the brothers decided to remain employed in Ecuador. They were not interned as enemy aliens (as was frequently reported), but remained on the mainland of their own free choice. After the war, the Ecuadorian ship *El Oro* brought them back to Academy Bay. Gus had married a girl in Guayaquil; Karl and Fritz married women residents of the island. The couples built their homes on the beach amidst the friendly iguanas; the creatures refused to relinquish their patch of lava and more or less moved in with the Angermeyers, tolerating the household dogs and cats and allowing themselves to be fed bread or rice out of a spoon. Like the iguanas, the Angermeyers have become an integral part of Academy Bay.

The Conways

Having inherited the pioneering spirit of their respective grandfathers, Frances and Ainslie Conway left Carmel, California, in 1937 with $500 in their pockets, a small steamer trunk, three suitcases, and a portable typewriter. Their destination was the land of history and mystery, the Encantadas, where they hoped to stay alive for at least six months.

Frances had taught high school English; Ainslie was a former newspaperman and writer of fiction who had fought the Moros in the Phillipines and

Mexican bandits on the United States border. The couple wanted to join a colonization project in Alaska, but it had a long waiting list. After perusing all available literature on the Galapagos, they packed their meager belongings, hoping to find a suitable secluded spot. "In a place where no one else had broken ground," they wrote, "we wanted to experience, at firsthand, what it is to bring into being a way of life from the very beginning. As for risks, we were willing to take them, so long as no other people were involved."

The Conways prepared a list of all items they could buy at Guayaquil in the way of tools and hardware, kitchen utensils, cloth, bedding, and groceries. From Dore Strauch's book they gleaned a general idea of what was needed, and with their limited funds managed quite well. All of the preparations and purchases are charmingly recorded in their book, *The Enchanted Isles*. Their purchase of an alarm clock is a puzzler, though. Who needs one on an isolated desert island where time is unimportant? Getting there is half the fun. For the magnificent sum of five dollars apiece, the Conways bought "first class" passage on the newly-painted *San Cristobal* whose "ravaged complexion" exposed her true identity as none other than the old schooner *Cobos*. The fare included the thrill of a four- to seven-day sailing excursion – with meals! Some first-class passengers occupied three tiny staterooms at the stern; the Conways were bunked in the dining room. The small galley had a sandbox fireplace; water came out of several large gasoline drums. The hold was filled with corrugated iron roofing, barbed wire, empty oil drums, old automobile tires (perhaps for the manufacture of sandals), and all the chattels of the passengers. Second-class passengers and livestock slept on deck.

Besides the Conways, the first-class passengers consisted of a Captain Castro with wife and eight children; a Captain Goya Rico, also with wife and eight children; a Hungarian named Grafi; and a German with an Ecuadorian wife. The rest of the ship was peopled with thirty-odd workers, and four convicts guarded by two policemen with rifles who were also keeping guard over Goya Rico.

The *San Cristobal* motored out of Guayaquil, then briskly proceeded to Chatham under sail, arriving at Wreck Bay without mishap. There the workers and convicts disembarked and were soon trudging up to the coffee plantation to pick the ripe coffee beans. The Conways went ashore to purchase fifty banana plants, fifty pineapple hijos, cane cuttings, two burros, several chickens, a pig, some bowls, green coffee, baking soda, and some warm Andean ponchos. They visited the mud and wattle village of Progreso, which they admitted should have been named Regreso.

With its decreased load of passengers, the schooner stopped next at Academy Bay. Grafi, the Hungarian, had lived there before, and related to the Conways the embattled existence the "helluva peoples" endured on the island. There were about thirty to forty individuals there, some with houses on the beach as well as small plantations in the hills.

The leading and most affluent citizen was Danish Mr. Rader, who had a white cottage on the beach. He and his wife were preparing to leave the island and were hoping the Ecuadorian government would purchase the spacious house for use as a garrison headquarters. Icelander Finsen was still there, sporting a long white beard.

Old Mr. Zeen, the Estonian Rasputin, as well as old-timer Estampa with his Norwegian wife and three-year-old daughter, were residents of Academy Bay. Another settler, described as "Jesus Christ with blue eyes," – a tall, emaciated, barefoot man with long yellow hair and a beard down to his chest – raised tobacco on his escapist hermitage. Other Europeans had their homes in the uplands, and smoke could be seen curling along the slopes halfway up the summit of the volcano.

Wurm-Muller, now seventy years old and "hairless as a peeled potato," was again living a bachelor existence. Originally, he and his wife had occupied the large Norwegian house abandoned by the fishing colony, but were deposed by a world-travelling Alsatian named Kubler who came to Academy Bay in 1934 with his wife and small daughter. It seemed that Kubler had a diplomatic passport and a great deal of influence with the Ecuadorian government. When the deposed Wurm-Muller moved into a chicken house, his wife moved to Guayaquil, leaving her husband and Kubler to squabble between themselves. Some time later, Kubler, whose influence with the government apparently had waned, was deposed by garrison officers. Eventually, the house burned down mysteriously. Some said Kubler was the arsonist who was getting revenge on the officers; others say Rader caused the fire so that the government would purchase Rader's fine house for the now homeless officers.

The Hungarian, Grafi, purchased Wurm-Muller's tiny dinghy, named *Sangre Azul,* and the schooner *San Cristobal* proceeded to James Bay.

The Conways, Grafi, the German, and the Goya Rico family had all decided to settle on uninhabited James Island, also called Santiago. On May 23, 1937, the schooner deposited them on the southern beach of James Bay, where there was an old house built by the defunct salt-mining enterprise of nine years before. All the settlers moved into the house, except the Conways, who spent the night under the stars. They wrote, "Our dream of paradise was not founded on a collective economy. We wanted our own spring, our own chacra, our own life. Close-knit intimacy with these others would soon result in disagreements over who owned what. A certain degree of cooperation, of course, but a much greater degree of independence."

The tall, slim Conways, endowed with a lot of energy and fortified with an excellent sense of humor to cope with vexatious problems, found a spring inland. There they cleared a space under a muyuyu tree and built a shack of branches roofed with grass and flowers. They learned to roast their green coffee over a lava fireplace, made cupboards out of packing boxes, set out their plant cuttings, and planted seeds. Ainslie cut a road from the garden to the spring, a ten-minute round trip each time they needed water. In little over a month, the Conways and their neighbors were quite well established in homes; gardens were planted; quarrels were started.

For years, the schooner *Cobos* had been bringing colorful characters to the Encantadas, and the Conways' neighbors were no exception. Grafi, the bachelor, was a tall, heavy Hungarian who had lived at Academy Bay three years. He spoke English, Spanish, and German, as well as Hungarian, seemed quite affluent, and could have gone anywhere he pleased; he never revealed why he selected the Galapagos. Twice he had sailed for the islands in a small boat, but his navigation was somewhat amiss. On the first trip he landed in Chile; the second trip brought him to Panama. He finally arrived via the schooner, bringing plenty of food, chicken wire, corrugated iron roofing, an iron bedstead, packing boxes, mattresses, and brandy. He shot hawks with poisoned arrows from his Jivaro Indian blowgun, and spent all of his time eating, sleeping, and hunting; his garden was a failure. He left the island after several months, on the next trip of the schooner.

The German, Alberto, staked out a claim next to Grafi and drew a boundary line. He built a crude shelter to house his two bedsteads and set of dining room furniture. His dusky young Ecuadorian wife, America, showed him how to plant his garden in crude Indian style without spading or hoeing, and soon beans, corn, melons, potatoes, and other vegetables were thriving. The couple had arrived with three dogs, six chickens, two turkeys, two guinea pigs, and two ocelots. The latter were to be sold to visiting millionaires who would arrive by yacht.

Captain-Engineer Humberto Goya Rico was a political prisoner who had caused a man's death by exploding a revolutionary bomb in Guayaquil. He was sentenced to six months stay in the Galapagos, and in Ecuadorian fashion was dumped on the islands with his wife and eight children, where they were expected to shift for themselves. Captain Maulme of the schooner generously donated rice, coffee, and sugar to the foodless family. Goya Rico had counted on getting food from the government, and brought only clothing, bedding, and cooking utensils.

Goya Rico was a Chilean of Italian ancestry who claimed to have been a flier in the Italian Army. He had also helped build the Panama Canal, was thrown out of Russia for political activities, fled Chile with a price on his head, and had piloted a fishing vessel to the Galapagos. He selected James as his island of exile because Mrs. Johnson (Ecuadorian wife of the late Londoner) had given him secrets of treasure buried there. He also would lay claim to the salt lake and sell salt to the government. After his entrepreneuring activities brought him a small fortune, he planned to move to the United States where his daughters would marry millionaires.

Goya Rico wrote letters to the Ecuadorian authorities, complaining of the slow starvation of his family. Meanwhile, the eight children, aged nine months to seventeen years, feasted on dove stew, goat's meat and milk, broth, tea from chala leaves, and handouts from fishing boats and yachts. The eldest daughter, Oslavia, (all of the children were named after Italian battles) was a budding seventeen, and as Frances Conway stated, "a working agreement which benefited all parties was patched together" with the bachelor Grafi. Fish were caught from Grafi's dinghy and shared with other settlers. There were arguments between the Goya Ricos and the Europeans; the Conways kept to themselves.

Goya Rico abandoned his salt venture after almost drowning in the salt lake; his new scheme was to start a cheese factory, and he experimented with goat cheese recipes. Various holes, which the Conways called "graves of blasted hopes," soon dotted the landscape as the captain-engineer dug for pirate treasure. His countless activities were matched by those of the German, Alfredo, who collected goat hides, sealskins, and salted fish, and raised pigs for sale. He scorned the offer of five dollars for the ocelots by a visiting yachtsman who was an American, but no millionaire.

Meanwhile, the Conways fought rats, ants, cockroaches, and birds. Finches attacked the bean, corn, and banana sprouts; weevils and grubs infested the sacks of beans and corn they had purchased in Guayaquil. Hawks killed their chickens, and Frances developed sores on her face which she thought were caused by contact with sap of the manzanillo tree as she photographed flamingoes near the salt lake. She shared the same experience as Basil Ringrose, the pirate, who in 1680 complained of red sores after he sought shelter from rain under a manzanillo tree.

One day, Estampa, the genial fisherman from Academy Bay, arrived with a boatload of taro, yuca, and camotes as a gift for the new settlers at James Bay. With him were his rosy, plump wife and little daughter, and "a tall bearded Frenchman of impeccable manners and villainous reputation, star convict of San Cristobal Island. "Here he was loose on our island," wrote Frances Conway, who had made his acquaintance on the schooner several months before. It seems that El Frances was an escapee of Devil's Island, a murderer who was sent to the Galapagos for illegal entry into Ecuador. He had a permit from the Governor to go fishing with Estampa.

Soon afterwards, sixty men were disembarked at James Bay to load fifty tons of salt, and they remained a few weeks. Goats, burros, and doves were slaughtered indiscriminately, firewood was burned, and flies multiplied in the garbage heaps of offal and fish entrails which the men scattered all over. To the relief of the Conways, the workers soon left on the *San Cristobal* accompanied by Grafi, Alberto, and America. In September of 1937, the Ecuadorian destroyer *El Calderon* removed the Conways and Goya Ricos to Floreana; the Captain-Engineer's complaints about starvation and thirst had taken effect upon the Governor, who felt a moral obligation to protect the welfare of his constituents. Santiago was once again uninhabited.

Floreana, 1937

In addition to the erstwhile Santiagans, the *El Calderon* carried a large number of scientists and biology students from the University of Quito. The Conways and Goya Ricos were delivered to their new home at Black Beach on Floreana, whose sole residents at this time were the Wittmers and Zavalas.

Señor Ezekiel Zavala had operated a coffee plantation on Isabela Island for fifteen years, but was transferred to Floreana to help control the growth of the excessive herds of cattle. He cured the hides and dried the meat of the wild animals which he shot periodically, sending the leather and beef to Chatham. He was also asked to keep a watchful eye on any squatters. After all the irregular doings among the gringos (foreigners) in the past few years, the Governor believed it prudent to keep an Ecuadorian citizen in charge. It was a case of locking the barn door after the horse was stolen; all the troublemakers were dead or gone.

In general, the Ecuadorian population in the islands was peaceful and loyal; most trouble arose from the exploits of adventurers and vagabond sailors. To bring the settlers under some semblance of protection, military outposts were established at Wreck and Academy Bays. They were manned by former Ecuadorian cavalrymen, who still sported spotless white uniforms, black cavalry boots, and jaunty blue caps – a sharp contrast to the rough garb of the settlers and the rugged terrain of the islands.

Zavala, the Governor's representative, was instructed to provide meat for the Goya Ricos; both families were soon squabbling as Goya Rico demanded fruit and vegetables also, and was disappointed at not being allowed to settle at the Ritter chacra, which Zavala had appropriated three months earlier. All residents of Floreana breathed a sigh of relief as the Goya Rico family once more boarded the *San Cristobal* in December of 1937, after the revolutionist had fulfilled his six month exile from Ecuador.

The Ritter chacra lay halfway between Black Beach and the rounded volcano called Straw Mountain; the former Friedo was now labeled "Asilo de Colonel Puente – Propriedad Zavala," and the dusty, winding trail leading from here to the beach was named "El Camino de la Muerte." Marked by bleached skulls of wild bulls, desert scrub, leafless bursera, and sharp-spined cacti, this road was the grisly reminder of the island's inglorious history and repeated tragedies.

The Ritter house under the ciruela tree had been dismantled and everything useful was taken away. Ritter's garden was neglected, but the fence still managed to keep out the jungle that was slowly strangling the old plantation. Coconut trees towered near the spring. Weeds almost concealed the lonely grave of Dr. Ritter, who had died only three years before, and whose companion was living with her memories in Germany, thousands of miles away.

About a mile east and a mile south of Friedo was the Wittmer Haven of Peace, where Heinz was now aged fifty and Margret about thirty-five. Harry was a robust eighteen, Rolf an active four, and little Ingeborg was four months old. The happy family lived comfortably in their neat stone house, which now boasted of a cement floor, bookcases, kitchen sink, and excellent hand-crafted furniture. There was an atmosphere of cheerfulness and sunshine about the place; Harry's bouts with rheumatic fever were the only cause for sorrow.

The Conways settled about a mile east of the Wittmers, on the old Hacienda tobacco plantation which now was a lemon tree jungle with a freshwater pool nearby. The guavas were spreading rapidly, and there were avocado and orange trees. The Conways say that Floreana oranges were the best in the world.

With some lumber from the dismantled house at Post Office Bay, and their iron roofing, the Conways soon had a comfortable shelter, and planted a vegetable garden which yielded cabbage, sweet potatoes, squash, and other delicacies in abundance. The greatest problem was fencing out the cattle; the couple were treed several times by rampaging bulls which occasionally had "agony fits" accompanied by grotesque bawling, grunting, and regular bullfights to which the Conways had ringside seats.

It wasn't long before the Conways were plagued with the nigua, a female flea which burrows into the flesh of the feet and lays her eggs under the skin. These fleas are carried by wild hogs which are badly crippled by the infestation of the pest. Constant digging with a needle, to remove the flea, resulted in inflammation, infection, and continuous soreness. Dore, too, had suffered from the nigua, the result of walking barefoot.

Frances also developed ulcer-like sores on her legs, which took about three months to heal despite all sorts of medication. In 1931, Roydon Bristow had remarked, "The only queer thing I noticed [in the islands] was that during the rainy season a cut would fester and would not heal until the end of the season. I was told that white men suffer from this disability until after a few years they become acclimatized."

The Conway jungle was seven to eight miles from Post Office Bay, so the struggling couple missed out on all the social life on the beach. Luxury yachts and destroyers came and went without seeing the Conways. At times, the proud couple purposely refrained from contacting the visiting American ships; they were not spongers and were making (and succeeding in) a strong effort to eke out a living from the unwilling lava without outside assistance. The Goya Ricos and Zavalas shamelessly begged for food and cigarettes, then flouted their "Lookies" and "Chestairfeels" as Ainslie Conway grimly smoked his ersatz muyuyu tobacco in silence. American warships had responded generously to the desperate pleas left in the barrel by the Goya Ricos. Once, Conway did request, and received, a much-needed American axe, but was either too bashful or too proud to ask for packing boxes, sacks, glass containers, and oil drums which ships ordinarily discard into the sea. On an insect-infested island, these things acquire a value in proportion to their scarcity.

For four years, the Conways battled the cutworms, ants, moths, rats, cockroaches, and mosquitos. Somehow they managed to raise sixty varieties of plants, an accomplishment praised by the new governor. Colonel Alvear was an enlightened administrator, who had built the first school and hospital in the Galapagos and helped the colonists secure legal title to the land which they had cleared. He established a small garrison of men and their families on Floreana, providing another market for the Wittmer vegetables, eggs, sausages, and bakery goods heretofore sold only to tuna clippers.

In November of 1941, Frances Conway sailed to Guayaquil on an Ecuadorian freighter to inquire about Ainslie's chances of obtaining employment at the new American air base at Baltra Island. She was unable to get transportation back to the Galapagos after the December attack on Pearl Harbor, and returned to the United States. Ainslie worked at the Baltra base for two years before he finally rejoined Frances in Oakland, California. The couple was destined to return to the Galapagos once more in 1946.

Perhaps the Conways can be considered the last real "pioneers" in the Galapagos. Settlers who came after them in the 1940's and 1950's found life much easier: mail and supply boats arrived at regular intervals, medical and dental care could be obtained on San Cristobal Island; patrol boats and wireless stations kept the authorities informed of activities in the entire archipelago. The lava cinders of the Encantadas harbored fewer mysteries than ever before.

17

A TOUCH OF WAR

∽◌∿◌∿◌∿◌∿◌∿◌∿◌∿◌∿◌∿

Beachhead on the Moon

Ever since 1850, when proposals were made to lease the guano fields of the Galapagos, the United States had cast covetous eyes upon these lonely isles which were economically unimportant to Ecuador. The little republic consistently resisted American intervention, and American efforts to lease the isles for protection of the Panama Canal came to naught.

The United States was fully aware that the Galapagos were the possession of one of the weakest republics in South America; Ecuador had not the means to prevent improper use of the archipelago, since it could not protect them from attack by European or Oriental power. The islands were considered a menace: raiders based there could attack Pacific trade routes; fleets of destroyers and aircraft carriers could rendezvous in the sheltered bays; submarines based here could threaten shipping to and from Panama. Suggestions were made in 1928 to establish a naval station similar to Guantanamo, which would still allow Ecuador, like Cuba, to keep her sovereignty intact, retaining the islands and their prestige value.

Ecuador had refused to permit large-scale alien enterprises in the islands, so it was a little surprising when, in 1940, the republic permitted Paul Foster, a former U.S. Navy commander, to conduct a four-month survey of Isabela before leasing it from the owner, Carlos Gil. Foster had obtained a $30,000 Reconstruction Finance Corporation loan to investigate the possibilities of exploiting the sulphur deposits, cattle ranges, and fertile lands of Isabela.

In the same year of 1940, numerous American naval vessels cruised about the islands. The U.S.S. *Lapwing* anchored in Post Office Bay for several weeks, as experts charted and photographed this island and others. The cruiser *Erie* arrived with high Ecuadorian officials as well as high-ranking Americans. In July, 1941, Paul Foster, head of the Pacific Development Company, was awarded a $500,000 loan for beginning operations on Isabela. He denied rumors that U.S. naval plans were behind his deal with the RFC.

In September, 1941, it was officially announced that the United States was leasing an island in what *Time Magazine* called "the fantastically storied haven of pirates and more modern escapists."

The settlers at Academy Bay claimed that Ecuador at first agreed to sell the island of Santa Cruz (Indefatigable) to the United States for $21 million. At the last moment, they said, the sale was cancelled, and the small island of Baltra (South Seymour) was leased instead. Also, a radar station would be permitted on Hood Island, and an outpost established on the westernmost tip of Ecuador at Punta Elena.

This was a good neighbor deal in which the United States would protect not only her interests in Panama, but also patrol the South American coast. A huge triangular area of ocean, from Peru to the Galapagos to Guatemala, would be closely patrolled by planes based at Baltra. A Dutch freighter sank in this area in the fall of 1941, and it was rumored that a raider was based in the Galapagos. The military strategists of Japan had their eyes on the islands; Japanese fishermen had frequented these waters long before World War II.

Baltra was selected as ideal for an air base, because it is four miles long, and low. It lies just north of Isla Santa Cruz, and is separated from it by a channel a half-mile wide and only three fathoms deep; geologists believe it was once part of Santa Cruz and had become separated by recent faulting.

When the first ships arrived, about September 9, 1941, bringing materials and equipment for the base, they were greeted only by goats and iguanas, the latter being a dull red color like the rocks they live upon. These iguanas were the same which Captain Hancock had tried to save in 1934, and which he thought were becoming extinct.

First, a huge pier of concrete and steel, several hundred yards long, was projected into the water to enable large ships to unload directly to the island. Over two hundred bungalows of United States pine were erected to house the laborers and future servicemen. Bulldozers began to carve out roads to facilitate movement of equipment. Reservoirs were built for fuel and drinking water.

No water is available on Baltra, so a ten-mile pipeline was constructed on Chatham Island, which would carry water from a 2,000 foot elevation to storage reservoirs at Wreck Bay. The water was then hauled by tugs, and stored in the reservoirs at Baltra.

Workers by the thousands from Ecuador, Peru, Colombia, Panama, and other Latin American nations began to work day and night to build the biggest base in South America. No expense was spared to make them comfortable. After all, the ever-suffering American taxpayer was footing the bill of ten million (1941) dollars to build the base.

The workmen were lodged rent-free in wooden houses complete with furniture, running water, radio, and refrigerator. A huge mess hall was built, in which they ate free meals; laundry service was free; wages were fabulously high. Each man received one carton of cigarettes per week and two bottles of beer every night. After three months of work, they received two-week's leave, with free transportation to Panama.

There were problems at the beginning. Heavy equipment got stuck in the volcanic dust. Wild goats gnawed communication lines, but soon they found another source of food and consumed tons of waste paper (in triplicate) discarded by personnel.

Work was begun immediately on the two macademized airstrips. The largest runway was over a half-mile long and could accommodate fighter planes and giant bombers. Taxiways surrounded the airstrips, and paved roads soon criss-crossed the island from one end to the other. In the amazingly short period of three months, the airstrips were ready. Planes of the United States Sixth Air Force landed on Baltra on December 11, 1941, only four days after the Japanese attack on Pearl Harbor in Hawaii.

A regular town sprang up on the "Rock." In addition to Quonset huts and bungalows, there was a church, mess hall, administration building, theater, an enormous club house dubbed "World's End," a luxurious officers' club, offices, and clothing stores. The first newspaper in Galapagos history was a mimeographed sheet called "The Rock." There was a power station, munitions depot, patrol huts, radio and signal station, and all the other appurtenances of a war base. Seaplanes were safely tucked away in a sheltered cove a half-mile wide, with a good anchorage for ships.

Baltra was not only an air base; it was also used as an acclimatization station, where troops and crews of planes and ships could become accustomed to the heat before they were shipped to the South Seas or the Far East. It is said that at least ten thousand men were trained here between 1942 and 1946. Elsewhere, a radar station was established on Hood Island, about one mile inland.

Despite all the comforts and recreational facilities, like tennis and basketball courts, loneliness took its toll. Out of sheer boredom, Mr. Hancock's precious iguanas were hunted down and shot. In this never-never land, some men went about greeting goats as friends and calling rocks by name. Servicemen could not spend any money here, so they saved it for the fleshpots of Panama on furloughs granted every three months. Dysentery laid many men low. Some died, and were buried in graves blasted out of igneous rock.

1944 and After

Aside from such excitement as a visit by globetrotting Eleanor Roosevelt, the Baltra base experienced an unusual event not connected with the war. In April of 1944, the peculiar odor of sulphur could be detected in the atmosphere. One night a terrific explosion was heard, as the awesome Cerro Azul on Isabela Island exploded, shooting flames into the blackness of the sky. The glowing mountain was then carefully watched, and ships were made ready to evacuate any islanders in danger. One plane flew too near the blazing crater and crashed into the midst of the flames. Planes dropped messages to the Wittmers on Floreana, keeping them informed of the eruption. Earlier, at the beginning of the air base construction, the Wittmers were cautioned not to build fires which might be misconstrued as signals to enemy submarines; they were not, however, deported as enemy aliens. In May of 1945, they were surprised as thirty planes flew over Floreana, and a message was dropped to them. The war was over; Germany had surrendered.

They were even more surprised in February of 1946, when a dozen American soldiers searched the Wittmer premises. A Panama City newspaper had reported that Adolf Hitler had escaped in a submarine and was being sheltered by the German Wittmers on Floreana.

In July of 1946, as a bugler blew a sad retreat, the United States flag was lowered from the flagstaff fronting the service club. Ecuadorian sailors presented arms as the flag of Ecuador flew alone over the airfield. The United States had no desire to abandon the airfield, but did so as a matter of protocol. The tiny Republic of Ecuador could well have benefited by an outright lease of Baltra, but that would have involved political risks at home. Ultranationalists had denounced the base as a violation of Ecuadorian sovereignity. A fifth column encouraged grumbling against the United States, and rumors were spread that the Yanquis were growing fat on Ecuadorian food. In reality, for the first time in the history of the island settlements, the base was actually an excellent market for their fresh produce and cattle. Ecuadorian laborers had also been the recipients of excellent wages.

A small contingent of United States technicians and military personnel were left on the island to train the Ecuadorian garrison to assume control and maintain the airbase. Soon Quonset huts were pulled down; heavy equipment and other substantial things were taken to the Panama Canal Zone. Bulldozers buried abandoned equipment in the red volcanic dust. The large buildings were left standing, as well as all the wooden houses. The munitions depot was emptied; seaplanes and ships left; huge bombers roared away. Only a few small planes were left for the small garrison.

Gradually the wooden buildings were being dismantled and hauled to other islands for use by the settlers. When an author, Arthur Eichler, arrived on Baltra about 1950, he saw a huge scrap yard instead of the former little town. Convicts were stacking bundles of lumber on the huge pier for shipment to Chatham, Santa Cruz, and Floreana.

Mrs. Wittmer had been allowed to choose any building she preferred, and selected an imposing structure which had served as a post office. With the help of Commander Baverstock, Rolf Wittmer was able to transport 120 bundles of timber on the *Inca,* and soon the Wittmers had a spacious home erected at Black Beach. It was quite fitting that the post office from Baltra should find its final resting place on the island famous for Post Office Bay.

When Eibl-Eibesfeldt came to Baltra in 1954, he found a deserted airstrip whose asphalt runways were cracking in the sun. Only rusty shutters, rattling in the wind, broke the utter silence. Some of the larger buildings were still there, but their windows were smashed and gaping.

The iguanas that Hancock wished to save were now reduced to skeletons with bullet holes in their skulls. Little tropidurus lizards were rare; their eggs were being devoured by mice. In fact, the whole place was overrun by mice scavenging for food. Eibl-Eibesfeldt predicted that soon, finding no other food, they would eat all the vegetation, and themselves become extinct. Baltra would become a barren rock, crisscrossed by asphalt roads and runways.

In October of 1960, Charles Hillinger of the Los Angeles Times found three Ecuadorian sailors as the sole residents and caretakers of the abandoned base. They were known as "treasure hunters," but were not searching for pirate gold. Instead, the Ecuadorian Navy had men uncovering all the valuable equipment and scrap iron bulldozed over and buried by the extravagant Norte Americanos.

18

1945 TO 1955

One of the first private yachts to visit the Galapagos after the second World War was the 70-foot brigantine *Varua*, built by William A. Robinson, shipbuilder from Ipswich, Massachusetts. Enroute to Tahiti in 1945, Robinson made his third visit to the Encantadas. He preferred not to anchor at any of the populated settlements, but spent some time in the remote coves of Isabela. When passing Marchena Island, he reported that the mummified remains of Lorenz and Nuggerud were still visible on the parched sand.

The Wittmers Revisited

In 1947, the 96-foot brigantine *Yankee* brought Irving and Electa Johnson to the Galapagos on their fourth visit. They found the Wittmers thriving exceptionally well on Floreana. Rolf, an excellent backwoodsman, was now fifteen years old. With brother Harry, he was experimenting with growing tropical wheat. Herr Wittmer proudly displayed his well-equipped workshop; Frau Wittmer and young Ingeborg were delighted with the new dishes, clothing, and mail order catalogue which the Johnsons brought.

The Wittmers were dependent on incoming yachts for flour, tools, clothing, and yard goods; for these they traded fruit and vegetables. Fruit was less abundant though, since a blight had destroyed lemon and orange trees, and the imported guavas were strangling other growth.

The Wittmers now had their own livestock and were no longer dependent on the decimated wild cattle herds. A severe five-year drought had dried the springs; rats proliferated, as there was no rainy season to drown the young. Several Ecuadorian families settled near the Wittmers and Zavalas, but left after much disappointment at the meager results of their hard labor. Suydam Cutting had observed, quite correctly, "The fact that the Wittmers are surviving does not dispute the fact that the Galapagos are a malignant abode for human beings." The Wittmers tried to discourage the Conways from making their second settlement in the islands. The indefatigable Encantadas were almost winning again.

Santiago Revisited

For two years, Ainslie Conway stayed at the American air base on Baltra during World War II. He rejoined wife Frances in California, and once more the couple decided to return to their beloved desert island of Santiago (James Island).

In December of 1946, the Conways left Guayaquil for the Galapagos aboard the same ship which once before had removed them from Santiago – the old gunboat *El Calderon*. After a disaster in 1940, during a war between Ecuador and Peru, *El Calderon* had been converted into a passenger vessel. Its only gun, not having been used for twenty years, exploded when fired, and, as a result, two seamen and half the decks were gone. The ship had then been relegated to more peaceful uses. The Conways met old next-island-neighbors on board – Carlos Gil of Isabela, Karl Kubler of Santa Cruz, and Hans Angermeyer, who was bringing his bride, Emma, to the Galapagos for the first time.

The port of Baquerizo-Moreno at Wreck Bay looked a little more prosperous to the Conways. There was a new hospital, schoolhouse, and a red-roofed barracks. There was no equipment in the hospital and no provisions in the commissary, "but the buildings gave dignity to the place, anyway."

Economic conditions had changed. Gringo warships from the still existent Baltra base had bought all available fruits, vegetables, pigs, tobacco, and rum. The Conways had to content themselves with such leftovers as red potatoes and camotes to add to their other purchases of three donkeys, four chickens, and one dog.

The Conways, duly deposited at James Bay, soon located their old spring. Animals had created a mess around the waterhole, but this was soon corrected, and once more the couple began keeping house on their lonely, seldom-visited island. Their first visitor after six weeks was a tuna boat looking for bait, but it did not stop and proved quite unsociable. Three weeks later, several more tuna boats arrived, very sociable and generous. A shark-fishing vessel from San Francisco – the *Pearl Harbor* – brought the only woman ever to visit the Conways on their island: Mrs. Thornton. An unexpected pleasure was the arrival of Tucker McLure's *Norseman* with Captain Baverstock on board. McLure, an old friend, was happy to find the Conways successfully pioneering away, and departed with a stack of letters to mail.

During their eight-month stay on Santiago, the Conways found many potsherds on what they called Pirates Flat. They searched in vain for Lieutenant Cowan's grave, and surmised that it may have been covered by a lava flow. Ainslie built some towers along the trail to the spring as a guide for future visitors seeking water. All in all, life on this former pirates' rendevous

was calm and peaceful as the Conways busied themselves with their gardening and cooking experiments, including several hundred recipes for pancakes.
One day, a plane dramatically dropped a message with shocking news:
a United States tug was on its way to evacuate the Conways from their
Galapagan Nirvana, because three desperate prisoners had escaped from the
penal colony at Villamil and were supposedly headed in the direction of
James Bay. The Comandante at Wreck Bay feared international repercussions if the two gringos on Santiago were harmed, and ordered the Conways
off the island.

After spending two months on Baltra, the Conways were permitted to
return to Santiago, but only to salvage whatever was left of their belongings.
Someone, presumably the convicts, had ransacked the camp. After cleaning
the place for its next future occupants, the Conways finally departed in
August, 1947, aboard a United States tug. Unwilling to settle in any of the
established colonies in the archipelago, the fiercely independent Conways
regretfully left the Galapagos.

Albatross

In September of 1947, the snow-white *Albatross* dropped anchor at
Wreck Bay. The huge, four-masted motor-schooner was a new training ship,
owned by a shipping combine and loaned to the Swedish Deep Sea Expedition for a fifteen-month voyage led by Hans Petterson.

Financed by Swedish donors without any governmental aid, the expedition had been planned at the University of Goteborg. The ship was equipped
with special coring devices to remove long sample cores of sediment from
ocean bottoms. Later, these would be analyzed for microfossils, minerals,
uranium, and radium. From the percentage of lime present in the cores, it was
hoped to determine the surface temperature prevailing at the time the layers
were deposited. This would be valuable in the study of climatic changes in
the earth's history. Also, depth charges would be exploded, and the sound
waves reflected by echoes through the layers would give information as to the
thickness of the sediment and whether the bed-rock was basaltic or granitic.
Cores, some as long as sixty-five feet, were collected from all oceans of the
world.

The work of the *Albatross* would perhaps some day lend a solution to
the puzzle about a land bridge to the Galapagos. From the character of the
sediment, the scientists hoped to determine whether sinking had occurred and
how much sediment had collected over the bed-rock. However, sampling
was not an easy matter; the coring tubes were often bent and almost ruined by
unexpected hard lava beds caused by recent eruptions.

At Wreck Bay, the port captain urged Petterson not to land anywhere on
Isabela because the deported criminals and notorious desperadoes of the

penal colony at Villamil were liable to seize their ship and slit their throats. Ainslie Conway, present at Wreck Bay when the *Albatross* arrived, also urged the Swedes to steer clear of Isabela, but encouraged them to visit James Bay.

While the *Albatross* was taking core samples south of the archipelago, Dr. Petterson and four men camped at James Bay. They crossed the river of pahoehoe lava which bisects the crescent bay. This solidified river of lava poured from a crater at a thousand-foot elevation and streamed down the mountain slope, forming a mile-wide barrier between the two halves of the beach. This recent flow of black lava, about fifty years old, "resembled a choppy sea suddenly transformed into black and very brittle stone," wrote Petterson. It cut the soles of their heavy boots and was "perfectly awful to traverse." Nevertheless, the group was reluctant to leave James Bay, which to them was "our Paradise Lost."

Kurun

A young Frenchman left Brittany in September of 1949 in a 33-foot gaff-rigged cutter. Jacques-Yves le Toumelin sailed the *Kurun* singlehandedly for the greater part of the voyage and circled the globe in three years.

The lonely voyager sighted the Galapagos on October 20, 1949, after a twenty-five-day trip from Panama – not too bad for a sailing vessel without an engine. He could not detect the chimneys of the sugar-works described in his nautical directions book as landmarks to Wreck Bay. They had vanished years before.

He walked through the streetless, shopless, "picturesque but poverty-stricken hamlet" of Baquerizo Moreno and observed, "The resources of the archipelago are exceedingly restricted, though this perhaps is a blessing in having safeguarded it from human cupidity. Happy are those countries without wealth; the world leaves them in peace."

However, the economy at Wreck Bay seemed destined to change. An enterprising American named Mann had started building a large refrigeration plant on the beach and owned a small fleet of motor boats equipped for fishing.

On a high rise of the sandy beach, a padre was putting the finishing touches on a new chapel, "a modest little edifice, touching in its very simplicity." The village itself, with its wooden cabins and corrugated roofs, "was interesting only in being bizarre."

Villagers pestered le Toumelin for magazines; the illustrations were used to decorate the inner walls of their huts. There also was a great demand for nails and shirts, which, unfortunately, the *Kurun* could not supply.

Le Toumelin visited Mr. and Mrs. Mann at their home at Sundown Beach. He also met the French-Canadian who decided to settle permanently at Chatham after a chance visit in a yacht. In the hills, Karin Cobos's sixteen-year-old daughter, Sylvia, entertained the mariner with tunes on her guitar. Not too far away, old Mr. Guldberg lived happily with his older daughter Snefrid on "a strange little corner of Norway in this tropical island." The old man had not been to the port for sixteen years, preferring to remain among the mountain lakes and clear streams, where the wild horses run free. It is interesting to note that a fresh-water mullet is found in some of these tiny streams at Chatham. It resembles the mullets of the mainland of Mexico and Central America – a fact which would strengthen the theory that the Galapagos had been connected to Central America at some time.

During the six weeks of le Toumelin's stay at Wreck Bay, other ships arrived: *Fleur D'Ocean* enroute to Tahiti, where the Argot family would settle permanently; the Norwegian ketch *Ho-Ho II*, with the Bryhn family sailing around the world; the old yawl of Captain Slemback, *Stortbecker III*. Mrs. Butler, secretary to the president of Ecuador, graciously took le Toumelin's mail on the yacht *Solana*.

"There is a saying that those who have tasted the island's guava will come back for more," said le Toumelin, as he regretfully sailed out of Wreck Bay, once more to pass Dalrymple Rock, named "Five Fingers" by Americans. At Academy Bay, he met the New Zealander Sanders, who had settled here after many adventures in the South Seas. Among these had been a nine-month stay alone on one of the Cocos Islands, hoping to salvage the wreck of the *Heather Glen* on which he had sailed from England. Another islander, Madame Coray, a Swiss lady whose husband had died a few years before, was successfully acting as mother, teacher, and breadwinner for her daughter in this desolate place.

Life would certainly have been duller at Academy Bay without one of the remnants of the "helluva peoples" of the early 1930's – the irascible, sixty-year-old Alsatian named Kubler. This eccentric recluse was a superb fisherman, mighty hunter, and phenomenal eater, but was said by some of his neighbors to be a raving lunatic. The powerful man had built his house single-handed, and reportedly allowed no one beyond the large room at the front door. His house was surrounded by a solid stone wall with a raised observation post from which he could guard the approaches. He was a crack shot and owned a veritable arsenal. Occasionally he fired his gun to let his neighbors know he did not lack ammunition. It was said, quite incorrectly, that the misanthrope detested children, and certainly there was enmity between himself and the locals.

After meeting so many exceptional people in the islands, le Toumelin wrote that the Galapagos were a haven for "amazing human types," illustrating man's natural tendency to carry on in spite of obstacles. In these islands, where modern man lives among prehistoric iguanas, le Toumelin suggested that this might be the place where the human race would end.

Scarcely a dozen years later, in October of 1960, Charles Hillinger wrote a series of articles about the Galapagos Islands which appeared in the Los Angeles Times.   Hillinger stated that an American, who lived alone at Iguana Cove on Isabela Island, had gone to the Galapagos out of fear of an impending atomic war.   When last seen, Hillinger reported, the man believed he was the sole survivor of a nuclear holocaust.

Miscellaneous Visitors

Another Peterson (this time from Brooklyn) reached the Galapagos in 1948.   Alfred Peterson left Europe in his small *Stormoway*, a cutter of Colin Archer design, and eventually sailed single-handed as far west as the Red Sea, where the boat was wrecked on the Yemen coast.

Reporter Rolf Blomberg came again to the islands and spent some time digging for treasure.   Karin Cobos had told him many credible stories of buried loot which could be located by various clues such as mystical inscriptions on a slab of marble, an old anchor chain, or a row of palms.   If any treasure was found in the Galapagos in recent years, it certainly has been a well-kept secret.

Count Von Luckner arrived again in June of 1950 on Commander Clinton Baverstock's *Inca*, bringing long-range radio equipment for the Wittmers.   Luckner took Rolf Wittmer to the abandoned Baltra base, where he spent six weeks dismantling the American post-office building.   The *Inca* returned for him and hauled the bundles of lumber to Black Beach.   In November of 1950, the Wittmers moved into their new two-story mansion which boasted of two guest rooms.

Two dozen young Americans spent a month cruising and fishing in the archipelago about February of 1951, stopping not only at the settlements, but also at lesser known coves.   Captain Charles Otterman had sailed his 136-foot gaff-rigged schooner, *Gloria Dalton*, down the coast of Mexico and Central America to Panama, proceeded leisurely down the coast of South America as far as Callao, Peru, then headed west to the Galapagos and the South Seas on an eighteen-month cruise.   The skipper made complete circuits of both Floreana and Narborough in an outboard motor boat.

Soon afterwards, an American couple (who prefer to remain anonymous because they don't like to see their name in print) arrived at Academy Bay in a thirty-seven-foot ketch and settled permanently, raising the total population to an even 200.

The 1950 census of the population of the entire archipelago totaled 1,329.   On San Cristobal (Chatham) Island there were 802 residents, equally divided between Baquerizo Moreno and Progreso.   Most of them were tillers of the soil, who came from the Ecuadorian highlands and were accustomed to the cool climate of the higher elevations of Chatham.

Isabela Island had 92 convicts and 216 other residents on the cattle ranch and coffee plantations near Villamil. Floreana Island had only 21 people near Black Beach, while Santa Cruz Island had 198 in and near Academy Bay.

The 70-foot *Arthur Rogers*, formerly a Brixham trawler and now rigged as an ordinary ketch, made two trips to the Galapagos in 1951, sailing from Panama in ten, and then in fourteen, days. At Progreso, W. I. B. Crealock, the naval architect and marine surveyor, found the settlement unattractive and unimaginative. The port captain at Wreck Bay tried to impose an unjustified "handling charge"; the *Arthur Rogers* had paid its forty dollars port charge to the Ecuadorian consul at Panama and refused to pay the additional fee. Ecuador at that time furnished no navigational aids to the islands; the high rate, based on tonnage and the number of persons aboard, was excessive.

After cruising to Barrington Island and Academy Bay, the ketch dropped anchor at Black Beach. The visitors were the first guests in the new house of the Wittmers. The Wittmer resourcefulness was indicated by a lathe operated by a homemade windmill. At the farm, Frau Wittmer was boiling sugar syrup, while Herr Wittmer busied himself with a homemade still, brewing some island schnapps. With their grown children helping with the heavier work, the elderly pioneers found life a bit easier.

After stops at Sulivan Bay and Tagus Cove, Crealock wrote that, even though at first all the islands look the same, each had something unique to offer. He admitted that he did not begin to appreciate the beauty of the islands until he had spent time exploring. "To the sailors of old," Crealock wrote, "the Galapagos were the Enchanted Islands because they were so hard to reach; to us they were the Enchanted Isles because they were so hard to leave."

In earlier history, many castaways were stranded in the Galapagos by unscrupulous pirate captains; the year 1951 had one such incident. Toward the end of the year, the Dutch yacht *Anna Elizabeth* anchored in Post Office Bay while two Europeans decided to call on the Wittmers. They were forced to spend the night on the island, having lost their way searching for the Wittmer house in the hills, apparently not aware that the Wittmers were living at Black Beach. The ship left without its passengers, leaving some of their luggage near the barrel. The unscrupulous skipper had absconded with their passports and $500 earnest money reserved for Tahiti. The Belgian and German then received shelter and food from the sympathetic Wittmers until the next island ship arrived. One of the two, a journalist, stayed with the Wittmers until February of 1952.

Another writer visited the islands about this time, and from him we received an account of the prisoners at Isabela Island.

Penal Colony

Arthur Eichler sailed to the Galapagos from Guayaquil on a "little nutshell eighty years old," named *Cinco De Junio*. Aboard ship, he conversed with an Italian who was returning to Chatham to liquidate a canned fish business which had gone bankrupt due to lack of transport of the canned product; the only "junk ship" available was completely unreliable. The refrigeration plant, which had been finished in 1950, was used for several months, then abandoned.

At Baquerizo Moreno, Eichler saw dark-skinned people wearing scanty garments and giving an impression of carelessness and indifference. There was no sign of activity at the beach, and the people "seemed to live as if every day were a holiday." They were more active in cooler Progreso, though.

At Villamil, Eichler watched cattle being loaded onto a freight ship. Each animal was tied to the outside of a shoreboat and floated to the larger ship. The half-drowned creature, with a rope around its horns, was then hauled onto the deck with a windlass. There were about forty thousand head of cattle on Isabela, as well as goats, wild burros, wild dogs, and rats.

Several days before Eichler's arrival, some of the wretched prisoners from the penal colony had seized a fishing boat and headed for the open sea with a small supply of rice and water. They were never seen or heard of again. A watery grave may have been preferable to the living death they had suffered on Isabela.

Only murderers and criminals of the worst sort were sentenced to this "island of sorrow," but nevertheless, Eichler felt compassion for the half-naked wretches who wore pieces of sackcloth as their only garments. They accepted his gift of cigarettes with touching gratitude at this unexpected kindness. Earlier at sea, Eichler had learned about the prisoners' miserable life.

At Guayaquil, six convicts, each guarded by two policemen, boarded the *Cinco De Junio* with their arms behind their backs and their thumbs tied together with twine. They were permitted freedom to converse with Eichler.

There were three prison camps on Isabela Island, they said. The first was on the beach at Villamil for the prisoners who had served their full term and were about to leave. The second camp was near the village of Santo Tomas, about two hours distant from shore and at a higher elevation. The last camp, located thirty miles inland, called "Alemania" (Germany) was "worse than Hell."

The unfortunates destined for Alemania had to carry a pack of fifty kilos (110 pounds) upon their back as they hiked the long distance over glass-sharp lava that cut their shoes to pieces. Calloused guards, armed with guns and whips, prodded the men forward despite their bleeding feet. The trip lasted several days, and at camp the wretches suffered additional atrocities. Eichler stated that "no prisoner sentenced to maximum penalty and sent to the Galapagos ever had a chance to see the end of his term alive." Mercifully, the penal colony on Isabela was abolished in 1957 by the Ecuadorian legislature.

Donald Green, a Canadian boy aboard the *Yankee*, had reported that, in 1951, he saw a huge steel barrel half buried in the sand at Wreck Bay. It had an opening in the side big enough for a man to pass through. At one time it had been used as a dungeon for solitary confinement of prisoners on San Cristobal Island.

1952-1953

On Febuary 10, 1952, Annie and Louie Van der Wiele sailed their forty-six-foot steel-hulled yacht, *Omoo*, out of Panama. Several years before, they had enjoyed a pleasant stay in the Galapagos aboard the *Fleur D'Ocean*, and had looked forward to renewing acquaintances with their friends there. But the arrogant conduct of the Ecuadorian consul at Panama had angered the skipper to such an extent that he decided to forego the pleasure.

In Panama, the Ecuadorian consul's office opens at 9 A.M. and closes at noon. Van der Wiele made four separate trips to get a visa before he finally encountered the consul at his office at fifteen minutes past noon. It seems that the consul knew only one English word – overtime – for which he charged double rates. After an impolite reception, the consul tried to charge $46 for the 18-ton boat. Pierre Suzanne had previously paid only $46 for a 46-ton ship, *Fleur D'Ocean*. Refusing to pay the exorbitant charge, Captain Van der Wiele "left the dear man to his islands" and decided to sail non-stop to the Marquesas.

Another mariner who greatly desired to visit the Galapagos could not afford to go there. He was Eric Hiscock, a young Englishman who had built and sailed the *Wanderer II* to the Azores, whence Howell and McNulty sailed it to Australia via Panama and the Galapagos.

Hiscock and his wife Susan left the Isle of Wight in July, 1952, in his newly-built 30-foot Bermudian sloop, *Wanderer III*. Arriving at Panama in January of the following year, they inquired about the Galapagos at the Ecuadorian consul's office. The two had planned to stop at the Galapagos Islands to take on water and supplies enroute to the Marquesas but found the permit fee to high. They considered stopping without a permit but were warned by Captain Baverstock the Ecuadorian gunboats had been known to seize fishing boats, and even yachts, which did not have their papers in order. That was a risk they were not pepared to take, so they bypassed the Galapagos.

The *Wanderer III* did visit the Galapagos seven years later.

A more affluent visitor arrived in the Galapagos at this time. James

S. (Pebbles) Rockefeller, Jr. and his friend Tony had spent a year rebuilding a rotten hulk named *Mandalay* and sailed from Connecticut on a merry jaunt around the world, sampling the life and coconut beer of remote islands. Three of the most delightful households they encountered in their travels were those of the Angermeyer brothers at Academy Bay.

They found the handsome Karl Angermeyer, who called himself the Duke of the Galapagos and who once turned down a Hollywood screen test, building a new stone house about fifty yards up from the ten-foot cliff off Angermeyer Point. He was married to flaming-haired Marga, who had been brought to the island by her first husband, the Alsatian Kubler.

Marga's daughter Carmen had married Fritz Angermeyer and now had two daughters. Fritz was presently engaged in building a plywood boat. He had salvaged a motor from a junk heap and, with his home-made foot-pedal lathe, was turning out bearings and bushings for it. He had also built a clutch and stern bearing, and had performed other feats quite remarkable, considering that machine shops and hardware stores were somewhat scarce on desert islands.

Gus Angermeyer and wife Lou were now the proud parents of five sons, the eldest being eight years old. Baking bread for this large brood was a problem, and Gus was engaged in building a box-like affair, not unlike a stove, which would some day bake six loaves of bread at a time. It was being made of surplus parts from an old engine, tractor, and air compressor from the Baltra base. Gus also tutored his children every day after breakfast. They were learning German, Spanish, and English. The crew of the *Mandalay* parted with their magazines because the children were hungry for new literature. "Reading matter is hard to come by here," said Karl.

Besides such activities as hunting goats and wild pigs, and skewering lobsters on pronged spears at night by the light of flashlights, there was time for art and music. Karl painted landscapes and iguanas in oil. Frequent concerts were given, with Gus at his accordion, Karl playing the harmonica, and Marga at her violin. Fritz thumped away on a drum made from a pelican pouch stretched over a nail keg.

For the Angermeyers, life was quite delightful, gay, and cheap, "if you don't count the labor."

Thor Heyerdahl

Toward the end of 1952, Dr. Robert I. Bowman was studying the Darwin finches in considerable detail, especially those near Academy Bay. So far, among scholars, the Galapagos Islands had attracted only biologists and a few geologists; archeologists and anthropologists paid scant attention to these islands which heretofore had never yielded any signs of permanent aboriginal habitation.

It was thus quite a novelty when Thor Heyerdahl, of *Kon Tiki* fame, arrived in January of 1953. He came not on a balsa raft as is his wont, but in a large sailing vessel named *Don Lucho*. His companions were Arne Skjols-vold of the University of Oslo and Erik K. Reed of the United States National Parks Service. The trio hoped to excavate Inca relics, and brought fifty-five crates of equipment plus a superabundant supply of water.

Their first order of business was to visit the Wittmers, to study the huge stone face which Phillips Lord had photographed near the old Wittmer farm. When shown at a lecture in New York, the carving had stirred up quite a controversy among archeologists; arguments arose as to whether it had Polynesian or Incan origin. Mr. Wittmer explained that he himself had carved the huge statue. Owing to a language misunderstanding, Mr. Lord had inferred that it was a prehistoric masterpiece.

As consolation, Mrs. Wittmer gave the archeologists of the *Don Lucho* some clay sherds and an old clay pipe which she found near her henhouse. Thor Heyerdahl at once declared them to be pre-Spanish, over 600 years old, and perhaps even predating the Inca civilization.

The expedition centered around James Bay in two valleys about two miles apart, and in minor sites at Santa Cruz Island. The sherds (which supposedly represented at least 131 pots and included a dun-colored ceramic frog) and sharp-edged flints were found several inches down in very scant soil. A few fragments were imbedded in frozen lava, and all finds were in areas close to a water supply.

In his monograph on the archeology of the Galapagos, Heyerdahl described the pottery as of Amerindian origin and dating back to Coastal Tiahuanaco times. However, he ignored the fact that the pottery's Peruvian and Ecuadorian beginnings did not prove that Incas brought them to James Bay. The pirates who looted the western coast of South America more than likely carried off the curiously-shaped ware to the islands. At Buccaneer Cove, on Plaza Island, and at all the other sites described by Heyerdahl, the artifacts were closely associated with pirate camps.

Using these bits of pottery to establish the fact that South American Indians discovered the Galapagos, Heyerdahl then expounded his theory that the Indians proceeded westward to settle the Polynesian Islands. In state-ments to the *New York Times* he contended:

> People able to go 600 miles to visit the isolated volcanic Galapagos and return to their base in South America could also with greatest ease continue their explorations and discover the Polynesias . . . . This strengthened my suspicion that a balsa raft, which was the only craft available to them must also be able to sail against the wind. We were wholly untrained for maneuvering *Kon Tiki* and only drifted helplessly until thrown

ashore in the Tuamotu Archipelago of the Polynesias . . . [The *Kon Tiki* did not touch the Galapagos.]

I concluded afterward that through the correct handling of the centerboards in relation to the sail that a balsa raft would be able to tack and sail into the wind like any keeled sailing craft.

It would have been a simple matter for the raft voyages to visit the Galapagos for fishing or catching giant tortoises or even to harvest some of the wild cotton growing there. This cotton is of the same species as that raised by South American Indians before the arrival of the Spanish and could not have reached the islands except by being transported there by man. The Indians who sailed to the Galapagos are as good sailors as the Vikings who sailed to England, and continuing to discover the Polynesias was only natural, for the Indians were also good navigators. The Galapagos were the missing link between the mainland and the Polynesias, but now I am convinced that the American Indians were the early settlers of the Pacific Islands.

If Thor Heyerdahl wishes to convince his readers, perhaps he should build a *Kon Tiki II*, and with proper manipulation of centerboard and sail, drift to the Galapagos from some port of Ecuador or Peru. Then to prove that his theory has some validity, he should sail the raft to windward back to its origin, just as he claims the Indians were able to return to their base. Even this would not be conclusive proof that the Indians did likewise.

Eminent anthropologists would like to know how Indians of the Tiahuanaco Period of 750 A.D. acquired sails whose use was not introduced to them until 1500 A.D. Robert C. Suggs wrote that the *Kon Tiki* type raft was developed by the Peruvians, but not until after the Spanish introduced sails to them. Prior to the white man, their rafts were propelled by paddles.

Six hundred miles is a long way to paddle a raft back and forth, especially when bucking the Humboldt Current on the return trip to the mainland.

As for the wild cotton, it could have been brought to the islands, but not necessarily by Indians. Many ancient, abandoned plantations attest to the fact that mainland crops were grown in the islands. In 1850, General Mena, and others before and after him, conducted agricultural experiments on San Cristobal, Santa Cruz, and Floreana. Besides cotton, there are many other domestic plantings which reverted to the wild state and thrived, like oranges, lemons, guavas, avocados, corn, yuca, and others.

Heyerdahl's discoveries and theories recall to mind the story told by William A. Robinson in his book, *To the Great Southern Sea*. Just before his famous appendicitis attack in 1934, Robinson had been filming the wild life on Isabela Island. At Elizabeth Bay, he constructed a complete miniature village, penguin size, around a tiny land-locked lagoon, using lava slabs for building material. Toy furniture was added to this movie set.

Years later, a scientific expedition from California reported finding this "mystery village," and pondered over its origin. The scientists decided, very seriously, that the village had been built by shipwrecked sailors deranged by suffering and exposure. This erroneous conclusion was duly reported in newspapers, to Robinson's "unspeakable delight."

Yankee

More ships arrived during the year: *Novia*; the thirty-seven foot *Nellie Brush* from California; *Observer* with the Krieger Expedition; the *Wanderer II* with Howell and McNulty sailing to Australia; and in December of 1953, the *Yankee* came again on its sixth cruise around the world.

Yankee's skipper, Irving Johnson, found that the port of Baquerizo Moreno at Wreck Bay had grown to three times the size he had seen on his last trip, but it was still a village of shacks, mostly constructed from lumber salvaged from the Baltra air base. The arable lands in the hills were gradually becoming settled, and a recent heavy rainy season had turned the islands into mud.

Santa Cruz Island had been flooded, but this did not dampen spirits at Academy Bay. The Johnsons were invited to a gay party at Karl Angermeyer's new stone house, and dined on lobster, which is plentiful there and easily picked with gloved hands. The Galapagos lobster is really a crayfish, without the wicked claws of the Maine variety.

On Floreana, the Johnsons were saddened to learn that their friend, Harry Wittmer, had drowned in October of 1951, after his fishing boat had capsized in a heavy sea. Harry died at the age of thirty-two, having enjoyed twenty years of contentment and freedom on the island. Several years before, Irving Johnson had helped Harry design the fourteen-foot fishing boat which Harry later built of Baltra lumber.

Before leaving the Galapagos, the crew of the *Yankee* refurbished the barrel at Post Office Bay by covering it with new canvas, painting it white, and adding a new roof.

Xarifa

In Europe, Hans Hass had started an Institute of Deep Sea Diving and Photography which made some interesting movies of under-water life in the Red Sea. Later, he purchased a dilapidated relic of a three-masted schooner which had been built in 1927 for the Singer Sewing Machine family. The steel-hulled 143-foot *Xarifa* had lost her sixty-ton keel and was degraded into hauling coal. Hass restored the ship to its original condition and sailed for the Pacific.

The Galapagos were sighted at sundown; in the morning they had disappeared. The currents of the Bewitched Isles had swept the *Xarifa* off her course. On January 5, 1954, the ship reached Wreck Bay, where fifty shacks of sheet metal and planks, roughly nailed together, graced the colorless beach. Darwin's monument had a neat little fence around it, and in a new and well-equipped military club, a gramophone scratched out a tune.

The *Xarifa* did not linger in this dismal place. "Our sailors wandered about sullenly in the open; they had seen everything that was to be seen in this god-forsaken place and they bought everything that was for sale," Hass remarked. However, the photographers and naturalists on board really had a field day in the islands.

Dr. Irenaus Eibl-Eibesfeldt, a specialist on animal behavior, was in his glory at Osborne Islet. He moved in with the sea lions, lived and slept on the beach, and had his meals sent to him by launch. Thus, he studied the whole daily routine of the animals' lives. At Seymour he found a sort of sea lion graveyard. In a small area were a half-dozen ancient, half-blind males, who had been conquered by younger fellows now ruling the harems. The old males, like residents in an old peoples' home, were peacefully waiting for death, and near them were the desiccated carcasses of those which had died.

For years, the Galapagos sea lion was mistakenly classified as belonging to a species of southern sea lion known as *Otaria jubata*. In 1953, the Norwegian scholar, Sivertsen, discovered the error while studying the mammal skulls at the Oslo Museum, and renamed this species *Zalophus wollbacki* after a Norwegian naturalist. The Galapagoan sea lions are a peculiar species occurring nowhere else in the world, and are closely related to the California species.

The *Xarifa* stayed about a week at Narborough, photographing the numerous iguanas, birds, sea lions under water, and coral fish. At least on this particular island, the fauna flourished unharmed because few boats went there; this was not true of other islands, especially those with settlements. Dr. Eibl-Eibesfeldt wrote that, on the populated islands, he and his crew found sea lions with skulls bashed in, birds with broken wings and beaks, and the sun-bleached skeletons of giant tortoises. They were openly offered living and dead specimens of protected animals, including penguins, young tortoises, tortoise shells, and the skins of fur seals and sea lions. He reported that there seemed to be no one to enforce the laws with respect to the protection of the wildlife.

Gloria Dalton

The mail deposited in the barrel by the *Yankee* was picked up by the crew of the *Gloria Dalton* at the end of March, 1954. Captain Charles Otterman and a group of young boys had sailed the schooner to the Galapagos on another trip to the South Seas. Their stay in the islands was brief, just long enough to enjoy some fishing near Post Office Bay. A supply of onions, radishes, and cabbages was purchased from the Wittmers at Black Beach, and there, too, the crew met the Governor from Chatham making his rounds of the islands.

The *Gloria Dalton* anchored at Post Office Bay for a week, and, during that time, a 57-foot schooner arrived. Aboard the *Windjammer* was Mrs. Peggy Poor, former New Orleans newspaper woman, and skipper James L. Cox, former first mate on a freighter plying between New Orleans and Africa. Visits were exchanged between the two ships. Captain Otterman marvelled at the inordinate supply of rice in metal cans aboard the *Windjammer*, which also carried about twenty to thirty cans of water strapped to its deck cabins. After making some tentative plans to rendezvous in Tahiti, the *Gloria Dalton* sailed to the Marquesas; *Windjammer* was to proceed to Easter Island.

About five months later, the *Gloria Dalton* was returning from the South Seas and was about fifteen hundred miles west of the Galapagos when its Portuguese mate translated a radio message by a Chilean or Ecuadorian destroyer: the *Windjammer* had been lost with all hands in a storm about one hundred miles north of Easter Island. Captain Otterman once more deplored the folly of sailing a round-bottomed centerboard schooner, unsuitable for open waters and heavy seas, into an area dangerous even for heavy-keeled ships. For ten years, he was unaware that Mrs. Poor and her skipper were very much alive.

Windjammer

Mrs. Peggy Poor, former New Orleans debutante and foreign correspondent for International News Service, had purchased the schooner *Windjammer* in 1948. Four years later, she left her native city to sail around the world, and, in Jamaica, James L. Cox signed on as skipper.

Panama Canal records show that the *Windjammer* sailed through the locks on February 27, 1954, with five persons aboard: Mrs. Poor, James Cox, two Chileans, and a seventeen-year-old cook, Gordon Nicolsey, from British West Africa. The ship arrived at Post Office Bay at the end of March with only two persons on board.

Instead of proceeding to Easter Island, the *Windjammer* lingered in the "freakish" Galapagos for four months, photographing the strange wild life and exploring interiors of the islands. While sailing along the western coast of Isabela, James Cox was attracted to the shore by a blinding white light.

Upon approaching closer, he saw a long strip of snow-white beach reflecting the sun's rays with a dazzling brightness. In the mixture of pure white sand and coral was imbedded remains of marine creatures in various stages of decay. The strong odor of decaying flesh was mixed with a suffocating smell of sulphur. Cacti and mangroves far to the rear of this beach indicated an obvious fact: the crew of the *Windjammer* was looking at new land which had risen from the sea to form a new coast line.

James Cox was curious as to the age of this new earth born out of the Pacific; flesh under the thick shells of dead sea turtles indicated it could hardly have been more than two months old. Fishermen at the nearest settlement fifty miles away had seen a blinding light about six or seven weeks previously, but knew nothing of the formation of new land. Irving Johnson had sailed along this coast four months earlier, in January, and would have noticed the unusual shoreline had it occurred before he arrived. Cox conjectured that a volcano had recently erupted under water but had not been strong enough to come to the surface and merely had lifted the ocean bottom.

Several months later, James Cox and Mrs. Poor sailed the *Windjammer* south towards Easter Island. About August 18, 1954, two radio amateurs at Oakland, California, intercepted a coded report that the schooner was lost at sea. One day later, the radio station on Easter sent out a message that the *Windjammer* was adrift, badly crippled, and that the crew was safe. Chilean authorities reported that the vessel had foundered at Port Hotuiti on Easter Island.

It was not until two months later that Mrs. Poor's plight became known as she registered a protest with the U.S. State Department. Her cable read, "A reign of silence and deceit followed the wreck of our schooner on August 23. We had run aground on jagged lava outcroppings on this volcanic island and two days later, while salvage work was taking place in the icy surf, a horde of natives attacked . . . . Nearly naked savages swarmed through enclosures on horses, galloped horseback over the hills, encircling the beach, dismounted, and swam through rough seas to loot the yacht." Mrs. Poor claimed that valuable cameras, jewelry, and food were stolen by these people who historically were notorious for pilfering visiting ships of anything not nailed down – just a friendly Easter Island custom.

Peggy Poor also charged that she had been marooned almost incommunicado for fifteen weeks, while her messages and cables were suppressed and distorted. On one occasion, the natives took potshots at her and Cox, while the military garrison could not cope with the situation. To add insult to injury, the Chilean navy billed her $1,000 for the use of cables in salvage attempts and for the food and shelter she had received for four months. Chilean authorities denied her allegations, and removed her from the island on a Chilean naval vessel making its infrequent scheduled stop at that remote outpost.

Such was the story of *Windjammer*, whose name is painted on a wall of gloomy Tagus Cove.

Upheaval at Urvina Bay

Unaware that James Cox had already reported the newly-risen land on Isabela Island in the *Roto Magazine* of the *New Orleans Times-Picayune* in October of 1955, three other Americans came upon this remarkable phenomenon, and a year later reported their find in a scientific journal.

Jack C. Couffer, Conrad Hall, and a third man named Doug lived for eight months in the Galapagos aboard their tiny 30-foot ketch *Highlander.* They were filming *Islands of the Sea, a True Life Adventure* for the Walt Disney Studios of Burbank, California.

"We found ourselves talking out loud to the wild things around us," said Couffer, as the creatures obligingly posed for the cameras. The extreme tameness of the fauna was a positive and convincing proof to the photographers that man had never settled in the islands before the arrival of the Spanish in 1535.

Inquisitive finches and buzzards followed them during the day; at night, small gnome-like herons watched them in the firelight. Curious owls went to sea and perched in the rigging of the boat. Iguanas were so numerous and tame that the photographers had to walk with caution for fear of stepping on them.

In late 1955, the *Highlander* sailed through Bolivar Channel between Isabela and Narborough Islands. As the boat approached Urvina Bay, on Isabela, the mariners became somewhat puzzled. As they took soundings, they found the depth of the water far shallower than indicated on their chart. Instead of a sandy beach or black lava blocks, they saw white coralline rocks. Dead mangrove trees, instead of rimming the water's edge, were located nearly a mile inland.

The men disembarked on the coralline but did not stay too long; the intense glare hurt their eyes and gave them headaches. Their skin turned fiery red as they studied the numerous skeletons of starfish, sea urchins, lobsters, eels, sea turtles, brittle stars, shellfish, and corals that were strewn about.

It soon became obvious to the men that they were standing on land that once had been ocean bottom. There was no evidence of geologic faults, but there were six-inch cracks at right angles to the beach and broken through solid lava boulders. It was apparent that a long stretch of coastline had risen about fifteen feet, forming a new land mass about two miles long and a mile wide.

The land mass rose quickly – many fish and sea turtles were trapped on ledges as the waters ebbed away. Although there was no sulphur odor, the men guessed that toxic volcanic products may have killed the creatures as the land rose. A great amount of the ocean bottom was exposed, and the marine creatures were dried by the intense heat of the sun.

Now the old beach-line was a mile away from the surf. The flightless cormorants, who like to live near their fish larder, had abandoned their old nests and started housekeeping anew on the raised land mass. Marine iguanas, larger and fatter than those seen elsewhere, thrived on the rich growth of algae now exposed. Less than two years after the upheaval, new life was replacing that destroyed by the cataclysm.

Here was positive proof that the earth can change suddenly. Jack Couffer did not regard the phenomenon as a pageant of death, but rather ''an infinitesimal episode in the age-long evolution of life – a geologic change that will continue as long as there is earth, and sea and sky.''

19

1955 TO 1960

cononononononononon

At the beginning of 1955, there were about eighty residents on Santa Cruz Island; Academy Bay even boasted of a small general store. Of the settlers, thirty were Europeans – a conglomeration of Swiss, Norwegians, French, Germans, Swedes, Canadians, North Americans, and a New Zealander. There was a small garrison, with a naval officer and his seven men, one of whom operated a radio. Sanders, the shipwrecked survivor of Cocos Islands, was still there.

A Norwegian, Hendricks, was a recent arrival. He was a frail-looking anchorite, about fifty years old. He lived alone in his hermitage in the hills and only mingled with others when selling fruit and vegetables. Dressed in shorts cut down from blue jeans, he wore a sort of skull cap made from jeans' remains to cover his long, flaxen hair. His lean body was toughened by his healthful outdoor existence, and perhaps by his diet – he was known as the "raw food eater." This man with the gentle porcelain-blue eyes and extreme embarrassed shyness was constantly jotting mysterious notes in a little notebook. His child-like simplicity and saintly aspect were in strange contrast to the more formidable Alsatian, Kubler, whose colorful personality was described by le Toumelin in 1949 and more recently by Gorsky.

Moana and Others

The forty-foot cutter *Moana* (the Tahitian word for "vastness of the sea") arrived at Darwin Bay on March 29, 1955. Bernard Gorsky and his friends, Serge and Pierre, had sailed from France to the Galapagos as part of their voyage around the world. Tower Island was known to them as "Hawk Island," a name which seemed appropriate when they found the island swarming with birds of all shapes and sizes.

Pierre bathed himself in the salty inland crater lake, hoping the sulphurous water would have a beneficial effect upon his painful boils, called "salt-water" boils and common to seamen. After dining on roast iguana and thrush, grouper steaks, and frigate-egg omelets, they sailed to Baltra and set up a tent on the beach while seals watched their every movement. In the distance, they saw a dilapidated triangular look-out tower and a mast with a flag. At night the flag was replaced by a light – Baltra was not deserted.

At Santa Cruz, the *Moana* anchored in Conway Bay. Nearby was an ancient fishing bark, manned by five young fishermen from Wreck Bay who were employed by a fabulous power, "The Company." Fishing and lobstering were extremely good there, and the fishermen cautioned the new arrivals to fear the seals as much as the sharks. Seals have sharp teeth and bite.

The *Moana* entered Academy Bay the next morning (entry at night is dangerous), and soon the crew split their last bottle of whisky with Gus Angermeyer, who was building himself a boat from the impervious matazarno wood of the island. The mariners were anxious to meet the dangerous madman described by le Toumelin of the *Kurun*.

Sure enough, they soon came to a house, inside a square wall surmounted by barbed wire. It bore a menacing notice (in Spanish) at the gate, signed by one Carlos Kubler and dated February 28, 1955: "A Los Ladrones Y Criminales de la Islande Santa Cruz: I declare myself tired of destructive acts and animosity. I would have you know that I have protected my property with traps dangerous to life. In the future any whom I find inside my boundaries, which I think are clear enough, I shall shoot like mad dogs."

The fierce Kubler turned out to be a kindly, gentle old man who greeted the visitors warmly. About age sixty-six, with flowing white hair, white beard, blue eyes, and no teeth, Kubler wore blue canvas shorts held up by a rope around his waist. He proudly displayed his date and fig trees, poultry house, concrete storehouse, a small house mounted on tall piles (from which he surveyed his domain), and his museum of curios fashioned from turtle shells, whalebones, pig skulls, and shark jaws.

It is said that Kubler had been deported with other German citizens to an internment camp on the mainland during World War II. He returned to the Galapagos with a slight persecution mania, aggravated to some extent by his mischievous neighbors. Kubler borrowed le Toumelin's book from the *Moana* and returned it later with marginal notes in blue and red attesting to the truth or falsity of certain statements in the book. He added his own personal appreciation of the author. He told Gorsky, "It's the people here put ideas in that Frenchman's head and he's put it all down, but it's all twaddle."

The "old billy goat" then trimmed his moustache and goatee and dressed in new clothes to pose obligingly for photographs of himself and house. Gorsky remarked that Kubler "was clearly something more than merely an interesting and entertaining hard-baked old misogynist hounded by a persecution mania," and added that Kubler had "withdrawn from man's universal disorder to create his own order, and ready, rifle in hand to take up its defense (whether goods or principle were in danger), asking of no man more than he was ready to give in return, considering every new day as the only real gift which we receive and enjoying the bounties of this earth in the way he desired. Yes, he was consistent and at least one knew where one was with him.''

After loading the *Moana* with goat meat, 110 lobsters in salt, haunches of beef, turtle meat, bananas, oranges, lemons, pumpkins, and sweet potatoes, the crew regretfully tore themselves away from the seemingly idyllic Academy Bay, where ''life is regulated solely by the rising and the setting of the sun.''

At this time, the population of Floreana Island numbered about fifty. A small radio station was operated there by a clever young man named Mario Garcia. He installed a generator at Black Beach and wired the Wittmer house for electricity. In 1957, his sister, Paquita, married Rolf Wittmer, and all the Europeans in the archipelago attended the gala wedding. Rolf was the first European born on Floreana, and the first European to marry there. Shortly afterwards, Ingeborg Floreanita Wittmer married her brother-in-law, Mario Garcia.

In 1959, Margret Wittmer, now a proud grandmother, flew to Germany for publication of her book, *Postlagernd, Floreana*, later published in the United States as *Floreana Adventure*, the fascinating story of her twenty-seven years on a desert island.

More visitors came from across the sea: *Solace, Tropic Bird, Elpetal, Zada, Nona, Presidente Alfaro, Arthur Rogers, Dirigo II, Stella Polaris,* Ralph Larrabee's *Goodwill* from California, *Hildur* from Toronto, and *Salmo* from Scotland.

It was an exciting day at Black Beach when Dr. Velasco Ibarra, President of Ecuador, visited the settlers of Floreana in April of 1956. After a talk with the Wittmers, the president promised the islanders a school building and a new radio station. These promises were kept. The following year, the new president, Dr. Camillo Ponce-Enriques, visited the islands and promised better connections with the mainland. Soon afterwards, the new ship *Tarqui* made regular monthly trips to all the settlements.

It was also in January of 1956 that Irving Johnson made his last voyage to the Galapagos in the *Yankee*. In past years, not only had he brought hundreds of young travellers to the enchanted Galapagos, but through his wonderfully illustrated articles in *National Geographic*, he brought the islands to millions of arm-chair travellers who never had the uncommon privilege of seeing the Encantadas in person.

UNESCO to the Rescue

For millions of years, the Galapagos Islands had been an isolated sanctuary for some curious reptiles and birds. Their counterparts on the mainland of South and Central America had disappeared or were replaced by modern stocks which arose under the stress of continental competition. The insular fauna thus represents a former geologic age, a lost world which somehow remained unchanged, a "miniature island cosmos where nature's processes could be clearly viewed in one small amphitheater," wrote Lincoln Barnett.

Perhaps the Galapagos land mass was much greater at one time, or ocean currents may have been different when a strait opened up at Panama during the Miocene and again during the glaciation period of North America. Whatever the cause of the freakish imbalance of the Galapagos animal population, its unusual species thrived undisturbed by natural enemies until destructive Man arrived.

Despite the pleas of many individuals like Von Hagen, Townsend, Swarth, and Hancock, in the last thirty years, slaughter of the priceless creatures continued unabated; their tameness had always been their death warrant. Fortunately, the complaints presented by Dr. Irenaus Eibl-Eibesfeldt in 1954 at Brussels brought about some positive action.

In the spring of 1957, Dr. Eibl-Eibesfeldt received an invitation to lead his own expedition to the Galapagos, to select a site for a future biological station. The International Union for Conservation of Nature and Natural Resources, working through the United Nations Educational, Scientific and Cultural Organization, appealed to the Ecuadorian government and received genuine whole-hearted cooperation.

On July 15, 1967, a Catalina Flying boat of the Ecuadorian Air Force landed on the hot, deserted airstrip of the Baltra base. The only sentries guarding the airfield were the red-barked tree cacti, as a distinguished company deplaned: Dr. Irenaus Eibl-Eibesfeldt, zoologist from the Max Planck Institute of West Germany; Dr. Robert I. Bowman, biologist from San Francisco State College; and *Life Magazine* reporters Rudolph Freund and Alfred Eisenstaedt.

The government supply ship, *El Oro*, was awaiting the visitors, and they were greeted by the president of the Ecuadorian Philatelic Association. A new series of stamps had been issued to commemorate the mission, and the four guests had arrived on the first day of issue. The stamps depicted the birds, animals, and scenery of the Galapagos, and were inaugurated by being flown back to Ecuador – the first Ecuadorian air mail service in the Galapagos.

The expedition made a complete survey of the islands and finally selected a site two miles west of Academy Bay for the location of the future Charles Darwin Station. The place was ideal in several aspects: it was an undisturbed area where flamingoes and iguanas thrived, and it was close enough to Academy Bay for provisions and military aid.

A special trip was made to the tortoise country in the hills of Santa Cruz (Indefatigable). Southwest of the settlement of Fortuna, some remnants of the giant tortoise still existed, and the party hiked over the confusing donkey trails and slippery substratum – a full day's journey. Led by Ecuadorian guide Cesar Moncayo, and with supplies loaded on a burro, the UNESCO team made their way through the dense underbrush, which dripped with red fire-ants at the 700-foot elevation. Forests of trees of the sunflower family towered as much as seventy feet above them. "But inconveniences fade after the first glimpse of the magnificent reptilian monsters plodding through the dense underbrush with the ponderous gait of a tank," said Bowman. A camp was established at this tortoise site, where they saw a huge 600-pounder and several smaller ones. Lying about were heaps of tortoise bones, "each an inglorious cairn to man's greed for a few quarts of cooking fat, . . . a sad example of man's misunderstanding of his place in the biotic community," commented Bowman.

It rained every morning during their three-day stay at the campsite, and Dr. Eibl-Eibesfeldt discovered a fat cockroach that behaves like a termite and dines exclusively on wood. He also learned that the little tropidurus lizards were becoming rare, ravaged by dog, cat, and rat populations. These lava-lizards are important, because they help the scientists learn how the islands slowly became detached from a main mass, which slowly sank, leaving its highest points as the present islands.

The little lizards differ from island to island. Those of the central group – from Indefatigable, Baltra, Barrington, James, Jervis, Albemarle, and Narborough – belong to the same species. Those further away, on Abingdon, Bindloe, and Chatham, are most divergent. On Hood, Floreana, and Duncan, the lizards are slightly different from the central group. But on the northernmost islands of Wenman and Culpepper, there are no lizards at all – nor any tortoises or snakes. Wenman and Culpepper were never part of the main mass of the archipelago and none of the creatures had reached them.

A study of the snakes reveals that the central mass had at first broken into two groups: Isabela-Narborough-Duncan and Indefatigable-James-Barrington. These later separated into the individual islands as they are today.

A visit was made to Dr. Ritter's Friedo. "A few palm trees were all that marked the site of his plantation and most of these had been beheaded by the winds. The tree-trunks rose up like telegraph poles in a melancholy tangle against the sky." A low mound marked the spot where Dr. Ritter found his final peace; a rude cross of two pieces of wood bore his name and the date of his death.

The survey revealed that the tortoises had suffered the most of all the Galapagan fauna and were completely extinct on Floreana and Barrington. They are extremely rare on Chatham, Hood, and Jervis. A small number can be found on James, Duncan, and Abingdon. They are common on Isabela, Santa Cruz, and, possibly, Narborough.

Land iguanas are numerous on Barrington, Narborough, and the Las

Plazas Islets. They are rare on Isabela and Santa Cruz, and are practically extinct on James and South Seymour.

Marine iguanas are plentiful on all islands except Floreana, and are scarce near all settlements.

Doves, ducks, and flamingoes are eaten by the inhabitants. Flightless cormorants and penguins fortunately breed in remote places and are spared.

Sea lions are plentiful everywhere, despite the fact that the tuna fishermen sometimes shoot them because they disturb live-bait fishing.

Wild cattle and burros run wild but do not seem to do much damage. Goats ravage seven of the larger islands: Chatham, Hood, Floreana, Isabela, Barrington, Santa Cruz, and James. Pigs and rats proliferate on Santa Cruz, James, Floreana, Chatham, Isabela, and Duncan.

Narborough is not plagued by any domestic animals gone wild, but there always is the danger that even a single pair of imported rats introduced on this island by settlers or fishermen could cause irreparable damage.

Besides the need to control the spread of domestic animals gone wild, there is also a necessity for controlling the importation of foreign plants. Guavas were strangling other growth on both Floreana and Chatham. In the higher regions of Santa Cruz, a sort of bean plant trailed all over the ground and shrubs, choking all other plants in the vicinity.

The following recommendations were made in July of 1957 and were approved by the International Zoological Congress in London:

> 1. A biological research institute, named Darwin Memorial Station, should be established either on Santa Cruz or San Salvador (James) island.
> 2. Twelve or more of the islands should be declared inviolable sanctuaries for the Galapagan wild life.
> 3. Laws for conservation should be strictly enforced by an appointed game warden.
> 4. A breeding and stocking colony for tortoises should be created.
> 5. The human population on the islands should be educated as to the priceless and irreplaceable value of the indigenous fauna.

Ascent of Narborough

The westernmost and uncanniest of the larger islands is Narborough (Fernandina). Hooded with dark, heavy clouds, the huge cone rises steeply to an impressive height of 5,300 feet with a base about twenty-five miles in diameter. Beebe had called it "the most desolate island of them all, it seems, with hardly any vegetation." From top to bottom is one seamed clinker covered with successive lava flows, some resembling frozen, black molasses candy, six-feet thick. A few strips of greenish-yellow vegetation relieve the eye, like unwelcome weeds in this unplowed Hell.

This pile of black evil is on the "hot" side of the archipelago and has had numerous eruptions, even in recent years. Of the black clouds which drape the crater's summit, Melville wrote:

> There is dire mischief going on in that upper dark. There toil the demons of fire, who, at intervals, irradiate the nights with a strange spectral illumination for miles and miles around, but unaccompanied by any further demonstrations; or else, suddenly announce themselves by terrific concussions, and the full drama of volcanic eruption. The blacker that cloud by day, the more you may look for light by night. Often whalemen have found themselves cruising nigh that burning mountain when all aglow with a ballroom blaze.

On September 5, 1957, the UNESCO team decided to explore the menacing crater of Narborough. Aerial photographs showed the oval rim to be five miles across, with a crater lake inside, as yet unvisited by man. Dr. Eibl-Eibesfeldt, Dr. Bowman, Rudolph Freund, Karl Angermeyer, and three Ecuadorians disembarked at a spot two-and-a-half miles east of Cabo Douglas, on the northern shore of Narborough, at a point where the distance to the crater is the shortest. Each man carried a fifty-five pound load of food, water, camping equipment, and cameras.

As they climbed the loose slag and rubble, they passed innumerable shrivelled grasshoppers and butterflies, mummified by the heat of this desert graveyard. Late in the afternoon, they reached the 650-foot level and camped on a patch of yellow grass. Just before sunset the air temperature was seventy-six degrees, but in the morning the hikers awoke with teeth chattering in the cold dampness. At noon, they reached the 2,300-foot level where little tropidurus lizards scurried about, mockingbirds attempted to steal their shoelaces, and huge yellow land iguanas over four-and-a-half feet long browsed on leaves of the scrubby croton bush.

By evening, the 3,285-foot level was reached, and there Dr. Eibl-Eibesfeldt was delighted to find the rare Galapagos rat, greyish-brown in color, with large naked ears. This is the only native land-mammal of the whole archipelago, and, unlike the imported black rats, is harmless to other species. It does not destroy lizard eggs, and the low birth rate keeps it from ravaging the plants in excess. Here, too, the hikers were bothered by ticks which normally feed on the iguanas, but found humans equally appetizing.

Clouds formed around the hikers as they hacked their way with machetes through dwarf scalesia bushes and a midget-height forest of sunflower trees. On the third day, at 4,500 feet, they broke through the northern rim of the crater. About two thousand feet below, the greenish-blue lake sparkled like a jewel. Near the middle of the lake was a small island volcano with a miniature lake inside. At one time, there was a huge rock in the center of this crater-lakelet, but it was bombed out by United States airmen who used it as a target.

Tired from stumbling into iguana burrows and hacking their way through creeping plants, the explorers eagerly plunged into the cool lake and drank the clean, fresh, but sulphurous-smelling water. Later, they all experienced gastrointestinal grief from drinking it. With difficulty, camp was pitched on a very steep talus slope.

The next morning, fish were seen swimming in the lake, and it was concluded that perhaps they reached it by being dropped by ducks, which often carry small fish in their plumage. These ducks are related to the Bahama ducks, but are a species peculiar to the Galapagos. A four-foot brown snake with a double row of light-colored spots was caught near the water's edge.

The eastern side of the island is more desolate than the north, and is "crinkled like the hide of an elephant." There were great hollows where the surface gave way, also deep tunnels several hundred feet long, and delightfully cool for resting. Feet were blistered, and their second pairs of shoes were cut to bits by the razor-sharp rubble. No land tortoises were encountered; these are more likely to be found in the moister areas on the southern side of the island.

In 1960, it was reported that the huge crater lake at Narborough had disappeared, leaving a dry crater bottom. Sulphur fumes arose everywhere, and an ominous rumbling could be heard.

Academy Bay, 1957

When the UNESCO team arrived at Academy Bay, they found about two hundred people eking out a meager existence at the little fishing settlement named Puerto Ayora. A few buildings constructed of lava boulders, or of lumber from the Baltra base, were scattered haphazardly along the cactus-covered coast. They were roofed with rusty corrugated iron, and most were merely miserable little huts. The old fish cannery, a relic of the Norwegian colony, had been reconstructed, and now served as headquarters for a government official.

The settlers were plagued constantly by food and water shortages, a fact which made Dr. Eibl-Eibesfeldt compare the Galapagos to an El Dorado and caution that settlers must be prepared to struggle continually for their "daily bread – and water."

The main occupation of the coastal dwellers was fishing; hand lines were used to catch groupers. The dried fish were shipped to Guayaquil at

Christmas and Easter seasons, bringing in a small income which was sufficient for the rest of the year. There was very little money in circulation, and
not much to buy in the few small shops. Each settler cobbled his own shoes,
built his own dwelling and furniture, and, more or less, cared for his own
needs.

Dr. Bowman questioned some of the immigrants and found their reasons for coming to the islands quite obscure: to escape the turmoil of recent
years, to find seclusion, to pioneer against innumerable odds, or to avoid
restrictions of their former homeland. However, it seems that life in the
islands presents even greater restrictions: limited occupation, confinement to
a small area, uncertain communication with the mainland, lack of educational, cultural, and artistic stimuli, and living under military rule.

Life in the upper farming regions was even more difficult. Tedious
trails led to the small plantations, where simple huts were raised on piles
above the mud and dampness of frequent rains. Mildew soon covered
anything that was not aired daily. The damp climate was good for bananas,
avocados, oranges, pineapples, potatoes, and other vegetables (for which
there was no market except on the island), but it also favored germs of
sickness.

Dr. Eibl-Eibesfeldt found the farming region in the hills above Academy Bay to be an unhealthy place, lacking proper sanitation. Most of the
settlers were Ecuadorians with a strong Indian strain, and he met an Indian
woman who had lost all of her children the week before. Only she and her
husband survived a severe attack of amoebic dysentery. Another malady was
the hookworm, which seems to thrive in this foggy place where the sky was
nearly always hidden by thick clouds. "All in all . . . life is hard, even
miserable," Dr. Bowman concluded.

Wreck Bay, 1957

Frank Rohr and three companions sailed to Wreck Bay in their 60-foot
topsail schooner, *Dirigo II*, and anchored near the old wooden dock. The
200-foot steamer *Guayas*, from Ecuador, was loading at the cannery, where a
generator could be heard whirring away. Four black fishing sloops were
anchored nearby.

Despite the activity at the cannery, the fifty wooden shacks of Baquerizo Moreno still wore an aura of poverty, and the ancient stone foundation of
the old warehouse crumbled away. The crude wattle-and-daub church now
summoned its worshippers with a ship's bell donated by California tuna
fishermen. The village barbershop sported an ancient wooden throne, and its
shelves were stocked with beer bottles instead of hair tonic. For twelve cents
(American), the customer received, besides a haircut, a powerful shot of puro

(sugar cane whiskey), which also is used as hair tonic and as liniment for rubdowns.

The pipeline installed by the United States Army in 1942 was still in operation, but the water was not safe for drinking; its use was restricted to showers and laundry. An impressive lava-stone administration building was located on the northwestern side of Wreck Bay.

Rohr climbed the weary five-mile lava-cobbled road to Progreso, past the orange trees and manzanillo to a full rain forest. About five hundred people lived in the clearing at Progreso, in dilapidated houses roofed with shingles, branches, or galvanized plates. Pigs rooted in the muddy streets everywhere, and mongrel dogs wandered about. Children played volleyball – a game learned from the United States Seabees. Meals were being cooked in iron cauldrons over open fires; a spring supplied pure water. The green spire of a 2,490-foot mountain formed the background for the village. The *Dirigo II* sailed away, and Frank Rohr commented after his brief visit: "The Encantadas are a strange interlude in the wanderings of small-boat sailors . . . . They seem to mimic the loneliness of the sea itself."

Salmo

The small yacht *Salmo* left Scotland in August of 1956 with Jill and Peter Hamilton honeymooning their way around the world. At Panama, they picked up a bundle of mail for the Wittmers, Angermeyers, Katsdalens, and Hornemans. Here, too, they learned that a permit for the Galapagos at the Ecuadorian Embassy cost eighty dollars, but would only cost fifteen dollars at Wreck Bay.

After a particularly rough passage from Panama to the Galapagos, which included four days and four nights of thundershowers and heavy downpours, the engine-less *Salmo* made its first landfall on Barrington Island. Here the couple filmed huge colonies of sea lions, which they at first had mistaken for dark rocks packed closely on the beach, motionless.

On September 10 at Post Office Bay, they saw "the remains of a Norwegian whaling station," referring to the concrete foundation of the old Norwegian Casa built in the late 1920's.

They studied the names of various yachts inscribed on every flat surface near the famous barrel. The yacht *Pandora*, from Green Bay, Wisconsin, had only one week previously painted its name on every boulder in sight. The couple immediately set to work carving an elaborate salmon, which was then attached to the roof like a weathercock.

With letters to deliver to the Wittmers, Jill and Peter hiked up the long road and came upon a small village of wood and corrugated-iron shanties. Some ragged Ecuadorians pointed out the green-painted Wittmer house.

Here, the couple added their name to the long list in the guest book and studied the photographs of ships and yachts which adorned the walls. At Academy Bay, the *Salmo* found the *Pandora*, a very well equipped staysail schooner carrying ten tons of gasoline. The Hamiltons listened patiently to the complaints of the small crew: Each had paid $2,000 for a trip around the world and felt they were not getting their money's worth. The skipper also complained that his passengers had no spirit of adventure and preferred to sulk aboard ship instead of going ashore to see the sights. Eventually, the skipper and crew settled their differences, and the *Pandora* left for Tahiti carrying an extra passenger, Joe Pachernegg.

Pachernegg was an Austrian, whose ship, *Sunshine*, had been wrecked on Santa Cruz several years before. He had hiked for four days to Academy Bay, drinking seal blood to stay alive. There he'd sold the ship's timbers, bought a shack with the proceeds, and settled down to write a book. Now he was off for newer adventures; years later he would return on the *Okeanos*.

Jill and Peter of the *Salmo* were a little apprehensive about the reception they would receive from the port captain at Academy Bay. The ship had not registered at the port of entry, nor had it an Ecuadorian flag to display. They were told that the last ship without a flag was fined $100 by the stern Comandante, who knocks off work at 11 A.M. and charges four dollars an hour for overtime for checking ships' papers. Surprisingly enough, the Comandante was kind and sympathetic, and endorsed their papers with the note: "Entered Academy Bay from stress of weather." He also gave them a letter which explained to the Governor at Wreck Bay that the *Salmo* had no engine, and that strong currents had prevented its entry into the said port.

The Hamiltons were told that the Katsdalen farm in the hills boasted of a bamboo grove, so they trudged up the steep road to obtain a twenty-foot pole to replace a broken spinnaker boom. Sloshing through the mud, pelted by avocado pears falling from high trees, and stung by little red fire-ants, they eventually reached the clearing and visited several farms.

They sampled the milk from the Katsdalen dairy herd, received fresh vegetables and pots of home-made jam from the Hornemans, and visited New Zealander Sandy, who'd bought a derelict farm next door to the Katsdalens. Both Friedel Horneman and Alf Katsdalen, on that very day, had teeth extracted, without benefit of anesthetics, by an American resident who owned the only pair of dental forceps on the island.

Back on shore, the Hamiltons caught a sackful of lobsters, aided by Gus Angermeyer and his son Johnny. The lobsters were pickled in salt, and the *Salmo* also added hunks of leathery, smoked goat meat to its larder.

After a short stay on Isabela Island, photographing the elusive penguins at Elizabeth Bay, the Hamiltons left for another remote outpost – Pitcairn Island.

Phoenix

On January 18, 1958, the Reynolds family left Panama on the *Phoenix*, carrying letters, food, a wood-and-coal stove, books, and magazines which they were requested to deliver to the Galapagos. Earle Reynolds, wife Barbara, daughter Jessica, son Ted, and a Japanese crewman arrived at Wreck Bay two weeks later.

Reynolds was an anthropologist who had been sent to Hiroshima to study the effects of radiation on human life. In Japan, he hired craftsmen to build the fifty-foot ketch, a double-ender of Colin Archer design, and sailed around the world in three-and-a-half years.

At Wreck Bay, the Reynoldses called on Karin Cobos for whom they had a letter. To their surprise, they found that the first two miles to Progreso were a fine road, and the last three miles were under construction. Reynolds learned that the island residents believed there would one day be a fine road built and that a jeep would be imported to use it.

Elderly, dark-haired Señora Cobos was now living in a "bleak shoe-box." She had divorced her Ecuadorian husband and moved high into the hills. Still managing her large cattle ranch, she was exporting beef to Ecuador, where her eldest daughter was at college.

When the *Phoenix* left Wreck Bay, the skipper was handed a bill for ten dollars to be paid in American money. This special charge was for entering the port at the extraordinary hour of six o'clock, local time.

At Post Office Bay, the adventurers hiked to locate the Wittmer house, but could not find it. They left some letters in the barrel, hoping that Mrs. Wittmer would cancel them with her official rubber stamp. "We had heard that mainland services all over the world honor this cancellation," wrote Reynolds. This is not true. The author once took forty-one pieces of mail from the barrel. On July 21, 1962, at the post office in Papeete, Tahiti, she paid $9.60 (American) to have the letters mailed to their destination. Somebody has to help pay for that brand-new post office building in Papeete.

The *Phoenix* anchored in Academy Bay just off the stone house of Karl and Marga Angermeyer, and the crew enjoyed a delightful eight-day visit: "The settlers we met in Santa Cruz," Reynolds wrote, "came nearer to fitting our ideas of true pioneers than any other group we had ever seen . . . . Life is lived very close to the subsistence level."

They learned how important it was to build a cistern and a properly-guttered roof in the islands. Washing and cooking was done with brackish water collected from a shallow well. Bread was sourdough, and at each baking time, a bit had to be kept back as starter for the next batch. The supply ship from Ecuador came infrequently; sometimes the captain forgot to bring the long-awaited mail and considered his lapse of memory a great joke.

Marga showed the visitors a bag of sand which had been substituted for the sugar she had ordered.

Up in the hills, the Reynoldses met the enterprising Katsdalens. Once a week, young Alf came down from the hills with a train of six burros, and distributed potatoes, carrots, onions, bananas, and fresh meat ordered the week before. He brought back flour, barbed wire, and other supplies ordered by boat from Ecuador. Mrs. Katsdalen had not been to Academy Bay for a year and had not seen her neighbor, Marga Angermeyer, since Rolf Wittmer's wedding.

The scholarly, gentle Mr. Jacob Horneman was still on his old plantation. His children, Friedel and Sigvart, were mature far beyond their years, extremely well-read, and had mastered five languages.

Several other yachts arrived at Academy Bay: the French yacht *Cle Du Sol,* which had been built around a grand piano that occupied one large cabin, and the American motor-yacht *Valinda.* The latter ship arranged to rendez-vous with the *Phoenix* at James Bay at a later date. Near the Angermeyer house down the coast, could be seen the wreckage of the yacht *Sunrise,* which was carefully being salvaged piece by piece by the needy islanders. Nothing is wasted in the Galapagos.

As a farewell gesture, the crew of the *Phoenix* gave a slide show for the Galapagoans at Academy Bay. At Buccaneer Cove, they caught a goat, which later was donated to a family in the Marquesas. They also collected pottery sherds for the Bishop Museum, but unfortunately these were lost when their dinghy capsized in the strong surf.

On board the *Phoenix,* besides the kid and several cats, was a young ten-inch Galapago named Jonathan Jr. This tortoise had been obtained quite legally – the Ecuadorian government had given the *Phoenix* a permit to take "two of every kind of animal." Jonathan Jr. had been bartered for some canned shortening, powdered milk, and hot pepper sauce. He was named after the famous Galapagos tortoise which they had seen at the island of St. Helena in the Atlantic.

The original Jonathan had hobnobbed with Napoleon and was over 250 years old. He resides in the governor's front yard and is fond of pears, lettuce, and bananas. On the croquet lawn, he often sits on the croquet balls as if they were eggs. He'd had a mate at one time, but she had died a hundred years before, when he was still in the flower of his youth, about one hundred fifty years of age. Nevertheless, he has not forgotten his lost love; each spring he becomes restless and embarks on a fruitless quest for his beloved.

The *Phoenix* arrived at James Bay on February 16, 1958, with letters for the *Valinda.* However, there was no yacht in sight, and the *Phoenix* waited until noon the next day before leaving the Galapagos. A month later, while reading the March 10 issue of *Life Magazine,* Skipper Reynolds learned why the *Valinda* had not kept its appointment.

Hijack of the *Valinda*

Scarcely four hours before the *Phoenix* arrived, a strange drama occurred at James Bay. It was just before dawn, and the 110-foot converted sub-chaser *Valinda* lay at anchor in the darkness. Owner William Rhodes Hervey, Jr., a Los Angeles attorney and yachtsman from Balboa, dozed on deck in the balmy weather. His wife Mildred, four crewmen, and friend Frank Olson of Seattle were asleep in quarters below.

Suddenly, two ancient fishing boats chugged alongside the *Valinda*, and twenty-one ragged men, armed with pistols, swarmed over the rail. The sleepers below were aroused by the shouts and rushed on deck, where they were promptly held at gunpoint. In the manner of the pirate Briones of 1850, the modern pirates demanded to be taken to the mainland.

As the yacht proceeded eastward, the pirates, clad in filthy blue denim or khaki trousers and soiled white undershirts, descended into the galley. Obviously famished, they at once began cooking rice and frying eggs. In the ensuing two days, they consumed sixty pounds of butter, thirty-dozen eggs, several cases of canned fruit and vegetables, and large quantities of rice and sugar. Starved for sweets, they made a thick syrup of sugar and water and ate the sticky mess with a spoon.

One of the yacht's crew spoke Spanish and gradually learned the story of the desperate men. The twenty-one raiders were convicts who had escaped from the penal colony at Villamil. This colony had been abolished in 1957, but sixty-one convicts were left on Isabela because all the mainland prisons were overcrowded. All of these men were serious criminals, convicted murderers, all trigger-taut and dangerous; the crew of the *Valinda* wisely did nothing to antagonize them.

Soon, the escapees began relating all the horrors of their prison island. They had been allowed food rations of fourteen cents per day, but these were stolen by their jailers. They were housed in crude shacks, clothed in filthy rags and forbidden to eat the crops which they harvested. They were beaten with rattan whips, and, for punishment, were hoisted by the armpits to hang in the blistering heat of the sun all day without water. Many had gold teeth forcibly yanked out of their mouths. Unable to endure their misery any longer, they mutinied on February 11, raided the arsenal, disarmed the few remaining guards, and looted the town of Villamil, which had a population of 200. Twenty-one of the convicts then crowded into two small fishing boats, taking several fishermen as hostages, and sailed twenty miles to James Bay, hoping to seize a larger and more seaworthy craft.

Not all of the convicts were Ecuadorians. One young white man spoke French; another was a powerful black who had received two bullet wounds during the escape. An Oriental, named El Chino, sported a heavy jacket with a fur collar, and a leather hat with ear flaps tied up.

Though physically unharmed, the Herveys experienced a harrowing sixty-three-hour nightmare. The convicts tore through the ship, stealing everything in sight: $2,000 worth of cash, jewelry, silver, and clothing. They found and drank two cases of rum and gin, but surprisingly enough, the liquor mellowed their disposition and put most of them to sleep.

After one of the wild-eyed escapees broke into the Hervey cabin, Mildred escaped him and refused to go below. She spent the rest of the trip in the wheelhouse. Meanwhile, the convicts played cards and danced to records, scattering food and cigarette butts in all the cabins. The ship's supply of 1,000 gallons of water was quickly exhausted, as the men showered, shaved, and dressed in stolen clothes.

The young convict leader of the gang called a meeting of everyone on board, and declared that all the convicts pledged to mend their ways if the escape succeeded. He apologized to the Herveys for the fear and inconvenience caused, and thanked them for the food and clothing. The convicts then sang the Ecuadorian national anthem and cheered Ecuador, the United States, and Liberty.

Instead of disembarking at Guayaquil, the convicts asked to land at some lonely beach close to the Colombian border. At five miles north of Punta Galera, the young leader embraced the Herveys, kissed their hands in gratitude, and motored ashore with his comrades in the ship's launch. The two fishermen hostages were left aboard the *Valinda*.

As soon as the convicts were gone, the yacht proceeded to Panama, and Hervey reported the seizure of his yacht to the Coast Guard. A few days later the Comandante at Villamil reported that order had been restored at Isabela Island. On the Ecuadorian mainland, ten of the fugitives were captured. Thus ended the saga of the *Valinda*.

Other Ships and Events

In the years through 1960, more ships came to the Encantadas: *Halcon*, *Gracious Me*, *Serai II*, *Triburun Dubloon*, *Shemara*, *Fortune*, *Azoreana*, *Presidente Alfaro*, and *Bali Hai*. There was *Phoebe* from Durban, *Si Ye Pambili* from Rhodesia, *Rundo* from Oslo, *Isabel May* from Australia, *Umitaki Maru* from Tokyo, and *Ben Gunn* from Connecticut. The *Gloria Dalton* came again but had been renamed *Collegiate Rebel*. The 38-foot ketch *Marachi*, manned by a young couple and their small son, stopped for a brief visit during their three-year cruise in the Pacific.

One ship didn't quite make it. Ships leaving Panama for the Galapagos are often requested to deliver cargos of supplies for the islanders. In November of 1957, the Carrs were asked to carry a load on their ship *Havfruen*.

Somehow they missed the Galapagos completely and the cargo was unloaded at the Marquesas. It was then shipped to Tahiti, then Hawaii and California, and finally returned to Panama to wait for another yacht heading for the Encantadas.

Finally, the little *Nellie Brush* made a visit in 1958 and again in 1960. Forrest Nelson, an American from California, had sailed his thirty-seven foot craft for eight years and 50,000 miles, before he selected Academy Bay as his permanent home. He claimed to have migrated from the United States to get away from restrictions. However, his marriage to the charming and talented Friedel Horneman, born on Santa Cruz Island, may have been a stronger inducement for him to stay in the bewitching Encantadas.

Nineteen fifty-nine was the one-hundredth anniversary of the publication of Darwin's *On the Origin of Species*, an opportune time for the creation of "The Charles Darwin Foundation for the Galapagos Islands." It receives grants from UNESCO, the Gulbenkian Foundation, and other sources; its seat is at the Palais des Academies in Brussels. Sir Julian Huxley was named Honorary Chairman, and V. Van Straelen became the first president. Dr. L. Jaramillo, permanent delegate of Ecuador to UNESCO, was named first vice-president.

In cooperation with Ecuadorian government research workers, the Foundation set up an international research station at Santa Cruz Island for studies on the conservation of the "most precious assembly of animals on the face of the globe." No longer are tortoises sold to visiting cruise ships, and resident biologists restrain the depredations of residents and visitors who are unaware of the damage they are doing by removal and slaughter of the odd creatures.

Denver Museum Expedition

The Museum of Natural History at Denver, Colorado, wished to prepare an extensive exhibit of plant and animal life of the Galapagos; reptiles, birds, and plants were to be incorporated into a habitat group. With information supplied by Dr. Bowman, and the financial support of the Tremont Foundation, a party of seven was dispatched to Ecuador. They left Guayaquil on July 25, 1960, aboard the *Cristobal Carrier*, a freighter which ran quite regularly to Wreck Bay. On June 30th, they were placed in the friendly care of the Angermeyer family at Academy Bay. Comandante Angel Benavides placed a naval patrol boat at their disposal to give them access to the remoter islands. Over a month was spent in the field, busily photographing and collecting specimens.

On Santa Cruz, the UNESCO biologist, Raymond Leveque, was making a census of the reptiles; a warden also was being paid to prevent residents from taking tortoises for food. The Museum Expedition selected a fine 300-

pounder for its exhibit, and a smaller one to be taken to Denver alive. Karl Angermeyer took some of the exploring party to Barrington Island to photograph the land iguanas, Galapagos hawks, sea lions, and fish. Gus Angermeyer took a second group to Hood Island, where Dr. Bailey photographed the rare Galapagos albatross.

Dr. Alfred M. Bailey had a lifelong interest in seabirds of remote places, and knew of thirteen species of albatross breeding on some of the most isolated islands of the world. The Galapagos albatross, considered one of the rarest of the thirteen species, was the eighth which Dr. Bailey had the privilege to photograph on nesting grounds. He was pleased to discover that the Galapagos species was far from extinct, and bred there from April to August.

The patrol boat took the party to Baltra, James, and Daphne Islet. At Plaza Islet, they photographed the endemic, swallow-tailed gulls and large herds of sea lions, as well as huge manta rays, fifteen to eighteen feet across. The giant rays, or mantas, float around like velvet carpets, about one foot underneath the surface of the water, with the tips of their ''wings'' turned up about six inches out of the water.

Back at Santa Cruz, a visit was made to the Horneman farm, where the two-story house stood in a setting of tropical plants surrounded by exotic fruit trees. Fourteen-year-old Sigvart Horneman took the expedition to the nesting sites of the little-known Galapagos petrel, a large species of seabird which builds nesting tunnels under rocks on the higher altitudes of the volcanic islands. On a later trip to Isabela, a rare discovery was made of the flimsy nest of water-worn sticks belonging to the Dusky Gull. Since Darwin's time, naturalists had searched in vain for the nest and eggs of this species. On a narrow peninsula of black lava, about a mile across the bay from Villamil, two olive eggs with gray splotches were photographed, as several pairs of gulls kept up a constant attack.

All specimens were carefully packed aboard the *Cristobal Carrier* and eventually arrived intact at the Denver Museum. Several thousand feet of motion picture film had been exposed, as well as hundreds of still pictures in color, and in black and white. A unique exhibit, the largest of its kind, was prepared for the public. Dr. Bailey also gave an illustrated lecture.

During the Museum's successful expedition, another group of Americans was in the Islands on a very different undertaking at Wreck Bay. Its results were far from rewarding.

20

AMERICAN FIASCO

Once in a while, a group of misguided Americans leaves the United States seeking greener pastures elsewhere. In the late 1930's, twenty-one adults, seven children, and a baby left Pasadena, California, to found a colony at East Caicos Island in the Caribbean, where they hoped to start a sisal plantation. Despite warnings that the island was uninhabitable and as arid as the Galapagos, the undaunted group chartered Captain Otterman's eighty-five-foot schooner, *Stormalong*, in Miami, Florida. They were duly deposited with their chattels (including a huge army stove) on the coral island which lies scarcely five feet above the water in an area plagued by tornadoes and hurricanes. The group stayed less than six months and left on a mail packet.

In mid-March of 1960, the old decrepit refrigeration ship *Alert* docked at the rickety pier of Baquerizo Moreno at Wreck Bay, San Cristobal Island, Galapagos. A sign scrawled in red paint with the words "Bienvenidos Millionarios!" greeted the thirty Americans who disembarked. Who were these rich people coming to the Galapagos? Were they eccentric millionaires who whimsically selected an old wreck instead of a palatial yacht for their visit to this favorite haunt of yachtsmen?

No, they were the advance contingent of an American cooperative community of hundreds of people, who hoped to begin a new life in a utopia based on working together towards building something worthwhile for their families. A misconception of their wealth arose when the colony's founder had spread rumors in Ecuador that some day the colonists would build a two-million dollar hotel and would develop an air strip for flying in multitudes of free-spending tourists. Anticipating a new era of prosperity, the islanders eagerly welcomed the newcomers. Perhaps the curse of the Encantadas against commercial enterprises would be broken.

The Dream

It all began in the summer of 1959, when a curious ad appeared in a Seattle, Washington newspaper: "Wanted – Swiss Family Robinson. Is your family one of fifty adventurous families with the spirit of America's early pioneers needed to establish a model community on a beautiful Pacific Island?''

Intrigued readers in the Pacific Northwest area immediately responded with letters and phone calls requesting more details. A flood of inquiries poured in after the newspaper printed an illustrated feature on Don Harrsch and his not-so-new idea.

The thirty-two-year-old adventurer was a small man of slender build, with regular features and a small mustache. Generally, he gave a favorable first impression of intelligence, ambition, potential energy, and high self confidence. He had tried logging and tugboat operating, and at one time joined the United States Army to get to Alaska. After a dishonorable discharge, he operated a tugboat in Puget Sound to support his wife and two daughters. During a period of unemployment, he began to formulate his plan of founding a colony in the Pacific.

Harrsch was a dreamer, a "loner" with no close male friends. He preferred reading science-fiction to mixing with people, and had a cynical view of life. He was critical of the government and the moral codes of society, and proclaimed himself an atheist. He believed in free love with a considerable privilege difference in favor of the male. He was highly prejudiced against blacks and Mexican-Americans.

Disenchanted with the United States and hoping to profit economically, Harrsch began to look for an island paradise. He had never been to the Galapagos, but to him they seemed ideal for a colony, being sparsely settled and open to aliens. For several months before placing his advertisement in the newspaper, Harrsch read every bit of literature available on the Galapagos. Whether he read anything about the luckless Norwegian colonies is not certain; if he did, knowledge of their failure did not stifle his enthusiasm. One of his brochures stated, ''The Galapagos Islands were chosen for the main reason that from our research, it seems they will bring in more income than any other available site.''

The original plan called for 50 families to invest $2,500 per family in the cooperative venture. The capital would be used for the purchase of ships, equipment, food, and all living expenses once the colonists left the United States. However, as the money began to pour in very rapidly, the number of families was raised to 100. More ambitious projects could be launched if the capital was increased to $250,000.

Clever publicity and salesmanship can easily entice persons seeking adventure and profit. No matter how impractical, any novel venture promising romance and riches will attract people with adventureless careers seeking escape from boredom and routine.

The mimeographed brochures sent out to inquiring prospects did not exactly promise huge financial rewards, but the company did hope to make "everyone a millionaire blessed with a wealth of knowledge, health, happiness, and, most of all, enable its members to create and leave for their children a better world to live in."

Other documents claimed, "Our aim is to make an above the average income and to live better doing this through agriculture, science and marine activities . . . . We hope to show that a pioneer colonizing group dedicated to furthering scientific research can succeed with this motivation replacing the religious or political motivations of many such new colonies in the past."

The first few members interested in the enterprise met in the basement of Harrsch's home to discuss organization plans. As more memberships were secured, an office was rented in Seattle, and the Island Development Company was off to a fast start. As of September, 1960, a total of eighty-three families joined the venture.

The people attracted by the plan were mostly young and of modest income. Of the first 106 who actually sailed to the islands, all were under the age of fifty except for a naturopathic physician. There were 14 single men, and 22 families with children ranging from eighteen months of age to teenagers. Various religions and nationalities were represented, and only one man had the equivalent of a college degree. Harrsch himself had never completed grade school. Several had been aircraft employees in Seattle; others were truck drivers, auto and insurance salesmen, mechanics, engineers, warehousemen, a state park ranger, fireman, janitor, sheet metal worker, plumber, and a rancher.

These people were all willing to sell their homes and automobiles at a loss; many relinquished secure jobs and pensions and took their children out of school. They left friends and relatives; they abandoned the comfort, luxuries, and high standard of living for an uncertain future in primitive surroundings. What induced them to exchange so much for so little?

A few sought travel and adventure. Some wanted to leave the hectic and competitive workaday world for peaceful and quiet surroundings – to exchange urban life for a rural environment. Others wanted to sample the pioneering spirit of their forefathers; one family admired pioneering life as portrayed by a program on television: "We decided this was the nearest thing to Wagon Train. Life in America can be pretty complicated . . . bills, bills, bills." Most of them thought they could achieve a far better life by working as a group instead of being individual entrepreneurs.

There were idealists who hoped to establish a model community "to demonstrate to all nations that it is possible to live together without selfishness and greed." By moving to the islands, none would be forfeiting their American citizenship, only substituting a free-enterprise system for a cooperative way of life similar in some measure to the Amish, Oneida, or Mormon cooperatives, without the religious aspect. Many felt that such a form of life was no longer possible in the tax-ridden and restiction-filled United States.

Others came closer to the truth when they stated, ''We had been told that before long we should be earning $300 a month . . . , that in not many years, each working shareholder should be averaging $10,000 a year.'' Here was a chance to be in on the ground floor of a new, budding Hawaii. Whether they admitted it or not, one of the strongest reasons for their exodus was their cupidity for greater material wealth and an exorbitant return on their initial investment.

Whatever the motives may have been, they soon had the company coffers filled to overflowing. Don Harrsch and two of the first members flew to Quito, Ecuador, and consulted Attorney Teodoro Crespo, a specialist in South American colonization. The four departed for the Galapagos, where Harrsch made a $30,000 down payment, picking up an option on the 64,000-acre coffee plantation selling for $110,000 and on the abandoned refrigeration plant on a twenty-four-acre site, selling for the exorbitant sum of $200,000. Both properties were on San Cristobal Island and were supposedly owned by Lorenzo Tous, Jr.

Attorney Crespo could have informed the organizers that far better land was available on the mainland of South America in places much better for farming and coffee-raising and close to markets. However, the isolated islands had the added appeal of tourism. Harrsch himself spread the word that eventually, under his leadership, the Galapagos would become a haunt for tourists, who would flock to the lavish $2-million hotel the colonists would build in the future.

The Ecuadorian government bestowed its blessings upon this plan which could revitalize the islands. Being one of the smallest and least developed countries in South America, Ecuador welcomed the investment capital coming from a foreign source. Attorney Crespo, who had been appointed leader of Ecuador's Institute of Colonization, said, ''We want the American colonists and hope they embark on realistic projects, perhaps to develop tourism for the first time in the history of the Galapagos.''

Harrsch left one of his men in Guayaquil to become the Island Development Company's Ecuadorian representative. Harrsch returned to Seattle to purchase several ships and to help frame a Constitution for the company.

Scientific Humanism

Influenced by his science-fiction readings, and perhaps hoping to give his project more prestige by having it treated as a scientific experiment, Don Harrsch had presented himself at the Department of Psychology at the University of Washington in Seattle. He explained that he wished to secure help in the selection of members for his company. He was directed to the Sociology Department.

Scholars immediately recognized here an opportunity to study a novel utopian movement from beginning to end. Harrsch readily consented to have the entire scheme treated as a case history. He agreed to an observer team that would interview people connected with the project and keep memos, documents, and minutes of all meetings in order to learn the psychological and other forces contributing to the eventual success or failure of the venture.

From the beginning, it was made clear that the Department of Sociology was not interested in promoting or endorsing the project, nor did it wish to be paid by the organization. Harrsch was enjoined not to use the University in his publicity. In return for being allowed to study the movement as an experiment, the sociologists would offer advice and help in organizing the company.

Harrsch was questioned about his objectives and beliefs. In a taped interview, Harrsch stated that he wished atheism to be the official doctrine of his community. He felt the world would be better without religion, because religious people tend to be lazy, dependent, and non-thinking. He was advised that such a radical approach would be unsuitable for the group, not only because most of the members had religious backgrounds, but also because the colony would be in close proximity with Ecuadorian Catholics. For some reason, Harrsch gave little thought to the Ecuadorians on San Cristobal, acting as if his colony would be starting in an essentially empty land.

Harrsch was advised to adopt a more tolerant policy, and finally accepted the "scientific humanist way of life," in which mature adults would use scientific methods increasingly to cope with their problems and not rely upon the help of supernatural forces. Dr. Stuart C. Dodd thus defined this belief:

> This philosophy of life leaves them free to practice the best of Christian brotherly love, or Moslem acceptance of what man cannot modify, or Socialist sharing of the means of production, or democratic equality of opportunity for all men, or American faith in progress for those who try it, or any other social policy that after fair trial and comparison proves that it works in satisfying more men, more fully, more of the time than do other available alternative policies. As adult human beings the colonists take full responsibility for coping with their problems for themselves and their posterity and will no longer depend like children on a fathergod. They are thus scientific humanists, whether aware of that label or not.

The research group of sociologists unanimously expected the colonizing scheme to fail, but as independent and impartial observers, they did nothing to influence the outcome in any way. They did offer a few words of caution to prospects who sent them letters of inquiry, especially to those risking their life's savings in the venture.

In meetings, Harrsch outlined his aims and principles and interviewed would-be colonists. At first, he was choosy, but later settled for anybody with money and a desire to join. He did express dissatisfaction with the quality of his fellow colonists, calling them narrow-minded. However, he believed that eventually he would succeed in imposing his own attitudes upon them. This egotistical belief later contributed toward helping this "controlled social experiment" go haywire.

The Constitution

The official name of the colony would be "Filiate Science Antrorse," an odd mixture of Latin and English meaning "Together with Science We Move Forward." Its aim was "to build a free cooperative community for ourselves and our posterity in the Galapagos using scientific means increasingly in pursuit of a better life, liberty and happiness."

"We do not intend to spend our efforts trying to acquire material wealth neglecting the essential needs of mankind," it stated.

Harrsch was named first president of the company, with an election for the office to be held every four years. The vice-president and secretary-treasurer were appointed by the president. The president could be deposed by a ninety-five percent vote, with each family head entitled to one vote. Foremen were to be appointed by the officers for two-year terms, and lesser officials would be elected by a majority vote of members. Special rules were set up: "No one may go directly to the president or any other officer without permission from his foreman, who in turn has to receive approval from the Chief Foreman.'

Each member would be given an acre of land and free housing. The initial settlement would be built around six homes used by the former plantation owners. A stipulation was made: "The company will own all real and personal properties except items purchased and used by individuals in a manner non-competitive with the company. No member of a company family will be allowed to be in business in competition with the company."

A school would be established, with grades from one through twelve, and it would be open to all who live in the islands. "Psychology, sociology, medicine and biology will be the main emphasis subjects." Some of the members had already availed themselves of the special course on animal husbandry offered to them at the University of Washington.

Hospitalization would be free to all members and their families, no matter where it might be; doctors, dentists, and medical supplies would be furnished free.

A tremendous amount of work was facing the colonists: land had to be cleared for small farms, new homes were needed, coffee had to be harvested, tuna and lobster would be caught to raise quick revenues, and then the island had to be surveyed for future development of tourism.

Members would receive monetary income in two forms: dividends as shareholders, and wages on a differential scale according to the job performed.

Profits would be shared according to a formula:

"One third of the income shall be used for the development of the community and industry – for schools, houses, roads, business expenditures, recreational facilities.

"One third to be set aside for research – at least one half of this spent in the fields of psychology, medicine and behavioral sciences. No money shall be expended by this company for researches in the sciences of war or related sciences." Sociology students would be invited to spend their summers in the colony to study its progress. Research money would not be allocated all at once, but gradually as the immediate needs of the colony were satisfied and there was a growing level of income.

"One third shall be distributed in wages. The highest paid worker's income shall never exceed an amount three times that of the lowest paid worker." To help resolve the everlasting conflict about the optimal distribution of wealth, it was decided to start with a spread of 1 to 1.25. This meant that the president's salary would be only 25 percent more than the lowest paid member of the colony. However, upon leaving office, the president was to receive a pension of two wage units.

A point system was set up to give different rewards for different abilities: 10 wage units for the medical officers and doctor; 9.5 units for chief foreman, teachers, dentist, and master technicians; 9 units for the accountant, foremen, and ships' officers; 8.5 units for leadmen; 8.0 units for unskilled workers. These points would be totalled and divided accordingly from the portion set aside for wages.

The company also introduced something new in pioneering a seven-hour day and thirty-five-hour calendar week. Working overtime in excess of three hours would also grant the worker extra time off at a rate of time-and-a-half. Old-fashioned pioneers like the Ritters, Wittmers, Angermeyers, Katsdalens, and Conways, who worked from sunrise to sunset, seven days a week, certainly would have appreciated this innovation. They also would have starved to death while enjoying their time-and-a-half leisure. In all fairness, it should be mentioned that Harrsch did tell the colonists that the first year would be tough, requiring a lot of extra work with no overtime pay at all, and that they should expect sub-standard housing and other inconveniences.

The final organization document was termed inconsistent and unworkable by the sociologists. Nevertheless, it seemed to satisfy the members, who were all set to embark on their novel enterprise.

Exodus

His pockets bulging with money, Harrsch searched the waterfront of Seattle for a vessel which would accommodate the colonists and their belongings on their long journey to the Galapagos. An ancient 100-foot tuna clipper with a refrigeration unit seemed suitable for their needs; Harrsch paid $13,500 cash for it and christened her the *Alert*. The colonists were told that they would sail in late 1959.

Harrsch also purchased an old 130-foot freighter for $32,500 cash. The *Western Trader* had been a refrigeration ship at one time and had seen better days; its tired Atlas engines were in bad condition. In fact, both the *Alert* and *Western Trader* needed extensive repairs. Both ships were placed in shipyards, and over $50,000 was spent to recondition them.

The first thirty colonists had planned to begin their new life and a new year by leaving Seattle on the eve of January 1, 1960. However, bad weather and leaky seams forced the wooden-hulled *Alert* back into port several times; the Coast Guard had questioned the seaworthiness of the vessel before. On January 8 the *Alert* made another attempt and promptly was caught in a thirty-six hour storm on its way to Coos Bay, Oregon. Pumps were manned continuously. Three women and four children were lashed to their bunks to keep from being washed overboard.

On February 11, when Don Harrsch skippered the *Alert* out of Coos Bay, only thirteen persons were left on board; the others had prudently left to continue their journey by car. The *Alert* reached Los Angeles Harbor on February 13 for a two-week stay and was joined by a four-car caravan.

Fifteen men, women, and children in this caravan later joined another family in Mesa, Arizona, and proceeded south through Mexico, Guatemala, Honduras, Nicaragua, and Costa Rica. Here they joined the group on the *Alert* and sailed south to San Cristobal Island – their beautiful Pacific Island. There were thirty people on board: seven families and five single men; there were eleven children.

One woman broke her hip during rough seas. After some rather questionable navigation – at times they were 300 to 500 miles off course – the modern pilgrims landed at Wreck Bay on March 16, 1960.

The New Life

At the small fishing village of Baquerizo Moreno, on Wreck Bay, over a dozen two-story houses graced the beach. Several dozen more immediately to the rear provided homes for 400 villagers. Over 800 people lived in the cooler highlands.

Several buildings housing the soldiers and officers were located at the southern end of the bay. About a mile north of the village was the new home of the American colonists. On a rocky bluff at the water's edge was the yellow sixty- to eighty-foot refrigeration plant; adjoining it was a dilapidated, reddish two-story building. Nearby were five empty frame houses soon occupied by the pioneers, who quickly busied themselves making living as pleasant, or at least as comfortable, as possible.

For the small children, San Cristobal was a veritable Eden of childhood delights. They walked barefoot on the long stretches of white beach, swam in the cool surf, fished, hiked, caught iguanas, rode burros and tortoises, learned Spanish from their new-found native friends, and at first had no formal school to attend.

After the initial novelty wore off, the teenaged children began to miss the good old days in the United States. They missed malted milks, American-type music, school dances, movies, television, cokes, and telephones. The highest grade in the local Spanish school was the sixth; no higher education was available except through self-study or parents.

Life for the women was far from idyllic – no modern electrical appliances, no supermarkets. There were no automatic washing machines; the dirty clothing that accumulated during the voyage was boiled in a community iron pot and hung on a community clothesline. Wood had to be chopped for the stoves on which such delicacies as goat stew were cooked in huge community pots. In accordance with the by-laws of the constitution, all meals were served in the community mess hall.

The housewives had one consolation: food prices were unbelievably low. A large stem of bananas weighing 60 to 80 pounds cost about fifteen cents. Oranges were ten cents for a 50-pound sack, avocados were five cents a dozen, and pineapples three cents apiece. Beef sold for twelve cents a pound on a first come, first served basis to early risers. If a steer was tied to a tree before the slaughterhouse in the center of the village the night before, there would be fresh meat for sale the next morning. The same rule applied for pigs and goats; pork cost six cents (one sucre) per pound and goat meat was three cents. Live chickens sold for three cents a pound. It would be interesting to know how many of the women in the American colony had ever killed and dressed a chicken before coming to the Galapagos.

Despite the low cost of living – a family of five or six could subsist on ten to fifteen dollars per month – the colonists soon realized that they must develop a source of income. The money in the company treasury was quickly being depleted; there were insufficient funds to transport the other 76 families who had paid to join and were to arrive in the future.

The Tous refrigeration plant, which could hold 700 tons of frozen fish, had been idle for years; it was badly deteriorated, roofless, and inoperative. Another plan to make a quick profit on frozen lobster had also been thwarted when the freezer unit on the *Alert* was damaged during the rough passage to the Galapagos. Immediately upon the colonists' arrival at their Pacific Paradise, Harrsch had planned to catch twenty tons of lobster which would be hauled to the United States on the return trip of the *Alert*. This was supposed to net a $40,000 profit.

There is some doubt that this plan could have been carried out even if the freezer on the *Alert* had been operative. There was no professional fisherman in the group, nor any lobster diver. Commercial lobstering is done with lobster-pots; the colonists had neither the lumber nor the know-how to construct any. Twenty tons of lobster is a lot of lobster, and obtaining them by diving would certainly require a long time. Then too, any large-scale commercial lobster enterprise would soon deplete the supply. The Galapagos Islands rise steeply out of the sea; there are few shallow banks for lobsters to thrive on.

There was no lack of non-profit work to be done. The water pipeline installed by American forces in 1942 was clogged and dirty, and the colonists met with the village leaders to discuss overhauling the system. Soon afterward, both islanders and Americans were working together dismantling and cleaning the pipes. The village reservoir was emptied and cleaned of muck and dirt.

At the plantation in the hills, an attempt was made at gardening. The irrigation system was reconstructed, and vegetable seeds planted. Pigs, burros, and chickens soon ate any crops that sprouted. A second planting was more successful after barbed-wire barriers and a fence of lava boulders were erected. But this planting too was completely washed out by a long spell of rain and lack of sunshine. After the end of the rainy season, a third planting did show some promise.

One farmer quickly realized that conditions on his farm back in Washington were not as bad as he had imagined. He applied for and received a repatriation loan from the U.S. State Department and soon was happily flying home. Where else but in the United States can a farmer get subsidies for not growing crops? It sure beats the Galapagos.

The colonists soon learned to obtain their own meat, and a main part of their diet was wild goat from Barrington Island, forty-five miles northwest of Wreck Bay. Some of the men detested the task of butchering, but it was something which had to be done. Roydon Bristow once wrote, "Since living this life I had encountered many tasks I did not like, and I had learnt that one must take them in one's stride if one wants to go on living . . . . It is surprising how quickly one can adapt oneself to the wilds when one has to; failure means hunger."

Another task confronting the colonists was to break down the barrier of suspicion which the villagers had toward the newcomers. The islanders erroneously believed that the "wealthy colonists" had purchased the entire island. However, after the villagers became aware that the Americans had invested their life's savings in the enterprise and had no intention of commandeering the island, relations became friendly.

American children enrolled in the village school – grades one through six – and quickly were becoming bilingual. They swapped stories about the United States for stories about life in the curious islands. The American parents were also learning Spanish, and classes were held on the beach. The eight Ecuadorian schoolteachers were learning English, and Spanish-English dictionaries were stuffed in the back pockets of all islanders, old and new. Originally, only one or two Ecuadorians spoke a little English, and only one American woman remembered a little Spanish which she had learned years before in two semesters in high-school.

A serious problem arose when almost every person in the American colony was laid low by an epidemic of infectious hepatitis. Many recovered very slowly; some had to be hospitalized in Guayaquil. Medical expenses further depleted the company treasury.

One American had a serious personal problem when his wife fell in love with a handsome Galapagoan youth. The romance budded as the two were studying Spanish in the hills. The husband was filing suit for divorce; the wife flew to the United States hoping the youth would join her. However, the Ecuadorian commander at San Cristobal would not permit the youth to leave.

Meanwhile, the colonists worked and amused themselves as best they could. One form of recreation very popular with the islanders was dancing at the Hotel Miramar, the one and only "hotel" on Chatham. Its only two rooms were converted into a dance hall, where, for sixty cents (ten sucres) an evening, a remarkable orchestra could be hired. The musicians helped to while away the monotonous evenings with their bongo drums, guitar, maracas, and a rattle quaintly fashioned from the jawbone and teeth of an ass.

Perhaps the greatest social event at Wreck Bay, though, was the arrival of the monthly mail boat from Guayaquil. As a matter of habit, islanders scanned the horizon daily for ships. When the *Cristobal Carrier* was sighted, the church bell rang, school was dismissed, and all villagers gathered at the dock.

From March, far into the summer, the colonists waited patiently for the arrival of the *Western Trader*, which would bring more families and much-needed equipment. Month after month they sought it on the horizon. It did not arrive until August 19, 1960, after being delayed by red tape of both the Ecuadorian and United States governments.

Political Repercussions

The *Alert* arrived at Wreck Bay less than three months before Ecuador's presidential election of June 1960, and the American "invasion" of the Galapagos became a hot political issue. Red agitators and a leftist press, supporting candidate Parra Velasco, gleefully declared that life in the United States was very bad, and the Americans were fleeing while still able. In the next breath they accused Yankee imperialists of trying to grab the islands. The small colony was the beginning of a major-scale invasion. Editorials carried the warning: "Don't let the same thing happen to the Galapagos that happened to Texas!" – a reminder that Mexico lost Texas to the Norte Americanos only one century before.

Parra Velasco, representing the Communists and left-wing Union of Ecuadorian Youth, spoke in the main plaza of Guayaquil shortly after the colony arrived at San Cristobal. He called the Americans invaders, and accused the incumbent administration of failing to take proper steps to halt the invasion. After the speech, a group of seventy Ecuadorian youths stoned the American consulate, shouting, "Americans, get out of the Galapagos!" Police broke up the demonstration, but only after many windows were broken and rocks landed on the desk of Consul-General Ward P. Allen.

Not too many Ecuadorians were impressed by the riot and speech; Parra Velasco received only 10 percent of the total vote. High-placed government officials and the new president Velasco Ibarra favored the colonization, hoping it would boost Ecuador's economy by opening a hitherto undeveloped area. Some thought the venture would bring publicity to the little-known archipelago. Others were puzzled by the exodus: "Imagine Americans leaving the United States to come to Ecuador. We must have something pretty good to lure them from their home."

Anticipating the arrival of 500 American colonists, the Ecuadorian government sent out 300 Ecuadorians – mostly Indians – to San Cristobal and Santa Cruz Islands to sustain an Ecuadorian majority in the settlements. This action was not exactly appreciated by the fifty European and other aliens residing at Academy Bay. Reporter Charles Hillinger quoted one of the islanders as saying:

> See what happened when Harrsch came out here and said there would be 500 American families eventually living on the Galapagos. It stirred up a hornet's nest. Fearful that the Ecuadorians would be outnumbered, there have been shiploads of people, mostly Indians, brought here.

> On Santa Cruz a year ago there were less than 200 living here. Now that number has doubled. New people have been dumped here without money, without homes. They are living in makeshift shacks, killing off our supply of meat, and slaughtering what few of the giant tortoises that are left on our island. They have been told that they will have to remain here at least a year before being returned to the mainland . . . . The Americans are creating unrest in our islands.

There was a great deal of unrest among the Americans themselves when they discovered that Tous could not produce clear title to the 64,000 acre, 17,000-tree coffee plantation. Nobody owns land in the Galapagos Archipelago, which has been declared a national park of Ecuador. Lorenzo Tous Jr. was merely leasing the land, and all settlers on the islands were considered squatters. After a month on San Cristobal, Harrsch left for the Ecuadorian mainland to clarify matters concerning the lease. He never returned to the Galapagos.

New Leadership

Dissatisfaction with president Don Harrsch increased after the *Alert* landed on San Cristobal. Suggestions by the sociologists that Harrsch tone down the special powers of the leader were ignored. He quickly made it clear that he expected a bigger and better house than would be available to the other members, and it should be provided with household servants. This was a notion he acquired from the Ecuadorian authorities, who assured him that the only way to retain the respect of the natives would be to adopt their class system and become another Cobos.

Harrsch also felt he should get a higher income, and there was some question about his bookkeeping of the company funds. Friction between himself and the members grew bitter.

Harrsch was no more successful in his relations with the Ecuadorian officials. Attorney Crespo announced publicly:

> I found the leader to be less than honest in his statements of his intentions. I helped establish the colony in the Galapagos, then discovered the leaders of the American group to be a bunch of adventurers with cockeyed ideas. They proposed to cure everyone in the islands of whatever ailed them, . . . to give everyone free dental care, . . . to re-educate the islanders to their way of thinking, . . . with belief in God relegated to a minor role and great emphasis placed on scientific achievement. They claimed to have 50 million dollars in assets, and that they represented at least 50 American companies.

The Island Development Company voted unanimously to dismiss Harrsch as leader. Votes were obtained from the colony on the island, the members in Seattle, and from those en route. Harrsch was replaced by young Alex Reuss, a twenty-five-year-old former insurance salesman. The new president was elected in May of 1960, but he did not arrive at the colony until September.

Meanwhile, the sociologists were preparing a highly technical abstract containing "a brief description of three possible explorations towards eventual controlled experiments on better ways of living." They urged the new president to reexamine previous policies of the company, and not to depend on what Harrsch as the founder thought or wrote. They wrote to the United Nations expressing the colony's desire to participate in the Darwinian Equatorial Laboratory in the Galapagos. The UNESCO officials sent a reply indicating their strong skepticism concerning the company's intentions.

Eventually, the sociological research effort drifted into various hands, becoming very loosely coordinated, and opportunities for potentially useful observations were lost.

Red Tape

At the end of March, 1960, the *Western Trader* docked at Pier 227, Terminal Island, at San Pedro, California, with 78 people aboard and was prepared to sail immediately for the Island Development Company's distant Pacific paradise. A cargo of tractors, farm equipment, a jeep, small boats for fishing, tools, and other supplies were stowed above and below deck. Captain Lloyd Van Kirk, a skipper in Alaskan waters for fifteen years, and a new member of the company, had everything shipshape for the long voyage. The only remaining problem was to obtain clearance and visas from Ecuador. Alfredo Donoso, Ecuadorian Consul-General in Los Angeles, assured the colonists that the visas would be forthcoming.

Week after week passed, and the colonists grew restless on the overcrowded ship. Tents were pitched on deck and on the beach to relieve the cramped quarters aboard ship. The *Western Trader* received a new coat of paint and a sundeck, as the men tried to keep busy during the delay. Some obtained temporary jobs in town to break the monotony and to refill their pockets with spare cash for cigarettes and personal items. The delay was proving costly to the company, as each member was guaranteed food, housing, and medical attention once he left his former home and became an active colonist.

After a woman, girl, and baby were stricken with infectious hepatitis, the entire group aboard ship received injections of gamma globulin from the Los Angeles Health Department to protect them from the disease. This was the same illness which had affected almost all thirty colonists who had reached San Cristobal via the *Alert*.

Aboard the *Western Trader* was a naturopathic physician and member of the colony who had been appointed official company doctor. A graduate of a chiropractic college, he used herbs and roots as medications but nothing in the line of drugs. He felt sure he could do an appendectomy if absolutely necessary. Some medical facilities were available on San Cristobal.

Meanwhile, time dragged interminably. It was quite obvious that the visas were being withheld purposely until after Ecuador's June election. A second influx of seventy-eight Americans would have created more pre-election incidents, which the present administration wished to avoid. It was not until August 2, 1960, (exactly two months after the election was safely concluded) that the visas were granted to the would-be colonists. The long four-month delay had taken its toll among the cooped-up passengers. Tempers flared, petty thievery of cigarettes and personal belongings caused arguments, and former well-mannered people became surly and quarrelsome. Captain Van Kirk was called "Captain Queeg" when attempting to restore discipline and order. The Seaman's Church Institute in San Pedro helped allay some of the tension by supplying books and magazines to while away the tedious hours of waiting.

More frustration was caused when tons of machinery, building supplies, and boats had to be unloaded from the *Western Trader* and stored in a warehouse. Ecuador exacted a 100 percent duty on all items except clothing and personal possessions. The duty on the heavy equipment would be rescinded provided certain necessary legal steps were followed, but these would take time to prepare. Apparently, these legal matters could not have been attended to prior to obtaining the visas. The colonists decided to sail without the equipment and fetch it later.

Another hitch arose when the United States Federal Communications Commission restricted the number of passengers aboard the *Western Trader* to fifty. That meant twenty-eight members had to disembark and proceed to the Galapagos by air, or wait for a later trip. The reason for the restriction may have been overcrowding and lack of proper radio equipment. Many boatmen in the Los Angeles Harbor expressed surprise that the Coast Guard allowed the ship to leave at all.

With sighs of relief, the colonists sailed from San Pedro for the Galapagos. Fortunately, no rough seas were encountered, the weather was pleasant, and Skipper Van Kirk was competent. With the help of a hired first mate and two of the company's engineers, the Skipper reached San Cristobal in seventeen days at sea, a good time for a power boat travelling 3,000 miles and towing a thirty-six-foot landing craft.

All was not well aboard the ship, however. The company office reported that some sort of a "blowup" occurred among the colonists aboard the *Western Trader* shortly before the vessel reached Wreck Bay. Three families and a Seattle man "refused to get off the ship" when the *Western Trader* arrived at the island paradise.

Another problem which plagued the twenty-five adults and twenty-five children (representing ten families and five single men) on board the *Western Trader* was a shortage of provisions. For several days before reaching the Galapagos, soft baby food was served. The goat stew of San Cristobal was quite welcome after this mushy fare.

Disenchantment

The *Western Trader* arrived at Wreck Bay on August 19, 1960. Soon afterward, the new president of the colony, as well as the other members who disembarked at San Pedro, came to Wreck Bay aboard the *Cristobal Carrier* from Ecuador. With them were reporter Charles Hillinger and photographer Frank Q. Brown of the *Los Angeles Times*, the only newsmen ever to visit the colony. In fact, the entire enterprise received little or no mention in newspapers of the midwestern and east-coast United States.

Including the latest arrivals, a total of 106 Americans (22 families and 14 single men) had descended upon San Cristobal. Some of the last families to arrive took one look at the settlement and decided immediately to return to the States on the return trip of the *Western Trader*. Several weeks later, they had their wish.

The initial settlers were extremely disappointed that the *Western Trader* brought none of the much-needed equipment for which they had waited five months. In general, the first group, who did the real pioneering of the colony, had managed extremely well with very little friction among themselves, and had established very amicable relations with the Ecuadorian villagers. Indeed, some of them had sent favorable reports to their cohorts in San Pedro, and this led to arguments.

The newer arrivals accused the first group of painting a false picture in their reports, which failed to mention that the refrigeration plant was useless and that Tous could not sell the land. Some balked at the community-style meals, and longed for the good old-fashioned dinners enjoyed privately by the small family circle. Others deplored the lack of medical and educational facilities. One man, who had been enthusiastic about the colony for seven months, was still optimistic about its future success, but felt that he was being unfair to his five children, (ages six to twelve). Their education, and perhaps their health, would suffer, and he reluctantly decided to return to the United States.

Reporter Hillinger saw other indications that all was not well in the island paradise. He met one colonist, accompanied by an Ecuadorian policeman and an interpreter, heading for the home of another colonist charged with theft. Disappointment and hostility were rife everywhere. One colonist told the reporter that it appeared the experiment was a failure: that their utopia seemed to have all the problems of their United States home, plus more. Another man complained, "We're all broke, financially bankrupt. My wife and children haven't had a glass of milk since August. Our drinking water is so dirty you can't see through a glass. Dysentery and hepatitis have weakened all of us."

President Reuss and five other men sailed to other islands in the archipelago searching for new undeveloped land which would cost little or nothing to lease. At Academy Bay on Santa Cruz Island, they hiked fifteen miles inland, up to the higher farmlands. After their return to the bay, they conversed with some of the members of the foreign community of forty-five Europeans and five Americans living at the shore. From Hillinger's report, it was quite obvious that the new colony was unwelcome at Santa Cruz.

A Belgian settler was quoted:

> This is a marvelous island. When we want meat, we go a few yards into the bush and kill a wild steer, a goat or a boar. There are avocados, oranges, pineapples, coffee and vegetables here. I know all the islands in the Pacific. I searched years for a place to live. This is my dream. The weather here is ideal; the water beautiful.

> It is a paradise for diving and sport fishing, for hunting. There are no dangers. It is an island free of everything bad, no malaria or other diseases. You have time to relax. There will always be peace in the Galapagos. But – if 100 families come to Santa Cruz, everything will be ruined. There is not enough for that many. Everything will be gone in a short time if you come here. The cost of living will go up.

An American, who had a comfortable income from investments in the United States, asked how the settlers expected to get rich off of the islands, as Harrsch had promised, when those who had lived there longer could barely make a living. The fishermen of Santa Cruz and San Cristobal then earned about one hundred to two hundred dollars each during the four months preceding Lent by selling their salted grouper in Ecuador.

Karl Angermeyer welcomed newcomers, but with this reservation: "We need new blood to strengthen our community, but not a colony." Gus Angermeyer added, "If you had taken your $2,500 you could have bought a nice house here and settled down to a good life as individuals." Forrest Nelson stated, "We do not want a close-knit community. You want to import the very thing we have come here to escape. Individuals are here because they fled restrictions."

Aware of the dissensions among the new colonists, Jacob Lundh, who came to Santa Cruz in 1932 with his father, Captain Lundh, offered this advice: "You have to run your company like a ship. If everyone pulls in his own direction, the whole works will fall apart. That's what happened to the Norwegians. That's what might well happen to you if you don't get better organized." A Swiss colonist suggested the colony move to San Salvador (James) Island, where there was good soil, an abundance of sheep, drinking water, and no other people.

After visiting the air strip at Baltra, and finally Barrington Island, the scouts returned to Wreck Bay. The president of the colony announced that the colony would remain on San Cristobal Island.

The Yankees Go Home

When the *Western Trader* raised anchor ten days after its arrival at Wreck Bay, there were 29 people aboard, including Captain Van Kirk, his wife, and the hired first mate. Only 55 colonists (12 families and 3 single men – 27 children and 28 adults) remained on San Cristobal to continue the enterprise under new leadership. The original total was 106.

Second president Reuss had resigned; his wife, bitterly disappointed, had urged him to return home with their three small children. Moreover, while waiting in Guayaquil for the *Western Trader* to arrive at Wreck Bay, Reuss had become seriously ill, and his family felt he should return to the States to recuperate. Another colonist, whose wife had broken her hip on the *Alert*, said, "Well, I've had it. Everyone here has a lot of courage; they're as determined a group of people I know. But I've decided there's nothing for us to do in the Galapagos. I'm getting out while I have a few pennies left. The people here are going to have to face up to reality or turn native." One of the colonists who elected to stay on the island said that they had expected to lose half of the population even before they started.

The new and third president of the Island Development Company – Seattle fireman Galen Kauffman – was an idealist who was optimistic about the future. He had come to the Galapagos for the psychological and sociological aspects of the adventure, and for the posibility of making the world a better place in which to live. Kauffman admitted that he doubted whether a utopia could ever be achieved and that the odds of success were against the group. He proposed temporarily closing the enterprise to new members and called for a full accounting of the company's books.

Another sixty or more families in the United States were still looking forward to their trip to the Galapagos; their money had kept the enterprise alive. The company had spent over $165,000, and at least two thirds of that had been spent on the ships. Equipment and airplane fares had been costly, and very little money was left in the treasury. In fact, the money was almost gone, with very little left for food. "There is plenty of fruit, and it's cheap, but we still have to buy it," one man remarked. Efforts to re-establish credit in Guayaquil failed when efforts to raise more money in Seattle were unsuccessful.

Kauffman, whose children were hospitalized in Guayaquil with serious cases of hepatitis, envisioned a Galapagos of the future which would be like the Hawaiian islands a century before. He thought the Galapagos could be a great tourist attraction with grand hotels and tours of volcanic eruptions, sea lion colonies, and the "most spectacular sea life on earth."

The Ecuadorian villagers of Baquerizo Moreno did not wish to see the Americans leave. They wired to President Ibarra of Ecuador:

The Americans on San Cristobal have had no cooperation from the government in Quito. Many are returning to the United States. Help them get a decent piece of land on San Cristobal so they will stay and bring new life to our community. They are good neighbors for Ecuadorians in the Galapagos.

Every time Americans come to the Galapagos something good happens to our island. They gave us our water system. The lumber our homes are made of came from the old American Air Force base on Seymour Island. We urge you to encourage the colonists to stay.

The *Western Trader* left San Cristobal at the end of August, 1960, and was due in San Pedro about September 20, but lost a propeller off the coast of Guatemala. It was abandoned in the port of Salina Cruz, at the southwestern tip of Mexico. Later, one of the colonists and his family claimed it as salvage and miraculously sailed it to San Diego. There it was ultimately sold at auction for less than a third of its cost to the company. The new owner purchased it for scrap and wished to motor it to Long Beach, but the old Atlas engines refused to work. Being in San Diego at the time, Captain Otterman offered to start the engines, which he did by pre-heating the cylinders with a blow torch. The *Alert* never returned to the United States; it sank in Panama.

Slowly, all the colonists began to trickle back to the United States. A family that returned to Seattle, early in October, told reporters that they felt no bitterness, but were having trouble getting re-established. Their children were busily catching up on their school studies, which they had missed during their long vacation and great adventure.

By late January of 1961, all but one of the colonists left the island. The last family to leave returned to Seattle in February, after an absence of one whole year, and after having lived ''like animals'' on San Cristobal for six months.

The lone survivor was Edward Niles, a single man aged thirty-two. After the colonists left, he attempted to run a charter-cruise business with a converted landing craft, and almost gave up in despair after the first year. Then, UNESCO and some scientific groups steadily chartered the craft. Niles moved to Academy Bay and rented a fine home on a private lagoon for the princely sum of six dollars per month. After two years in the islands, he returned to Seattle for a visit, bringing his Ecuadorian fiance, a talented concert soprano who wanted to share his life in the Galapagos. He thought it was the perfect place to retire. He had no regrets over leaving the States: ''I wasn't fed up. It was a good life. But I know every day is a step into the unknown. I've always admired people who crossed the plains in covered wagons. So I left my television and stepped back fifty years. But I don't have to face the dangers the pioneers faced.''

Failure of the colony was inevitable, and predicted early. The injudicious use of funds; red tape; a psychotic leader; an impractical goal, in view of the low potential of the island; adjustment to a strange and primitive environment; illnesses and all these factors led to a speedy demise. The sociologists lamented, ''The hypothesis that men could live more harmoniously by devoting a third of their resources to science and limiting their personal income differential to a range of 5 to 2 remains untested.''

And what happened to the leader who started the whole business?

In October of 1960, reporter Charles Hillinger found Don Harrsch in Garden Grove, California, planning a series of colonies to be scattered throughout Central America and in the most primitive sections of the Amazon. Apparently he found no takers for his new plan, because in the summer of 1961 he was working as a caretaker of a refrigeration ship in Los Angeles Harbor and getting ready for lobstering in the Galapagos. Any fisherman could have told him that lobsters were plentiful closer to home off the coasts of Baja, California, and for a cheaper license than that demanded by Ecuador. Perhaps the bewitched Encantadas had become an obsession with Harrsch, for he was determined to see them once more. The strangely different, misshapen lava heaps – ''remote, grotesque, formidable, unconquerable'' – have a haunting fascination for those who bother to explore or study them more than superficially.

21
LATER YEARS

∽∽∽∽∽∽∽∽∽∽∽∽

Ships

Ships are mobile bridges between continents and islands; ships and far-away places like the remote Galapagos are inextricably linked. Previous chapters have shown that the unreal and bizarre Encantadas had attracted many adventurous boatmen, and almost every ship which anchored in the archipelago had an interesting tale concerning itself.

Susan and Eric Hiscock, on their second trip around the world, left England in July of 1959 and arrived at Wreck Bay the following February in their little thirty-foot *Wanderer III*. The port captain boarded the yacht at 1:55 P.M. to grant clearance. Because his lunch hour had been shortened by five minutes, he fined the skipper ten dollars extra for overtime. The fine was reluctantly paid, because there was a rusty, but formidable-looking, gunboat in port.

During the forty-mile crossing to Post Office Bay, the compass on the *Wanderer III* proved quite useless because of abnormal magnetic variation in the area – not too unusual in the magically bewitched Encantadas. Hiscock had written an article for a yachting magazine, and the manuscript and some letters were encased in a plastic bag and put into the barrel, together with some shillings for postage. None of this mail ever reached its destination, even after a period of three years. The *Wanderer III* left the Galapagos much sooner than they had intended; Hiscock did not wish to use up his scant supply of fuel. The Comandante at Wreck Bay had not permitted him to replenish his petrol supply.

On March 13, 1960, a thirty-seven-foot gaff-rigged ketch dropped anchor at Wreck Bay. The ship was immediately fined ten dollars for arriving on Sunday. The port officials said the fine would "compensate them for the extra trouble of getting out of bed and putting on their uniforms."

The *Si Ye Pambili* ("Let Us Go Forward" in the Rhodesian language) had sailed from Africa. The ship had been purchased by five Englishmen, all of whom were ex-Rhodesian policemen. Three of them left the *Pambili* before it reached Panama, and were replaced by two women.

Skipper Roger Gowen, and his friends Bill, Shirley, and Pauline, left Panama after meeting two other vessels also bound for the Galapagos. One of the two was the yacht *Ben Gunn* from Mystic, Connecticut, with Hank and Niki Horn and their eight-year-old daughter. They later met the *Pambili* again at Wreck Bay. The second yacht, *Secret*, was later wrecked on a reef at Wreck Bay. Peter and Helen Dohm managed to salvage only a few of their possessions before the boat sank.

The *Pambili* made the journey from Panama to the Galapagos in seven days, but they had motored 511 of the 864 miles, deeming this to be the most sensible way to cross this difficult reach.

There were about thirty residents at Black Beach on Floreana, where the crew of the *Pambili* were told of a mysterious tunnel reputed to be the burial place of the notorious Baroness. The foursome from the *Pambili* experienced eerie feelings – an atmosphere of evil and a sense of doom – as they lowered themselves straight down a twenty-foot shaft and then crawled on hands and knees along forty yards of descending tunnel past another drop of twenty feet. Gowen wrote:

> We could hear lapping water in the darkness and realized that we were crawling toward the sea. In the light of torches we could pick out the skeletons of giant tortoises who must have stumbled into the shaft to die of starvation . . . . After more scrambling and stumbling among the skeletons we came to an alcove, almost like a grotto, formed by the rock and sand falling away. There was a grave without a cross – the alleged last unhonoured resting place of the Baroness. In great haste we made our way back – we all felt we had rather a large ration of evil and needed the sun to dispel the lingering morbidity of the legend.

The *Pambili* left the Galapagos on March 29, 1960.

The early 1960's had their share of boats coming to the islands: *Argo*, *Manabi Esmeralda*, *Juan Kohn*, *El Buzo*, *Myonie*, *Bojac*, *Dwyn Wen*, *Marpatcha* from California, *Dorothea* from Oslo, and *Salty* from Germany. The brigantine *Yankee* came once more, but without Captain Irving Johnson. The ship had been sold to Windjammer Cruises of Miami, Florida, and Captain Johnson was now skippering another ship through the intriguing rivers and canals of Europe.

The Ill-Fated *Albatross*

Another old brigantine, about the size of the *Yankee*, spent several weeks in the Galapagos in the spring of 1961. The ninety-two-foot, steel-hulled *Albatross* had a colorful history. She was built in 1921 in Holland for use as a pilot ship, and became a radio station for German submarines during World War II. Seized by the British, she was sold to the Dutch as a cadet training vessel. Later, author Ernest Gann rigged her as a brigantine. Having survived a tidal wave in Honolulu, the *Albatross* was deliberately set on fire for the Hollywood production entitled *Twilight of the Gods.*

Eventually, the *Albatross* was purchased by young Dr. Christopher Sheldon for use as a floating classroom. His wife, Dr. Alice Sheldon, M.D., taught botany and mathematics to the young boys who signed on as crew for an eight-month voyage from Bermuda to the Galapagos and then back to Mystic, Connecticut.

At Post Office Bay, the crew of the *Albatross* re-painted the mail barrel, just as the cadets of the Polish *Dar Pomorza* had done twenty-five years before. The name of the ship was painted in huge letters on a low rock at the head of Tagus Cove. After a glorious two weeks studying the wild life and plants of the Galapagos, the boys sailed homeward through the Panama Canal. They had reached the coast of Yucatan, and were headed for the Bahamas, when disaster struck at the Dry Tortugas near Florida.

Without warning, a sudden white squall caught the highflying topsail and toppled the ship on its side with the sails soaking up tons of sea water. More water filled the hatches, and the ship sank quickly, righting herself as she went down. Those on deck were hurled overboard, and two boys below deck managed to swim through open hatches. Dr. Alice, four boys, and the cook perished; in the short space of two minutes, the skipper lost his ship, his wife, and his home. The thirteen survivors swam to the rubber life raft which floated up, and to the lifeboat which they tore loose from its moorings.

Instead of being bitter about the loss of their son, the parents of one of the crew thanked the skipper for having given their son the happiest year of his life, as indicated by his letters home.

Survival of the Fittest

Early in 1962, the United States training ship *Golden Bear* brought an expedition sponsored by the New York Zoological Society. Representatives from the New York Zoo, Zurich Zoological Gardens, National Geographic Society, and Lafayette College of Eaton, Pennsylvania, gathered information concerning the habits and needs of giant tortoises, and of the iguanas of both land and marine species. More facts were needed by the zoos for the creation of environments which would promise successful breeding in captivity.

A study of the periodic migrations of land tortoises was made; the creatures travel seasonally from the abundant vegetation of the moist upper regions to lay their eggs on the dry lower levels. The land iguanas were found to require not only abundant vegetation, but also proper soil for burrows. It was learned that marine iguanas could be retrained to feed on unaccustomed food other than algae and seaweed. Six specimens are now thriving well on zoo fare in New York.

The biological station on Santa Cruz Island, entrusted to M. Raymond Leveque by UNESCO in 1960, was progressing well, mapping out an ambitious research program and diligently painting numbers on the backs of the remaining tortoises. Besides conservation of the priceless fauna, studies were also planned of the invertebrates, soil biology, and geology.

It is important to conserve this little world of the Galapagos, which followed its own evolutionary laws after being cut off from the outside world. In the Galapagos, these laws were much easier to distinguish because of the simplicity of the fauna. Elsewhere, the tracing of relationships is complicated by the complexity of natural phenomena and the multiplicity of ancestors. The paucity of Galapagoan fauna and flora thus serves to make the islands Nature's experiment station.

Even the lowly cactus proved the occurrence of a remarkable inter-island evolution. Dr. E. Yale Dawson, Secretary for the Americas of the International Charles Darwin Foundation for the Galapagos Islands, wrote that, hundreds of thousands of years ago, prickly pear cacti (genus *Opuntia*) floated to the Galapagos from Central America. That was long before the tortoises arrived. Some plants managed to survive and develop on islands too small and dry to support families of tortoises. On other islands, the armored plant and the armored animal evolved together.

In places where there are no tortoises or iguanas, *Opuntia* developed scrubby species with short stems, and spread low over the ground. Where there were tortoises or iguanas, only the fast-growing *Opuntia* with long trunks survived. Giant cactuses evolved that were adapted for protection from the browsing creatures. The stems of young plants are so spiny that the tortoises and iguanas are discouraged from eating them. As the plant grows taller, the spines are replaced by a coarse papery bark on the woody trunk, which is not relished by the reptiles. The juicy pads are out of reach and form a leafy crown on the upper branches. The reptiles must be content to dine on the fallen pads which break off after acquiring a maximum weight of water. Not to be outsmarted by the clever cacti, some species of tortoises developed longer necks.

Actually, it is the least abundant and smallest cactus – *Brachycereus nesiaticus* – which may have contributed to the survival of the first reptiles to arrive in the Galapagos. This cactus is green during the dry season and grows at lower elevations. Though it has an extremely spiny stem, it is low enough for the creatures to reach the pads, providing food even in the driest climate.

The largest cactus in the Galapagos is *Opuntia megasperma*, whose trunk often achieves a diameter of four-and-a-half feet; it resembles a pine tree when viewed from a distance. A smaller species, *Opuntia ochos*, achieves a two-foot diameter and is abundant on Santa Cruz Island. The juvenile plants of both species are heavily armed with spines.

Perhaps the finest and most picturesque cactus forest in the entire archipelago is found near the Darwin Station on Santa Cruz Island. It stands near the seashore but is undisturbed by the seaweed eating marine iguanas which are plentiful in this area.

One of the most interesting cacti was described by Abel du Petit Thouars, of the French *Venus*, in 1841. It is the giant candelabra cactus *Jasminocereus*, whose purplish-brown blossom, with its creamy white interior, blooms at night and is pollinated by nocturnal insects like the hawk moth.

As early as 1812, humans found the fruit of the prickly pear cactus edible. In 1815, Captain David Porter wrote, "Their juice, when stewed with sugar, made a delicious syrup, while their skins afforded a most excellent preserve with which we made pies, tarts, etc."

Luther Burbank experimented for years in California, trying to develop a spineless cactus; he was unaware that a spineless form of *Opuntia* could be found on the Galapagos. There is nothing new under the sun.

Dr. Robert I. Bowman of the San Francisco State College returned to the Galapagos in late 1961 and early 1962. This time he and Stephen L. Billeb took thousands of tape recordings of the calls and songs of the Darwin finches. The scientists discovered "dialects": the song of a species on one island differed from the song of the same species on another island. Further experiments seemed to prove that young birds placed in sound isolation from their parents did not develop the typical adult song. Once more, the isolated oceanic archipelago proved useful because of the limited number of species involved, and because of the uncomplicated environment of what Dr. Bowman called "a natural laboratory" where "the original biota is still more or less intact."

Myonie

In February of 1962, Doctor Al Gehrman and his wife, Helen, arrived at Post Office Bay in the sturdy thirty-six-foot ketch *Myonie*, a double-ender. The young couple had sailed from Miami, Florida, and was on the first leg of their journey circling the globe – a voyage which eventually took three years and included riding out a typhoon near New Guinea and having all their possessions pirated in the Philippines.

The *Myonie* was asked at Panama to deliver packages to the islanders, including a twelve-volt battery. The Galapagoans were no longer permitted to order items from mail-order catalogues to be delivered via the *Cristobal Carrier*. Ordinary items like aspirin, tennis shoes, detergents, peanut butter, and oleomargarine, which we take for granted, were hard to come by in the Galapagos.

The *Myonie* also carried a package for a school teacher in the islands, unwittingly delivering to him some fresh Communist propaganda. Even the remote Galapagos were not free of agitators, and there they constantly strived to drive out all the gringos from the archipelago. Consequently, the large foreign community at Academy Bay had insecurity added to its other problems.

On Floreana, the Gehrmans found the genial Wittmers busily operating their supply store and small hotel, which brought a modest revenue, especially from visiting scientists. At the Wittmer house, Al and Helen were treated to a special delicacy of popcorn, which was served as a dessert and eaten with forks.

A message was radioed to Black Beach, ordering the *Myonie* to sail to Wreck Bay to put its papers in order. Al Gehrman had obtained a permit in Panama and had no intention of paying a second time. He had avoided the port of entry because the port captain was known to exact special fines from each vessel. At each clearance, the officials are known to exact cartons of cigarettes and canned goods for their services. Perhaps all yachtsmen who paid for their permit in Panama or elsewhere should have had the Ecuadorian consul wire to Quito for a wireless receipt, which would have forestalled future arguments with Galapagoan port captains.

The *Myonie* also reported seeing a small sailing vessel being towed to port by an Ecuadorian destroyer. The lonely voyager and his remaining twenty dollars were soon parted; the poor devil proceeded to Tahiti with no funds at all. To this very day, the Galapagos seem to be a haven for pirates. However, the motor vessel *Explorer* encountered no trouble in late 1964, and had to pay only a very modest fee.

Post Office Bay, 1962

On May 7, 1962, the staysail schooner *Marpatcha* lay at anchor in Cormorant Bay, Floreana, where fishing was excellent. Captain Otterman and three of his crew went ashore and decided to hike to Post Office Bay, a distance of about four arduous miles. Following a marked trail past the salt flats, they saw two flamingoes and a graceful gray heron. After two hours, they came to the famous barrel, about two feet high, painted white with red bands. The name *Albatross* had been painted in white on the little blue metal roof sheltering the door at the side of the keg.

Inside was a stack of mail, each piece bearing a rubberstamped picture of the barrel as a postmark and the words "Post Office, Galapagos." On the back of the larger envelopes was a stamped, stylized drawing of a land tortoise, and the message: "Come and see the Enchanted Islands, Galapagos,

Ecuador.'' Some of the letters and postcards bore Ecuadorian postage stamps in the upper right corner; obviously the senders were not aware that no stamps were necessary.

A typewritten message from Mrs. Wittmer was tacked to the inside of the door: ''The book *Voyages of 20 Years* left by yacht *Salmo* you will find in B.B. [Black Beach] in Wittmers house to save the book of destroying by the rainy season. Come and sign here. Margret Wittmer. Black Beach, Floreana.''

Below the barrel, on a rock base, were various wooden plaques, some extremely artistic, bearing ships' names and dates. Bleached skulls of cattle were added for decorative effect. Names of ships were also written on the barrel itself; none was older than eight or nine years. Older names had been painted out.

Near the barrel, a concrete bench, gaudily painted in red, white, and blue bore the message ''Compliments of the Brigantine Albatross,'' with *Yankee* painted on the seat. In all directions, pathways outlined with black lava stones led to nowhere. Further back, several huge rusty water tanks, dating back to the hapless Norwegian colony, had names (like: Marty Munson, Dwyn Wen) scrawled on them. On the ground, stones were arranged to spell out ships' names, and wooden stakes set in the ground announced some previous visitors. One of those bore the name *Cristobal Carrier*.

Further inland, in direct line with the barrel, were three or four concrete steps leading to a concrete foundation of what had once been a large structure. This is all that is left of the Norwegian Casa. Rectangular pillars scattered about were the concrete posts on which the frame structure of the house had rested. Whimsical visitors had converted them into benches and sign posts.

The forty-one pieces of mail from the barrel consisted of twenty-nine letters and twelve postcards. Eleven letters were destined for Sweden, five for Alemannia (Germany), and the rest were going to the United States, Bolivia, Argentina, Ecuador, Denmark, Austria, and Inglaterra (England). Two letters were addressed to a Colonel in the Panama Canal Zone. Six of the letters were empty envelopes containing no messages; they were intended for postmark collectors. One letter to Los Angeles had the following request on the back: ''Please write name of yacht who [sic] mailed this letter.''

There were several identical postcards which had a photograph of the barrel with the steamer *Stella Polaris* in the background. On each was printed in English: ''Post Office Bay. To be had only from M. Wittmer, Isla Floreana, Galapagos, Ecuador, S.A.'' These cards were addressed in European-style handwriting, one of them containing a message in Polish, which translated, read: ''Greetings from the island of Floreana; the only Postoffice on earth which accepts letters without stamps.'' It was dated March 10, 1962, and was destined for Inglaterra. A similar message was sent to Buenos Aires. There were some picture postcards of scenes in Ecuador; one was entitled ''Transporte de azufre en la Galapagos,'' and showed pack burros on the beach. These cards were addressed to Minnesota, Illinois, Wisconsin, Virginia, and Washington, and signed "Margaret and Ray."

The letters were mailed in Papeete, Tahiti, upon payment of the regular postage rate. The Galapagos postmarks were not honored and French Oceania stamps had to be affixed to each piece of mail – quite a problem because the Galapagos emblems left insufficient space for the French stamps.

Tunny-boats

The waters around the Galapagos Archipelago are considered one of the richest fishing grounds in the world. The vast abundance of marine life in these waters is caused by a freak of nature known as the Humboldt Current.

Tradewinds blow offshore from the continent of South America and set in motion a surface drift of sea water. To replace this, Antarctic water wells up from great depths, stirring up with it various nutrient salts which were formed by dead matter sinking to the ocean floor. This vast belt of fertile water, about thirty to forty miles wide, moves northward along the coast of Chile, then northwestward to the Galapagos, and diffuses itself in the mid-Pacific along the Equator. Rich in oxygen and carbon dioxide, it nourishes microscopic plants which are food for minute crustaceans, which in turn attract larger fish, whales, and sea birds. Consequently, fishermen are always assured of a bountiful harvest of fish in this area.

Ecuador never exploited these waters herself, but did benefit financially from payments for fishing rights paid by foreign companies. When the tax levied on the fishing boats was low and not too well enforced, tuna clippers were a common sight around the coast of Ecuador and among the Galapagos Islands. A yachtsman sailing into any one of the island harbors or coves invariably found several California boats from San Pedro or San Diego already at anchor there.

An increase in the tax, to as much as $5,000 to $10,000 per trip, discouraged fishermen by making their hauls unprofitable. Tax evasion became rife. Fewer boats came to the Galapagos, especially after the following incident:

On June 1, 1963, the Ecuadorian navy seized the vessels *Ranger* and *White Star* from San Diego and impounded them in Guayaquil. Nineteen other United States clippers followed them into port in protest. An allegation was made that the tuna boats were fishing without a license in Ecuadorian waters; the boats claimed that they were 13 to 14 miles offshore in international waters. Ecuador then announced that her territorial jurisdiction extended 200 miles out to sea.

The boats were fined $26,272, and were to be confiscated unless the fine was paid within five days. The charges were: contempt of moral authorities, illegal fishing, smuggling, attempted bribery, and willful disobedience. A United States ambassador flew to Quito to confer about the fishing dispute, and the decision reached left the commercial fishing associations howling with rage.

The State Department urged the boat owners to pay the fine, which would be reimbursed if the charges were proven invalid. The boats were released on June 11 after payment of the fine. The fishermen were angered because the United States did not borrow Britain's technique in a similar dispute. When Iceland declared a twelve-mile limit, British gunboats immediately went out to protect British trawlers that continued to fish within the disputed new limit. On June 14, a third tuna clipper, the *Espiritu Santo*, was seized, and released promptly upon payment of a fine to Ecuador.

"The sea is the last free place on earth," said Hemingway. Maybe so, but not for long if countries keep setting up arbitrary limits. Meanwhile, fishermen would shun the Galapagos waters, and the lonely Encantadas would become a bit lonelier.

Expedition, 1964

Perhaps the Galapagos will not remain so lonely after all – if scientists keep coming in ever increasing numbers. With so many scientific expeditions in past Galapagos history, it would seem that all scientific data on the islands must have been recorded by now, and all knowledge exhausted. But no: new discoveries are being made continuously; the Encantadas are indeed a fabulous wonderland for science.

On January 10, 1964, a barrage of sixty-six scientists left San Francisco for the Galapagos to make "a multi-discipline assault on still unsolved mysteries of evolution," also for formal dedication ceremonies of the Darwin Research Station on Santa Cruz Island. Dr. Robert I. Usinger declared this group to be the largest ever assembled on the islands "to develop a science of the relations between all the animals and the environment of a single area." In addition, about fifty diplomats were flown in by Ecuadorian and United States Air Force planes.

The project was conducted by the University of California Extension Service at Berkeley, and supported by a $121,650 grant from the United States National Science Foundation. The scientists and the latest scientific equipment were placed aboard the large power vessel *Golden Bear*, a training ship of the California Maritime Academy. The facilities and helicopters of the U.S.S. *Pine Island* were also available.

Five weeks were spent on this "living museum of past ages." Tiny Culpepper Island was completely explored for the first time in its lonely history. Many species of tortoises feared extinct were found on some of the smaller islands; these isles had been inaccessible because of the steep cliffs rising on all sides from the sea. Helicopters landed scientists on islands that had never before been visited by human beings.

On one island, studies were made of the evolution of wild tomatoes and wild cotton which grew in undisturbed isolation from pressures and forces found in environments in other parts of the world. Dr. Dawson reported that the wild tomatoes looked and tasted like the ordinary, familiar "cherry tomatoes" bought in markets in the United States. However, all efforts to grow these tomatoes from seed in the laboratory failed, despite diligent watering and fertilizing. Later, the botanists discovered accidentally that the plant had a curious life cycle. The seeds will not sprout unless they have passed through the digestive system of a tortoise.

Drs. Bartholomew and Carpenter noticed a peculiar sight: thousands of marine iguanas sunning on the rocks, all facing in precisely the same solar direction – a form of iguanid air conditioning. When the weather gets too hot even for these desert creatures, they lift their heads and shoulders, and face directly into the sun. Cooler air flows under their shaded bodies and thus helps to regulate their body temperature.

Some of the marine iguanas have a third eye in the middle of their forehead; its use is unknown. Scientists think it may be either a developing eye or one that is disappearing in the evolutionary scale. One of the projects undertaken during this expedition was the removal of this third eye from iguanas which were tagged for future study. Over the years, the behavior of those tagged lizards would be observed to determine whether the removal of the eye has any effect upon their life habits or gives a clue to its use.

Skin divers reported that the marine iguanas could be found forty or more feet below the surface of the water. It was surmised that these iguanas learned to stay under water for long periods in order to forage for the abundant seaweed that sprouts on the ocean floor. Large populations of seaweed-eating crabs and reef fish in the shallower water and on the rocks forced the iguanas to feed in deeper waters. Their cousin, the land iguana, cannot stay under water and confines his diet to cactus and greens, even though he can swim a little.

In order to determine the geological age of the archipelago, Dr. Allen Cox of the United States Geological Survey drilled cores from the lava flows. His samples were taken from various rugged and desolate areas, a task made arduous by difficult climbing over rocky terrains carrying a heavy diamond drill with a gasoline motor to drive it and two water tanks to cool it.

When lava cools, the crystals orient themselves to the magnetic pole of the earth. Dr. Cox reported finding crystals which lined up with the pole about one million years ago. Since then, the magnetic pole has changed its location, and the crystals are at an angle from it. The deviation from the pole can be measured and the geological age computed.

Hawks are generally considered ferocious; those in the Galapagos have a gentle disposition, allowing people to stroke them. Their cruel flesh-tearing beaks are used mainly for catching little lava lizards that scurry in and out of the rocks. In strange contrast, though, are the tiny finches which belong to the meek canary, gold-finch, and linnet family. Some of the little rascals live on the blood of live boobies!

It seems that the boobies of Wenman Island are pestered constantly by louse flies. Dr. Robert I. Bowman theorized that, at first, the finches were helpful to the boobies by attacking the parasitic flies. However, the finches acquired a taste for blood, "possibly by eating blood-engorged flies, or by overzealous stabbing at flies amidst the plumage, causing an accidental puncture of the booby skin." Now the finches can be seen deliberately attacking uninjured boobies. They perch on the back and stab at the tender elbow region of the booby until the blood flows. This blood-feeding habit of the sharp-beaked ground finch has been observed only on Wenman Island.

Another curiosity is *Dialommus fuscus*, a little known fish with four eyes. Actually, it has two eyes which are divided vertically into four sight organs, perhaps for viewing all four corners of the sea. The scientists have not yet determined the purpose of this multiple vision adaptation. Another rare species are the anableps, whose eyes are divided in half horizontally, perhaps to see above and below the surface of the water simultaneously.

I am reminded of some queer fish I saw in the tidal pools of Darwin Bay. The small antennarius crawls around the rocky pools like a clumsy toad, using his fins as feet; they even have toe-like digits. He dangles a little antenna with a bulbous tip before his nose to attract little fish, which he promptly gobbles up. There just seems to be no end to the wonders in what Dr. Dawson calls, "Natures's Old Curiosity Shop."

New Mystery

As the last chapter of this history was being written, the following headline appeared in the *Miami Herald*: "Woman Disappears on Island." The news story went on to detail how 70-year-old Sarah Reiser had vanished two weeks earlier from the brigantine *Yankee* while on a world cruise. The Galapagos island of Floreana, the newspaper reported, was one of the first stops.

The following day, a more detailed report was given. The *Yankee* had left Miami and sailed through the Canal where, at Panama, a Dr. Swanson disembarked from the ship. He described Miss Reiser as "one of the most adventuresome passengers aboard the ship. For a 70-year-old woman she seemed to be having the time of her life. Any place we landed she was one of the first to go ashore, and she took part in any activity or exploring that was to be done."

The *Yankee* stopped at several islands in the archipelago before anchoring at Floreana on April 5, 1964. Details are very slim, but it seems that the ship anchored either at Post Office Bay or Black Beach, because a group of three men and three women decided to visit Rolf and Floreanita Wittmer, who live alternately at Black Beach or their farm in the hills. As the group hiked along the island's rocky coast, Miss Reiser and a second woman separated from the others. While her friend stopped to remove a stone from her shoe, Miss Reiser walked on ahead – and vanished.

Unable to locate their elderly companion, the hikers reported back to Captain Derek Lumbers of the *Yankee*. The crew, passengers, and forty Ecuadorian settlers then combed the entire eight-by-ten-mile island from its rocky shores to its 2,000-foot peak. After four days without a trace of Miss Reiser, the *Yankee* sailed to Academy Bay, seventy-five miles away, and brought back two hundred Santa Cruz residents to continue the search.

"Word somehow filtered through to a third island, San Cristobal, where the Ecuadorian Navy maintains a token base," stated a newspaper, possibly unaware that there are radio stations on both Floreana and Santa Cruz. An Ecuadorian navy vessel was dispatched to the search, and the first word of the mysterious disappearance was radioed back to the mainland.

Ambassador Maurice Bernhaum, at the United States Embassy in Quito, appealed to the United States Air Force for help, and a G-135 Globemaster flew 1,000 miles from Panama to the air strip at Baltra. A helicopter was disgorged from the Globemaster's enormous insides and joined the search parties.

After two weeks, no trace of the spry adventuress was uncovered. Had she been attacked by wild dogs or bulls, or been injured or killed in a fall, her body and garments would have been found. Chances are she fell into some deep unknown crevasse, either inland or possibly underwater along the coast, or was swept out to sea. The newspaper accounts did not relate whether she walked inland or was lost near shore.

On April 20th, the Air Force Rescue Headquarters at Orlando, Florida, announced that everything humanly possible had been done to find Miss Reiser, and that now the futile search was being abandoned. Miss Reiser's personal effects were removed from the *Yankee* and sent to her brother in California.

It was exactly thirty years before that the Baroness and her lover disappeared under similar circumstances. Perhaps this mystery will also be just another unsolved riddle in the mystic and bewitched – some claim accursed – Encantadas.

Captain Lumbers' troubles were not over. Several months later a South-Pacific gale left the *Yankee* badly damaged on a coral reef off Rarotonga Island, stranding the remaining twelve passengers and seven crewmen. The ship was abandoned eventually and, left to disintegrate, battered by the surf

– an undeserving fate for the sturdy little brigantine that proudly sailed seven times around the world under Captain Irving Johnson.

22

EPILOGUE

Melville described the special curse of the Encantadas: "To them change never comes; neither the change of seasons nor of sorrows." He was referring to both their climate and their tragic history. He was wrong about the weather; there are periods of drought and periods of heavy rain. In fact, most of the residents and writers have extolled the cool invigorating climate of the upper regions, as contrasted with the desert atmosphere along the beach. Melville was correct about the tragedies. Percentage-wise per area (the entire archipelago is scarcely 150 miles in diameter) and population, perhaps no other islands have had as many wrecks, uprisings, unsuccessful settlements, and personal vicissitudes.

Beebe, too, had said that the Galapagos are "the one place in the world that remains unchanged." Geological changes, like the land elevation of Urvina Bay on Isabela Island, the disappearance and reappearance of the crater lake at Narborough, and occasional eruptions are sudden and perceptible changes. However, more subtle changes are occurring due to the influence of man.

The arable lands are being cleared and settled, their trees used for building huts or burned in cook stoves and campfires. Green slopes are being denuded of their skimpy vegetation by rats, pigs, goats, donkeys, and cattle; the original bizarre animals are reduced or even almost gone.

Perhaps the only change for the better is the fact that Ecuador and the United Nations recognize the uniqueness of the archipelago, which once was known as "the islands nobody cares about." The establishment of the Darwin Station was a step in the right direction toward conservation of the Galapagoan natural heritage. No effort should be spared to save this "little world within itself," if only for the reason given by Dr. Eibl-Eibesfeldt: "Slowly but surely we men are covering our planet with asphalt and concrete and we can see how, in a few decades, natural beauty which has lasted for millions of years has been destroyed forever. It may be that this sad state of affairs cannot be avoided in the fruitful, agricultural areas of our earth. Let us, then, do our best to see that at least the economically worthless Galapagos

Islands, that are so rich in natural marvels, are kept undisturbed for ourselves and for those who come after us.''

We read how every commercial scheme to exploit the islands ended in revolt, disillusionment, and tragedy. We learned that farming is difficult in the thin soil, that coastal settlements are plagued by a scarcity of water, that commercial fishing is hazardous in the variable currents, and that the great distance from markets makes any project unprofitable. So the only possible use of the islands would be to display them as a showcase of evolution, and develop tourism. A visit to the eerie atmosphere of the Galapagos would certainly afford the jaded traveler a taste of the unusual. Maybe some day there will be a Galapagos Chamber of Commerce urging travelers hither.

If so, perhaps it will not get much support from the alien population of Academy Bay. Chances are, most of them prefer the isolation; that is why they went there in the first place. An onslaught of tourists would be the last thing they desire. For over fifty years, the islands were a refuge to a queer assortment of humans: colonists, nudists, transients on their way to the South Seas, hardy pioneers, neurotics, escapists, and just plain people disgusted with the foibles of civilization. People seeking indolence and ease do not go to the Galapagos.

The islands never had any indigenous human population, and their history does not contain the usual tales of the conquest of natives who later died of white man's diseases. Much was said of the stragglers who drifted there, but not enough of the Ecuadorian settlers who comprise more than ninety-five percent of the total population. The omission was not intentional, only based on the author's lack of information. The Indios who hunted, fished, and farmed in the isolated Encantadas had no chroniclers to extol their heroic struggles for survival in the cruel Galapagos. No one recorded the dramas which occurred among these humble folk, many of whom were born and died here without having ever seen the mainland.

With the exception of the writings of Dr. Ritter, Dore Strauch, the Conways, and Mrs. Wittmer, all information about the Galapagos was furnished by outsiders peering into these unreal and curious islands for only brief glimpses. By no means is this book a comprehensive record, but it represents much research into scant literature and proves that appearances are deceiving. There is much more to the bleak Encantadas than meets the eye.

It would take months to see everything there is to see in the Galapagos. No mention was made of the chocolate-brown beaches of Jervis Island (Rabida), its salt-water lagoon, giant cacti, or numerous, foot-high, conical mud-tower nests of the flamigoes. Cowley's Enchanted Isle (Tortuga), which guards the approach to Villamil, would be ideal to photograph. It towers 300 feet straight up from the sea and is formed of a third of a volcanic crater, then a gap, then another eighth – the rest is missing. There are numerous other islets – for example, Guy Fawkes, Las Plazas, both Daphnes, and Duncan. In all, there are over sixty islets and isles in the archipelago, each with its own peculiar characteristics and beauty. If you have seen one, you have not seen them all.

In 1835, Darwin wrote a letter home from Lima, Peru, in which he stated, "I look forward to the Galapagos with more interest than any other part of this voyage." This represented my own sentiments exactly as I prepared for a second trip to the South Seas via the Galapagos in the 150-foot cruiser *Explorer*.

As a result of Darwin's subsequent voyage, man's conception of his place in the world has never been the same. My own brief trips inspired me to write this history, giving the Encantadas the publicity they rightly deserve. Darwin's "islands of a sombre phantasmagorical aspect" are worth another glance.

Galapagos Revisited

My second look at the Encantadas was more eye-filling than the first.

When the motor vessel *Explorer* arrived at Wreck Bay on December 23, 1964, Captain Otterman skillfully maneuvered the vessel past the unmarked, submerged Schiavoni reef. The masts of the wrecked steamer *Carawa* had disappeared years ago and no longer served as a warning to incoming mariners of the peril which lies beneath the waves. The port captain boarded the ship and very quickly and courteously cleared the ship's papers. The port fee was astonishingly low – a mere seventeen dollars for the 150-foot, 273-ton vessel. Perhaps the authorities had inaugurated a new policy to encourage yachtsmen and tourists. Or perhaps it was the holiday spirit – the entire ship's company of twenty-nine was invited to a dance to be held in town the following evening.

The wooden pier still jutted out into the bay, but the narrow-gauge tracks had been removed. Burros galloped freely along the beach, which was somewhat littered and messy in appearance, in keeping with the careless, unswept condition of the waterfront street. However, the two-story houses along the beach were gaily painted, and their occupants warm and friendly.

Negotiations were conducted for a bus trip to Progreso the following day, as well as getting some laundry done. The islanders seemed hungry for American dollars, but prices were not exorbitant. Supplies could be bought at several stores and a bakery; tasty omelettes were served at several beach cafes, along with Ecuadorian beer. The local orange wine was extremely sweet and syrupy.

The next morning, eighteen of the *Explorer* crew motored ashore for the Progreso excursion. The "bus" turned out to be a rickety old General Motors truck, converted to haul twenty-four passengers on its uncushioned wooden benches. Some doubts were expressed as to whether the bus would ever reach its destination – all the tires (filled with sand instead of air) were badly worn and carried heavy patches held in place by bolts. However, in the spirit of adventure we paid our dollar apiece and proceeded up the bumpy road, past cactus and scrub trees into the fertile highlands.

Progreso was a village of shacks, burros, cattle, chickens, and dogs; it was surprisingly clean. Movies were taken of some of the children playing with tortoises in a pen. Villagers eagerly accepted American cigarettes and chatted, telling us that Karin Cobos still lived in the distant hills. We made no attempt to disturb her chosen isolation, but proceeded upward toward the crater whose lake furnishes water for the islanders. The pipeline installed by the United States during World War II was still in existence and could be seen during most of our journey upward. Eventually, the bus stopped at an elevation of about two thousand feet, and we hiked several hundred feet steeply up to the crater's edge. The lake sparkled a hundred feet below us, and frigate birds hovered overhead. Somehow, after a wild ride downhill, the bus brought us back safely to Baquerizo Moreno.

Another trip was made to the derelict cannery on the northern edge of the bay about a mile north of town. There were no traces of the defunct American colony of 1960, but plenty of evidence that a thriving business had been conducted there in the earlier 1950's. Thousands of labels –"Enchanted Isles Sea Bass Fillets" – littered the floor, along with various memoranda and receipts issued by the Sociedad National de Galapagos. There were requisitions in "quadruplicado" for hardware and supplies. Letters and radiograms indicated an extensive correspondence with the Gubernacion Maritima, Archipielago de Colon, Armada de Ecuador. The machinery and equipment were stored in a locked room on the ground floor, but the second story rooms were vacant, seemingly unoccupied for years. A lot of capital had been invested in the structure.

In the evening, a dance was held in a large hall near the naval station. All of my preconceived notions about the lowly peons and unschooled fishermen of the lonely Encantadas were quite shattered as I saw these people doing the latest dance steps to fashionable South American tunes. It seemed strangely incongruous to see young ladies in spike-heeled shoes, fancy modern gowns, and the latest hair styles doing the "twist" on these clinkered shores. Despite their isolation, the young people managed to keep in close touch with the mainland.

Darwin's monument still occupied a dignified place in front of the impressive naval station at the edge of town. The eyes of the naturalist were directed toward the heart of the archipelago, gazing towards Santa Cruz Island, our next stop.

The *Explorer* anchored off Angermeyer Point, and visits were exchanged between islanders and crew immediately after the port captain cleared the ship. Another fee of seventeen dollars was paid – a small price for what the island had to offer. The brigantine *Beagle* and the schooner *Okeanos* were also anchored in the bay.

The skipper of the ancient *Beagle* was none other than Karl Angermeyer, the dashing and gallant Duke of the Galapagos. The sturdy bark had been purchased by the Darwin Foundation in England, arriving at Academy Bay in May of 1964. The vessel was to serve the needs of the Darwin Station, located about a mile east of the village. The crew of the *Explorer* was shown through the laboratories and tortoise corral, and viewed the bird, animal, and plant collections being studied.

The *Okeanos* was on its way to Australia, skippered by Joe Pachernegg who had left Academy Bay in 1956. In Australia, he had married a charming nurse, Bonita, then worked in Miami for Windjammer Cruises – "Burke's Fleet" – as skipper of the *Mandalay*. Now he was sailing again to Australia. Bonita was able to render medical assistance to the ailing engineer aboard the *Explorer*, who also had worked for Burke's Fleet. It's a small world.

Gus Angermeyer, Joe, and several of the *Explorer* crew went goat-hunting and paid a visit to Turtle Bay. Some hiked inland to visit Mrs. Horneman at her farm. Aged and ailing Mr. Horneman was in Norway with his daughter Friedel. Mrs. Horneman's request for glass jars and magazines was immediately granted, and a box of supplies was soon packed and shipped off the *Explorer*. The ship also promised to deliver a package to Post Office Bay.

Forrest Nelson operated a small hotel at Academy Bay, but business was very slack in these seldom-visited isles. Several days before, at Wreck Bay, Jacob Lundh had mentioned that the freighters had discontinued the unprofitable business of hauling tourists.

A most genial and delightful host was the sprightly, longbearded patriarch, Karl Kubler, who proudly took all visitors on a tour of his rocky domain. He displayed his private lagoon with fish trap (high tide brings the fish in, he closes the gate, and fish are trapped as tide goes out), date and coconut trees, extensive gardens, and stone house. He seated his guests on a concrete bench in front of the children's playground which he had built. Then they were treated to refreshing coconuts and regaled with stories in a mixture of German, French, English, and Spanish. Kubler received letters from friends in all corners of the world and was happy in this little kingdom which he seemed likely to enjoy for many years in the future. Despite his old age, he was in extremely good physical condition, was completely self-sustaining, and had a keen mind and lively sense of humor.

Another person who enjoyed world-wide renown was Karl Angermeyer, the colorful skipper of the *Beagle*, a real character ship. Karl's portrait has appeared on the front covers of adventure magazines of the United States and Germany. Some years earlier, he had scored quite a sensation in Germany, lecturing about his Swiss Family Robinson or Robinson Crusoe life at Academy Bay.

Karl's charming wife, Marga, invited all of us to tea at her lovely stone house built of lava blocks on a rocky point, where iguanas frolicked around. Karl had a workshop where he did his painting, and had quite an impressive display of large paintings of the bizarre creatures and landscapes of the Encantadas. I gave him my library of books about the Galapagos, and, in return, was delighted to receive one of his paintings.

In the evening aboard the *Explorer*, Joe and Bonita Pachernegg showed colored slides of their travels; Karl Angermeyer and his English mate from the *Beagle* sang sea chanties and German beer songs. It was with extreme regret that we of the *Explorer* had to leave delightful Academy Bay and its even more delightful people. The ship left with an added crew member, whose name became Galapagos Tom to distinguish him from First Mate Tom Sylvain. The new Tom had been stranded at Academy Bay for nine months after arriving on a French yacht, which, for reasons unknown or not admitted, left without him.

Our pains of departure diminished as we approached scenic Sulivan Bay.

Of course, the seals took most of our attention; we were able to get some excellent movies and photographs, because the tame seals allowed us to take close-ups and to touch them. The bubble caves of Bartholomew Islet were explored, and we cruised to Buccaneer Cove and James Bay. There we saw the immense black lava flow which divides the beach. Several huts were seen – the homes of workers at the salt lake; some of our crew were invited for a truck ride to view the salt mining operations there.

After cruising round the northern end of Isabela Island, the *Explorer* spent New Year's Eve at Tagus Cove. Though nursing hangovers after the wild costume ball of the night before, some of the more agile crew scaled the steep precipice to add "*Explorer* – 1965" next to "*Marpatcha* – 1962" on the wall of the cove.

After a short stay at Elizabeth Bay, we sailed to Cormorant Bay on Floreana Island to do some fishing and to see the flamingoes near the salt flats. The ship then moved to Post Office Bay, and letters were deposited in the barrel, which happened to be empty when we arrived. Shoreboats took us to Black Beach, where gracious Frau Wittmer squeezed fourteen of us into her dining room and served delicious Galapagos coffee and holiday cookies. We brought her a box of goodies and a large tin of dry yeast which she needed badly: the monthly mailboat was overdue and supplies were low.

Rolf Wittmer related how his father had died of a cerebral hemorrhage the year before. Because of a radio failure, it was three days before a doctor could be reached, and Heinz Wittmer succumbed, surrounded by his children and grandchildren.

Margret Wittmer sold us a copy of her book *Floreana*, which is available in fifteen languages. The English edition was sold out, so crew-member Juanita Opstein had to be content with an Italian version. A new house of concrete blocks was being built for Margret's sister, a visitor from England, who apparently was planning a permanent stay. Rolf, his charming wife Paquita, and their son and daughter posed for pictures. But time and tide wait for no man, and, regretfully, we returned to the shoreboats without having visited the Ritter homestead and grave. Twelve days later, we were in the Marquesas Archipelago.

*   *   *

In November of 1974, Virginia and Carlton Schammel had arranged an impromptu get-together at Ralph Irming-Geissler's home in San Francisco. With Juanita Opstein and Peter Goodewagen, we reminisced over our adventures in the Galapagos as shipmates aboard the MV *Explorer*. Virginia and Juanita still kept in touch with some of the Angermeyers living in California. I was saddened to learn the *Beagle* had been deliberately destroyed because of some tax hassle with Ecuadorian bureaucrats. The island of Floreana had acquired a new name – "People Eater Island" – and fishermen refuse to anchor offshore at night. No doubt Sarah Reiser's disappearance in 1964 served as a reminder of the island's sinister past. Nonetheless, we all wholeheartedly expressed a desire to return once more to the South Sea.

Chances of visiting all of the islands are getting slimmer, though. In 1975, the government of Ecuador declared the Galapagos off-limits to most cruise ships and yachts – a disappointment for those seeking off-beat places to visit. Reasons for the ban were environmental and conservation concerns to deter unauthorized visitors from carting off valuable animal and plant life. Many iguanas are now spared the ignoble fate of being converted into souvenir belts. Only 12,000 tourists per year are now permitted to visit, but only on guided tours.

It is possible to fly from Guayaquil to Baltra Island, then board one of several authorized cruise ships like the MV *Santa Cruz* or the MV *Buccaneer* for 4-day or 8-day guided excursions to scenic places in some of the islands.

No one who has been to the islands will ever forget the eerie enchantment of that weird lost world – the Galapagos Islands.

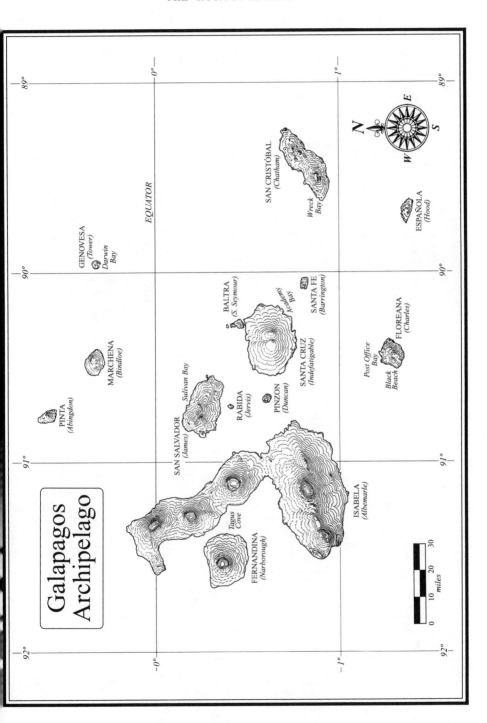

Galapagos Archipelago

Cross on ridge between Tagus Cove and Tagus Lake.

Sulivan Bay as seen from Isla Bartolomé with Pinnacle Rock and M/V *Explorer*.

Schooner *Marpatcha* in Tagus Cove. Tagus Lake in background.

Village of Baquerizo, Wreck Bay, Chatham Island.

Crater Lake above the village of Progreso, nearly 2,400-feet above sea level.

Dr. Ritter, Dore Koerwin Strauch, and Captain Hancock. *(photo courtesy of Allan Hancock Expeditions)*

The Wittmer family, Heinz, Rolf, Harry, and Margret, December 1933.
(photo courtesy of Allan Hancock Expeditions)

The Baroness (second from right), Philippson (right), and the scientists from the *Velero III. (photo coutesy of Allan Hancock Expeditions)*

Dr. Ritter, the Baroness, and Captain Hancock. *(photo coutesy of John S. Garth)*

Dr. Ritter and Dore Kerwin at their sugar press, Floreana. *(photo coutesy of John S. Garth)*

Captain Allan Hancock at the barrel post office, Floreana. *(photo coutesy of Allan Hancock Expeditions)*

Ainslie and Frances Conway. *(photo coutesy of Allan Hancock Expeditions)*

Author John Kefauver and Lillian Otterman with the only bus in the Galapagos, in front of the church at Progreso, Chatham Island, December 1964.

The Wittmer house at Black Beach, 1965. (Mrs. Wittmer second from right, son Rolf directly behind his mother with wife and children center, Lillian Otterman left.)

ACKNOWLEDGMENTS

The author wishes to express her grateful appreciation to:

Captain George Allan Hancock for his encouragement and gift copy of *Voyages of the Velero III*;

Sir Julian Huxley for his helpful suggestions;

Dr. Robert I. Bowman of the San Francisco State College for his constructive criticism and for valuable research material;

Dr. Stuart C. Dodd of the University of Washington for research material on the American social experiment in the Galapagos;

George Healy, Jr. of the *New Orleans Times Picayune* for clippings about Mrs. Peggy Poor and her Windiammer;

Florina Conklin of the *Seattle Times* for clippings about the Galapagos colony of 1960;

Many sailor-authors who wrote of their adventures in the Galapagos, whose books are out of print and unavailable to the average reader;

And finally, to my late husband, Captain Charles H. Otterman, who made my voyages to the Galapagos possible.

BIBLIOGRAPHY

Agassiz, A. 1892. General sketch of the expedition of the Albatross from Feb. to May 1891. *Bulletin of the Museum of Comparative Zoology* 23:1-89.

Anderson, Isabel. 1937. *Zigzagging in the South Seas.* Boston, B. Humphries, 262p.

Arnoldy, Julie. 1955. The first human eyes to look upon this land. *New Orleans Times-Picayune Roto Magazine* Oct. 9.

Bailey, Alfred M. 1970. *Galapagos Islands: Narrative of the 1960 field trip of the Denver Museum of Natural History to the Galapagos Islands.* Museum Pictorial No. 19, 85p.

Banning, George Hugh. 1934. Little Dragons of the Galapagos. *Travel* 62:21-3.

Barnett, Lincoln. 1958. Darwin's World of Nature: The Enchanted Isles. Paintings and photographs by Rudolph Freund and Alfred Eisenstadt. Text by Lincoln Barnett. *Life Mag.* 45:56-68 Sept. 8.

Baur, Georg. 1897. New observations on the origin of the Galapagos Islands. *Am. Naturalist* 31:661-680, 864-896.

Beck, Rollo H. 1903. In the home of the giant tortoises. New York Zoological Society. *Seventh Annual Report.*

Beebe, William. 1924. *Galapagos: World's End.* N.Y., G.P. Putnam's Sons, 443p.

Beebe, William. 1926. *The Arcturus Adventure.* N.Y., G.P. Putnam's Sons. 439p.

Blomberg, Rolf. 1951. Strange reptiles of the Galapagos. *Natural History* 60:234-9.

Blomberg, Rolf. 1959. *Buried Gold and Anacondas.* Tr. by F.H. Lyon. London, Allen. 144p.

Bowman, Robert I. 1963. Evolutionary patterns in Darwin's finches. *Occas. Papers Calif. Acad. Sci.* 44:107-140.

Bowman, Robert I. 1965. Darwin's finches. *Pacific Discovery* 18:10-13.

Bowman, Robert I. and Stephen J. Billeb. 1965. Blood-eating in a Galapagos finch. *The Living Bird* 4:29-44

Burney, J. 1950. *History of the Buccaneers of America.* Reprinted from 1816 ed. New York, W.W. Norton. 293p.

Byron, George A. 1826. *Voyage of the H.M.S. Blonde to the Sandwich Islands in the years 1824-1825.* London, John Murray. 260p.

Cavagnaro, David. 1965. Exploring the Galapagos on foot. *Pacific Discovery* 18:14-22.

Chubb, Lawrence John. 1925. The St. *George Scientific Expedition. Geol. Mag.* 62:369-373.

Colnett, James. 1798. *A Voyage to the South Atlantic and Round Cape Horn into the Pacific Ocean, for the purpose of extending the Spermaceti Whale Fisheries in the Ship Rattler.* London, W. Bennett. 179p.

Conway, Ainslie and Frances. 1947. *The Enchanted Isles.* New York, Putnam, 280p.

Conway, Ainslie and Frances. 1952. *Return to the Island.* London, Bles. 199p.

Couffer, Jack C. 1956. The disappearance of Urvina Bay. *Natural History* 65:378-83.

Couffer, Jack C. 1956. Galapagos Adventure. *Natural History* 65:140-145.

Cowley, Ambrose. 1699. *Voyage Around the World.* London.

Crealock, William I. B. 1955. *Cloud of Islands: by sail to the South Seas.* New York, Hastings House. 254p.

Crocker, Templeton. 1933. *Cruise of the Zaca.* New York, Harper. 238p.

Cutting, Suydam. 1940. *The Fire Ox and Other Years.* New York, Scribner. 393p.

Dampier, William. 1968. *A New Voyage Round the World.* New York, Dover Publications. 376p.

Darwin, Charles. 1845. *Journal of Researches into the Natural History and Geology of the Countries Visited During the Voyage of the H.M.S. Beagle round the World under the command of Capt. Fitz Roy, R.N.* Second revised edition. London, John Murray. 496p.

Darwin, Charles. 1959. *The Voyage of the Beagle.* New York, Harper & Row. 327p.

Darwin, Charles. 1968. *Origin of Species.* New York, Viking-Penguin. 477p.

Dawson, E. Yale. 1962. The Giants of the Galapagos. *Natural History* 61:52-57.

Delano, Captain Amasa. 1817. *Narrative of Voyages and Travels in Northern and Southern Hemispheres.* Boston, E.G. House. 598p.

Dodd, Stuart C. 1960. *The Galapagos Experiment on Ways of Life.* Abstract. Washington Opinion Laboratory. Univ. of Washington. May 16, pp.60-83

Durham, J. Wyatt. 1965. Geology of the Galapagos. *Pacific Discovery* 18:3-7.

Eibl-Eibesfeldt, Irenaus. 1957. Challenge of the Galapagos. *Nature Mag.* 50:405-7.

Eibl-Eibesfeldt, Irenaus. 1961. *Galapagos - Noah's Ark of the Pacific.* Garden City, N.Y., Doubleday & Co. 192p.

Eichler, Arturo. 1955. *Ecuador, Snow Peaks and Jungles.* New York, Crowell. 216p.

Fahnestock, Bruce and Sheridan. 1938. *Stars to Windward.* New York, Harcourt. 335p.

Faris, Robert E. L., William R. Cotton, and Otto N. Larsen. 1964. The Galapagos Expedition; Failure in the pursuit of a contemporary Utopia. *Pacific Sociological Review* Vol. 7, No. 1, Spring.

Flynn, Errol. 1960. *My Wicked Wicked Ways.* New York, Putnam-Berkeley Group, Inc. 438p.

Garth, John S. 1946. Distribution studies of Galapagos Brachyura. *Alan Hancock Pacific Expeditions.* Vol.5, No.11, pp.608-638.

Gerbault, Alain. 1930. *In Quest of the Sun: the journal of the "Firecrest".* Garden City, N.Y., Doubleday & Co. 303p.

Gifford, E. W. 1913. The birds of the Galapagos Islands. Proc. Calif. Acad. Sci. series 4, 2:1-132.

Gorsky, Bernard. 1957. *Vastness of the Sea.* Boston, Little. 258p.

Gowen, Roger. 1960. *Voyage to Paradise* (by) Roger Gowen as told to Bernard McElwaine. London, Muller. 191p.

Green, Donald M. 1953. *White Wings Around the World.* Toronto, Ryerson Press. 187p.

Grey, Zane. 1925. *Tales of Fishing Virgin Seas.* New York, Harper. 216p.

Hall, Captain Basil. 1824. *Extracts from a journal written on the coasts of Chile, Peru and Mexico in the years 1820, 1821, 1822.* Philadelphia, Little. 2 vol. in one.

Hamilton, Alastair Gavin. 1961. *The Restless Wind* (by) Peter Hamilton. New York, St. Martin's Press. 335p.

Hass, Hans. 1959. *We Come from the Sea.* Garden City, N.Y. Doubleday. 288 p.

Heller E. 1903. Papers from the Hopkins-Stanford Expedition. 1898-1899. XIV. *Reptiles. Proc. Washington Acad. Sci.* 5:39-98.

Heyerdahl, Thor. 1961. Extracts from an interview. Archeology Section, *New York Times.* Aug. 25.

Heyerdahl, Thor. 1963. Archeology in the Galapagos Islands. *Occas. Papers of Calif. Acad. Sci.* 44:45-51

Hillinger, Charles. 1960. Galapagos Ho! *Los Angeles Times* series appearing daily from Oct. 9 through Oct. 19.

Hiscock, Eric C. 1956. *Around the World in Wanderer III.* London, Oxford Univ. Press. 275 p.

Hiscock, Eric C. 1963. *Beyond the West Horizon.* London, Oxford Univ. Press. 205p.

Howard, Sidney. 1934. *Isles of Escape, being the adventures of Roydon Bristow.* London, Bell. 304p.

Johnson, Irving and Electa. 1936. *Westward Bound in the Schooner Yankee.* New York, Norton. 348p.

Johnson, Irving and Electa. 1949. *Yankee's Wander World.* New York, Norton. 277p.

Johnson, Irving and Electa. 1955. *Yankee's People and Places.* New York, Norton. 332p.

Johnson, Irving and Electa. 1956. A Cruising Guide to the Galapagos. *Yachting.* 99:58-61, Mar.

Johnson, Irving and Electa. 1959. Lost World of the Galapagos. *Nat. Geog. Mag.* 115:680-703, May.

Kauffman, Ray. 1940. *Hurricane's Wake.* New York, Macmillan. 248p.

Kemp, Peter K. 1960. *Brethren of the Coast.* London, Heineman. 248p.

Kuschel, Guillermo. 1963. Terrestrial Faunas of Easter, Juan Fernandez and Galapagos Islands. *Occas. Papers Calif. Acad. Sci.* 44:79-95.

Le Toumelin, Jacques Ives. 1955. *Kurun, Around the World.* New York, Dutton. 300p.

Lewis, Oscar. 1949. *Sea Routes to the Gold Fields.* New York, Knopf. 286p.

Maury, Richard. 1939. *The Saga of the Cimba.* New York, Harcourt. 245p.

Melville, Herman. 1940. *The Encantadas; or Enchanted Isles*, with an introduction by Victor Wolfgang Von Hagen. Burlingame, Ca., Wreden. 118p.

Melville, Herman. 1970. *Great Short Works of Herman Melville.* New York, Harper. 510p.

Meredith, De Witt. 1939. *Voyages of the Velero III.* Los Angeles, Ca., Brookhaven Press. 286p.

Mielche, Hakon. 1950. *Let's See if the World is Round.* London, Hodge. 330p.

Morell, Benjamin. 1832. *A Narrative of Four Voyages to the South Seas and South Pacific Ocean.* New York, Harper. 492p.

Muhlhauser, George H.P.   1924.   *Cruise of the Amaryllis.* London, John Lane. 316p.

New York Times. 1958. News Item: Valinda Hijack. p.29, col.2, Feb. 18.

Nicolas, W. H. 1946. American pathfinders in the Pacific. *Nat. Geog. Mag.* 89 617-40.

Petterson, Hans. 1953. *Westward Ho! with the Albatross.* New York, Dutton. 218p.

Pinchot, Gifford. 1930. *To the South Seas.* Philadelphia, John C. Winston Co. 500p.

Porter, David. 1815. *Journal of a Cruise made to the Pacific Ocean in the U.S. Frigate Essex in years 1812, 1813, and 1814.* Philadelphia, Bradford & Inskeep. 8 vol.

Puleston, Dennis. 1955. *Blue Water Vagabond.* London, Hart-Davis. 352p.

Reynolds, Earle and Barbara. 1962. *All in the Same Boat.* New York, McKay. 310p.

Rick, Charles and Robert I. Bowman. 1961. Galapagos tomatoes and tortoises. *Evolution* Vol. 15, 4: 407-417.

Ritter, Friedrich. 1931. Adam and Eve in the Galapagos. *Atlantic Monthly.* 148:409-18, Oct.

Ritter, Friedrich. 1931. Satan walks in the Garden. *Atlantic Monthly.* 148:565-75. Nov.

Ritter, Friedrich. 1931. Eve calls it a day. *Atlantic Monthly.* 148:733-43, Dec.

Roach, Peter, 1952. *Voyage in a Barquentine.* London, Hart-Davis. 272p.

Robinson, William A. 1929. Mystery man of the Galapagos. *Literary Digest* No. 9, pp.50-51.

Robinson, William A. 1944. *10,000 Leagues Over the Sea.* New York, Harcourt. 383p.

Robinson, William A. 1956 To the Great Southern Sea. New York, Harcourt. 320p.

Rockefeller, Jr., James S. 1957. *Man On His Island.* New York, Norton. 358p.

Rogers, Captain Woodes. 1970. *A Cruising Voyage Round the World.* Printed from the original edition of 1712. New York, Dover Publications. 320p.

Rohr, Frank. 1957. We Sailed to the Galapagos. *Travel* 108:46-50.

Rydell, Raymond A. 1952. *Cape Horn to the Pacific.* Berkeley, University of Berkeley Press. 213p.

Schmitt, Waldo L. 1935. Galapagos Islands one hundred years after Darwin. *Nature.* 26:264-71.

Seligman, Adrian. 1947. *Voyage of the Cap Pilar*. New York, Dutton. 360p.

Shumway, George. 1954. Carnegie Ridge and Cocos Ridge in the east equatorial Pacific. *Journal of Geol.* 62:573-586.

Shumway, George. 1963. Bathymetry in the Galapagos region. *Occas. Papers Calif. Acad. Sci.* 44: 11-20.

Shurcliff, Sidney H. 1930. *Jungle islands – The Illyria in the South Seas*. New York, G.P. Putnam's Sons. 298p.

Slevin, Joseph R. 1931. Log of the Schooner *Academy*, on a Voyage of research to the Galapagos Islands, 1905-1906. *Occas. Papers Calif. Acad. Sci.* 17:1-162.

Stock, Ralph. 1921. *The Cruise of the Dream Ship*. Garden City, N.Y., Doubleday, Page & Co. 292p.

Strauch, Dore. 1936. *Satan Came to Eden*, as told by Dore Strauch to Walter Brockman. New York, Harper & Bros. 274p.

Strout, Edith B. 1939. At home on the océans. *Nat. Geog. Mag.* 76:33-86.

Suggs, Robert Carl. 1960. *The Island Civilizations of Polynesia*. New York, New American Library. 256p.

Time Magazine. 1938. Senior Shellback (Pres. F.D. Roosevelt). Aug. 8.

Townsend, Charles H. 1925. The Galapagos tortoises in their relation to the whaling industry. A study of old logbooks. *Zoologics* 4:55-135.

Townsend, Charles H. 1930. The Astor Expedition to the Galapagos islands. *Bull. N.Y. Zool. Soc.* 33:135-55.

Townsend, Charles H. 1925. The whaler and the tortoise. *Scientific Monthly* 21:166-72.

Townsend, Charles H. 1931. Giant tortoises. *Sci. Am.* 144:42-4.

Utley, Temple. 1938. *A Modern Sea-Beggar*. London, Peter Davies. 341p.

Van Denburgh, J. 1914. The gigantic land tortoises of the Galapagos Archipelago. *Proc. Calif. Acad. Sci.* 2:203-274.

Von Hagen, Victor Wolfgang. 1937. Sea Iguanas of the Galapagos. *Nature* 29:147-9.

Von Hagen, Victor Wolfgang. 1940. *Ecuador the Unknown*. New York, Ryerson. 296p.

Von Hagen, Victor Wolfgang. 1943. Curse of the Galapagos. *Travel* 81:12-16 May.

Von Hagen, Victor Wolfgang. 1949. Ecuador and the Galapagos Islands. Norman, Oklahoma. Univ. of Oklahoma Press. 290p.

Wafer, Lionel. 1903. *A New Voyage and Description of the Isthmus of America.* Reprint of the original edition of 1699. Cleveland, Burrows Bros. Co. 212p.

Wiele, Annie Van De. 1956. *The West in My Eyes.* New York, Dodd. 288p.

Williams, Howel. 1966. *Geology of the Galapagos Islands.* The Galapagos Proc. of the Symposia of the Galapagos International Scientific Project. Berkeley, Univ. of Calif. Press.

Wittmer, Margret. 1990. *Floreana, A Woman's Pilgrimage to the Galapagos.* Mt. Kisko, N.Y., Moyer Bell Limited. 240p.

INDEX